WRITING CREATIVE NONFICTION

Fiction Techniques for Crafting Great Nonfiction

Theodore A. Rees Cheney

Ten Speed Press
Berkeley / Toronto

Ten Speed Press
P. O. Box 7123
Berkeley, California 94707
www.tenspeed.com

Distributed in Australia by Simon and Schuster Australia, in Canada by Ten Speed Press Canada, in New Zealand by Southern Publishers Group, in South Africa by Real Books, in Southeast Asia by Berkeley Books, and in the United Kingdom and Europe by Airlift Book Company.

Cover and text design by Betsy Stromberg
Cover photograph by Theodore A. Rees Cheney

Library of Congress Cataloging-in-Publication Data

Cheney, Theodore A. Rees (Theodore Albert Rees), 1928–
    Writing creative nonfiction: fiction techniques for crafting great
nonfiction / Theodore A. Rees Cheney.
    p. cm.
    ISBN 1-58008-229-7
    1. Reportage literature—Technique. 2. Nonfiction novel—Technique.
    3. Journalism—Authorship. 4. Narration (Rhetoric) 5. Creative writing. I. Title.

PN3377.5.R45 C46 2001
808'.02—dc21   2001003095

First printing, 2001

Printed in Canada

1 2 3 4 5 6 7 8 9 10 — 05 04 03 02 01

DEDICATED TO
DIDION, McPHEE,
TALESE, AND WOLFE

They had the courage to break away
and report the world to us in words more vivid,
more dramatic, and more accurate.

ACKNOWLEDGMENTS

I acknowledge here the women who helped, each in her own way, with the production of this book: my mother, Ruth Rees Cheney, who made my life possible and creative; my wife, Dorothy Bates Cheney, who has allowed me the necessary freedom to write; and Meghan Keeffe, who edited this new edition.

CONTENTS

1   CREATIVE NONFICTION

When I wrote the first edition of this book, in the mid-1980s, creative nonfiction was a fairly new kid on the block. Since then, much has changed. The Internet explosion has opened up avenues for research a writer could once only have dreamed of having. That, along with the ease of in-depth research, done from the writer's desk on the now ubiquitous home computer, has contributed to the growth of the genre we now enjoy in books and articles of all kinds.

So, what is this genre of writing, variously called Personal Journalism, Literary Journalism, Dramatic Nonfiction, the New Journalism, Parajournalism, Literary Nonfiction, the New Nonfiction, Verity, the Nonfiction Novel, the Literature of Fact, the Literature of Reality, and—the name we know best—Creative Nonfiction?

Creative nonfiction tells a story using facts, but uses many of the techniques of fiction for its compelling qualities and emotional vibrancy. Creative nonfiction doesn't just report facts, it delivers facts in ways that move the reader toward a deeper understanding of a topic. Creative nonfiction requires the skills of the storyteller and the research ability of the conscientious reporter. Writers of creative nonfiction must become instant authorities on the subject of their articles or books. They must not only understand the facts and report them using quotes by authorities, they must also see beyond them to discover their underlying meaning, and they must dramatize that meaning in an interesting, evocative, informative way—just as a good teacher does.

When you write nonfiction, you are, in effect, teaching the reader. Research into how we learn shows that we learn best when we are simultaneously entertained—when there is pleasure in the learning. Other research shows that our most lasting memories are those wrapped in emotional overtones. Creative nonfiction writers inform their readers by making the reading experience vivid, emotionally compelling, and enjoyable while sticking to the facts.

This book discusses how creative nonfiction differs from traditional journalism and how techniques used in fiction—characterization, writing dramatically, using scenes, compressing information ("clumping"), developing character portraits and including character snapshots, using active instead of passive verbs—contribute to good creative nonfiction. Excerpts from the work of many fine writers are used in each chapter to illustrate the various techniques discussed. Many of the excerpts are from highly respected writers of the late 1960s, 1970s, and 1980s, when this genre was just beginning to take root, and some are from more recently published works. The authors may not have considered themselves writers of creative nonfiction, but the style of their work falls into that genre. The excerpts are teaching tools, just as the books they come from can be: As with all kinds of writing, one of the best ways to learn to do it well is to read the works of the masters in the field.

Some writers are well aware of the genre they represent and have the goals of the creative nonfiction writer in mind when they sit down to compose. Dan Wakefield, in a 1966 book about the New Journalism, *Between the Lines,* wrote:

> I am writing now for those readers—including myself—who have grown increasingly mistrustful of and bored with anonymous reports about the world, whether signed or unsigned, for those who have begun to suspect what we reporters of current events and problems so often try to conceal: that we are really individuals after all, not all-knowing, all-seeing Eyes but separate, complex, limited, particular "I"s.

Gay Talese, one of the first and best creative nonfiction writers, wrote in his 1961 book *Fame and Obscurity*:

> The new journalism, though often reading like fiction, is not fiction. It is, or should be, as reliable as the most reliable reportage, although it seeks a larger truth than is possible through the mere accumulation of verifiable facts, the use of direct quotations, and adherence to the rigid organizational style of the older form. The new journalism allows, demands in fact, a more imaginative approach to reporting, and it permits the writer to inject himself into the narrative, if he wishes, as many writers do, or to assume the role of a detached observer, as other writers do, including myself.

In the early days of this genre, writers were required to defend their practices. Tom Wolfe, one of the primary pioneers of creative non-fiction (then called "The New Journalism"), reported in his 1973 book of the same title that he had entered this strange arena with an article in *Esquire,* entitled, "There Goes (Varoom! Varoom!) That Kandy-Kolored (Thphhhhhh!) Tangerine-Flake Streamlined Baby (Rahghhh!) Around the Bend (Brummmmmmmmm)...."

Some people said it was a sort of short story, but Wolfe defended himself:

> This article was by no means a short story, despite the use of scenes and dialogue. I wasn't thinking about that all. It is hard to say what it was like. It was a garage sale, that piece... vignettes, odds and ends of scholarship, bits of memoir, short bursts of sociology, apostrophes, epithets, moans, cackles, anything that came into my head, much of it thrown together in a rough and awkward way. That was its virtue. It showed me the possibility of there being something "new" in journalism.
>
> What interested me was not simply the discovery that it was possible to write accurate non-fiction with techniques usually associated with novels, short stories. It was that-plus. It was the discovery that it was possible in non-fiction, in journalism, to use any literary device, from the traditional dialogisms of the essay to stream-of-consciousness, and to use many different

kinds simultaneously, or within a relatively short space…to excite the reader both intellectually and emotionally.

Creative nonfiction, though relatively new as a recognized genre of writing, has actually been done by some of the best writers for many years. Close to a century ago, in the May 1906 issue of *Collier's Weekly,* Jack London wrote an exemplary piece of creative nonfiction to tell "The Story of an Eyewitness," an account of the San Francisco earthquake. Here is a paragraph from that article, as it appeared in, Donald McQuade and Robert Atwan's *Popular Writing in America*:

> By Wednesday afternoon, inside of twelve hours, half the heart of the city was gone. At that time I watched the vast conflagration from out on the bay. It was dead calm. Not a flicker of wind stirred. Yet from every side wind was pouring in on the city. East, west, north, and south, strong winds were blowing on the doomed city. The heated air rising made an enormous suck. Thus did the fire of itself build its own colossal chimney through the atmosphere. Day and night this dead calm continued, and yet, near to the flames, the wind was often half a gale, so mighty was the suck.

Although he injected himself only once—"I watched the vast conflagration"—we feel his continuing and guiding presence. Through him we feel more closely the dead calm and the strong wind. Many newspapers, even today, would not allow even this single descriptive detail. Traditional journalism seeks neutral, impersonal, "objective" reportage.

Ernest Hemingway is another early writer of what is now known as creative nonfiction. In 1937 he wrote "On the Shelling of Madrid" for the North American Newspaper Alliance. Here is an excerpt from that article, as it appeared in Shelly Fisher Fishkin's *From Fact to Fiction,* a study of imaginative writers who began as reporters of fact:

> MADRID—At the front, a mile and a quarter away, the noise came as a heavy coughing grunt from the green pine-studded

hillside opposite. There was only a gray wisp of smoke to mark the insurgent battery position. Then came the high inrushing sound, like ripping of a bale of silk. It was all going well over into the town, so, out there, nobody cared. But in town, where all the streets were full of Sunday crowds, the shells came with the sudden flash that a short circuit makes and then the roaring crash of granite-dust. During the morning, twenty-two shells came into Madrid.

They killed an old woman returning home from the market, dropping her in a huddled black heap of clothing, with one leg, suddenly detached, whirling against the wall of an adjoining house. They killed three people in another square, who lay like so many torn bundles of old clothing in the dust and rubble when the fragments of the "155" had burst against the curbing.

Although Hemingway never mentioned in the article that he was right there, we feel his presence, most intensely when he provides the reader with concrete images: First there was that gray wisp of smoke, but then there followed the images of an old woman dropped in her tracks—"a huddled black heap of clothing"—and the three others lying in another square "like torn bundles of old clothing in the dust and rubble," and the cold insertion not of simply an artillery shell but more specifically, of a "155." Although unsaid, we find it believable that someone there on the ground would likely call such a shell with a diameter of 155 mm., a "155."

Newspapers still have the corner on the market of objective reporting, but more and more, editors are making room for this newer genre of reporting. Similar to magazine features in their depth of reportage, and more like fiction in their use of scene setting, character profiling, and use of dialog, these creative nonfiction articles tell stories that go far beyond coverage of incidents and analysis of a collection of facts. A good example of this is the *New York Times'* series, "How Race Is Lived in America," which ran for six weeks in 2000.

The series did not purport to be creative nonfiction, but that was the approach, and the effect made for a very successful, thought-provoking exploration of the topic of race. The *Times* editors instructed the writers to focus not on the rhetoric and policies of race but on the daily experience of race relations in America. The writers were not to interpret for the reader what something meant but to let the reader figure it out from what the reporter observed in the field and by what people said. The writers were not limited to using only direct quotes but rather were allowed to use indirect quotes where appropriate, something you would never see in traditional reporting. More than twenty *New York Times* reporters and photographers worked for a year researching their stories.

In one of the articles, "The Minority Quarterback" (*New York Times*, July 2, 2000), Ira Berkow wrote about the first meeting between the Jacobys and the white coach trying to recruit their white son for a black university:

> That day in his office, the Jacobys said they were impressed by his [coach Richardson's] quiet intellect, the way he measured his words, his determination. Indeed the president of Southern [University], Dr. Dorothy Spikes, often said that she had hired Mr. Richardson over better-known [black] candidates not just because his teams had been winners but because of his reputation for integrity, for running a clean program....
>
> Coach Richardson pointed out that there were other minorities on campus. He meant that of the 10,500 students, 5 percent were not black, but Mrs. Jacoby kept thinking about how it would feel to be in a stadium with her husband and 30,000 black fans.

In a traditional piece of reportage, those two paragraphs would have been riddled with quote marks—quotes by the Jacobys, quotes by Dr. Spikes, quotes by coach Richardson. Berkow would never have included what Mrs. Jacoby was thinking, especially because her thought was so politically incorrect and so personally revealing. But personally revealing is exactly what Berkow was after here: His goal was to uncover and expose the real people living the experience of race issues.

In another article in the same series, "Why Harlem Drug Cops Don't Discuss Race" (*New York Times*, July 9, 2000), Michael Winerip wrote:

Feelings ran deep. No case in recent years has hit the police closer to home. As Sergeant Brogli said, "There but for the grace of God...." Every officer with any sense, white or black, fears mistakenly shooting an unarmed man like Amadou Diallo. Talk about jamming up a career.

A reader may well believe that the last two sentences were a continuation of the previous, direct quote of Sergeant Brogli, but they're not. These are indirectly quoted words said to Winerip by Sergeant Brogli probably during a much longer interview. Used here, they accurately convey the tone and general sense of that interview. The final sentence sounds very much like what a police officer might say, but those could also very well be the words of Winerip writing carefully in the voice of the sergeant.

Winerip, toward the end of the article, wrote:

If the police can be too quick to label, Detective Gonzalez says, they are only reflecting society.

   On a warm afternoon, dressed in plain clothes, he met downtown with a prosecutor about a case, then stopped in a deli near Chinatown for an iced tea. One sip and he nearly spit it out. He knew immediately it was the extra-sweet tea that heroin addicts on Methadone often crave. "Sorry," said the Asian woman behind the counter, exchanging the drink. "This is junkie iced tea." An honest mistake? Or had she assumed he was a junkie from a nearby Methadone clinic because he is brown skinned?

We can probably safely presume that this story came during an interview with Detective Gonzalez. In traditional journalism, Winerip would have been expected to quote directly what the detective told him. Here, he told the story largely through indirect quotes. Perhaps, for variety, he switched to directly quoting what the vendor said about the junkie iced tea. Winerip then asked those rhetorical questions, making, in a fresh, *involving* way, important points about so-called profiling and how race is lived in America on a day-to-day basis.

Kevin Sack opened his article, "Shared Prayers" (*New York Times,* June 4, 2000) *in medias res*—right in the middle of things—with a scene in an integrated church on a Sunday morning:

> DECATUR, Georgia—Howard Pugh, head usher, is on patrol. May the good Lord have mercy on any child, or adult for that matter, who dares to tread across the lobby of the Assembly of God Tabernacle with so much as an open Coca-Cola in his hand. Because first he will get the look, the alert glare of a hunting dog catching its first scent of game. Then he will get the wag, the slightly palsied shake of the left index finger. And then, the voice, serious as a heart attack and dripping with Pensacola pinesap: "Son, this is the Lord's house. And they just shampooed that carpet last week."
>
> It goes without saying that Howard Pugh knows what is going on in his lobby. So when Mr. Pugh, a white man with a bulbous pink nose, spots 81-year-old Roy Denson slipping out of the sanctuary, he doesn't even have to ask. He just knows.

Sack led off with a scene that sets us up for what comes later by his use of "on patrol...." A traditional reporter might not use "on patrol" because this was not factual. This was not a military or police patrol: This was a church's alert head usher. I imagine that Kevin Sack knew that "tread across the lobby" would resonate in many readers' minds with that militant flag that declared, "Don't tread on me." Editors of traditional journalism don't condone this kind of resonance; after all, what resonates with some readers may clang the wrong bell for others.

As you will learn in later chapters, a writer gains authority by using realistic details readily recognized by readers, words like "Coca-Cola." Even though this particular detail may have been created in Sack's mind rather than in Pugh's, it is a detail that resonates clearly in most readers' minds and paints a clear picture of what is being described. The creative nonfiction writer also has devices such as rhythm in language and useful repetition in phrasings to draw upon, devices the author uses well in this article.

An editor of traditional journalism would object to that wonderful repetition of "the look," "the wag," and "the voice." Editors also usually frown on metaphors, which are viewed as more artistic than accurate. But who needs absolute accuracy when you can come up with a voice "serious as a heart attack and dripping with Pensacola pinesap"? Add to that, traditionally, editors would have had a fit about the use of the alliterative *p* in "dripping with Pensacola pinesap."

Articles like those in this series provide good reason to believe that this kind of writing is well on its way to greater acceptance in daily journalism. And why shouldn't creative nonfiction still be gaining in popularity? In addition to the fact that there is a broad interest today in reading factual material presented in a vivid, dramatic, and entertaining way, readers also turn to nonfiction because it's often stranger than fiction. Who needs fiction in a world so strange? As far back as 1966, Seymore Krim wrote:

> Reality itself has become so extravagant, in its contradictions, absurdities, violence, speed of change, science fiction technology, weirdness, and constant unfamiliarity, that just to match what *is* with accuracy takes the conscientious reporter into the realms of the Unknown—into what used to be called "the world of the imagination." And yet that is the wild world we live in today when we just try to play it straight.

Let's look now at some of the key techniques for writing good, compelling, creative nonfiction.

2 OPENINGS: DRAMATIC AND SUMMARY METHODS

This book will discuss techniques for telling a story, whether fiction or nonfiction, that grow out of two basic methods: the dramatic (or scenic) method and the summary (or narrative) method. Like so many great truths, the methods may sound too pat, too simple, but they're simple only in that they are so fundamental.

I had never heard about these methods until I read Leon Surmelian's book, *Techniques of Fiction Writing*. I am forever in his debt—and you, too, will soon be. Surmelian wrote about these methods as applied to fiction, but I've since found that they may be the missing link that binds fiction to nonfiction, the link that makes some nonfiction more creative than some other nonfiction and thus increases the potential of journalistic nonfiction to aspire to art.

A creative nonfiction writer will typically conceive of his or her story as a series of scenes connected by a series of summaries—drama connected by narrative. He or she will plan an article or book around a series of scenes, selecting only those events that seem to have the greatest dramatic potential and then organizing them in what seems the best sequence (not always chronological). The writer will then accomplish other of his or her purposes in between with what we'll call "summaries." We'll use "summaries" here to mean the typical narrative journalists write, summaries of what happened, as distinct from a running account of what is happening at the moment.

One writer might tell a story largely by scenes, while another might approach the same event using the summary method. The latter might have an occasional scene, but summary predominates. The former almost certainly has some summary material between scenes, but the method remains predominately dramatic. Most creative nonfiction writers today blend the two methods, but with more scenes than the traditional journalist. As we'll see in a later chapter, this business of writing scene by scene is one of the many techniques borrowed by the nonfiction writer from the fiction writer.

Writing in the dramatic method (in scenes) is appropriate in creative nonfiction. As fiction writers know, scenes give vitality, movement, action—life—to a story. Scenes show people doing things, saying things, moving right along in life's ongoing stream. Even when reporting about the past, writers may place scenes in present tense, giving the reader the feeling of being eyewitness to the action. Traditional journalists usually have to report what's happened; they are secondhand witnesses lacking the credibility of the eyewitness.

The creative nonfiction writer aims to be an eyewitness on the scene. If that's impossible, the writer researches a past event in much greater depth than the daily reporter has time to do. The creative nonfiction writer may then write a credible scene in present tense, making the past seem present. Of course, this places a great responsibility on the creative nonfiction writer; the reader must not be deliberately made to think the writer was actually present at the scene if that isn't true.

The dramatic method is the cinematographer's close-up shot; the summary method, in contrast, is the long shot. As readers, we believe the close-up shot because that's how we see most of life, particularly when dealing with people. Not that we totally distrust the long shot, but, as in life, we take with a grain of salt what we haven't seen or heard for ourselves—we await corroborating evidence from other sources before believing what we're told. We typically don't like being told—we like to find things out for ourselves.

You've probably heard (and have perhaps even wisely heeded) the advice given to writers to show, don't tell. Dramatic method is show; summary method is tell. In reminding writers not to rely so heavily on the summary method, I do not intend to say, "Always show, never tell." For the best effect, the two methods merge. A single paragraph may use the techniques of both scene and summary. A scene may well have some short narrative summary interspersed through it. Even in the midst of a long summary passage, one or two lines of quoted conversation may occur in a kind of tiny scene. No rigid rules exist—only the general rule that the techniques used must serve to accomplish part of the writer's purpose. Let's begin by demonstrating how some of our best writers use these methods for article and book openings.

We'll first look at the dramatic method as applied to openings, and then discuss in more detail the summary method and several techniques to apply it to openings.

DRAMA IN CONTEMPORARY FICTION

For the nonfiction writer, advice to show rather than tell means *put more drama into your nonfiction writing.* Show the reader what's happening. We believe what we see; we distrust what we're told. That's the secret to writing, whether fiction or nonfiction: Capture your readers' attention through the eyes and ears—the senses.

For most people, the most used sense is the visual one. In writing, "showing" means much more than offering visuals for the mind's eye. You can also show something about a person by letting the reader "hear" him or her speak. You may show us one thing when we hear a man speaking before the Rotary Club; you may show us something quite different when you let us hear him talk with a waitress when he's out of town on business. Unless you have also described him for us, we can't "see" him, but the scene will have certainly "shown" him to us just the same as we will have had several views of him through his conversations.

Good, dramatic nonfiction openings tend to move; they have life within them, life that moves, that gets somewhere. In a good piece of nonfiction, if life doesn't get somewhere in the opening lines, the reader must at least sense movement or the promise of movement, sense that the freeze-frame will soon launch into action. Readers will not wait long for this. Playgoers may not walk back up the aisle if they don't like the first few words of the play on stage, but the article reader can easily flip to another article if the movement of life is neither present nor promised.

Many years ago, readers would stay with the writer, sometimes for many pages, while the writer warmed up to telling the actual story. That was the style of the day; it fit the slow pace of life in that time. Today, the reader faces many demands on his or her time. This is complicated by an ever-shortening attention span in people of all ages. A shortened attention span would seem to spell nothing but negatives about the future of reading—and, closer to our hearts, writing—but fortunately, there is another side to the coin. As the result of television, the Internet, and the increasing pace of life in general, most people today are quicker on the uptake. They're ready to receive and process concentrated bursts of information much more rapidly than could readers several generations ago. This two-sided coin (or is it a two-edged sword?) influences our writing—or, at least, our thinking about writing. On the one hand, readers can generally accept high loads of information because of increased abilities, but on the other hand, they're quicker to put aside a piece of writing that isn't sufficiently interesting, entertaining, or informative. This means that writers can be more direct, creating an impression with a few bold strokes, a single exemplary, vivid incident, and some carefully selected concrete details. If the writer intends to have readers, he or she must grab them and do everything possible to stretch that short attention span. The first 250 words must do it. Good openings make us feel we're there, in the infield, involved in the double play.

Poor openings resemble a professional baseball pitcher's motions: a long, involved, often self-conscious wind-up punctuated partway by a furtive look to check first base, another squeeze of the rosin bag, and then another tug at the visor, another hitch of the pants, and finally, the pitch itself—sometimes three pages too late to catch the reader. The skilled nonfiction writer steps to the mound, checks out the batter, and hurls the word directly at the reader. It may end up a curve, but the game's begun—we're hooked, we're grabbed, we're involved in the game.

Like much good fiction today, nonfiction articles often begin *in medias res,* in the middle of some action, some event. An opening can begin in the midst of some very dramatic action with people talking about things we may not at first understand (but are intrigued by), or it can begin with very little or no conversation. Many nonfiction pieces start out with conversation.

In nonfiction, as in fiction, when people appear, and particularly when they begin to converse, the story comes to life. Until then, it's largely promise. Knowing this about fiction inspires many creative nonfiction writers to open with conversation. The reader comes down the aisle looking for his or her seat while taking in the dialog progressing on stage and is engrossed, before turning down the upholstered seat to get settled in.

DRAMATIC OPENINGS

With the following dramatic scene, George Orwell opened a book about his early years, *Down and Out in Paris and London.* It puts us immediately into the environment he's about to discuss. Not content with "telling" us about his street, Rue du Coq d'Or, he "shows" us the street by letting us hear some of the inhabitants speak. And he doesn't have them speak just so we can hear their speech patterns, he has them speak of things that show us what life was like on the street of the golden rooster.

> The Rue du Coq d'Or, seven in the morning. A succession of furious, choking yells from the street. Madame Monce, who kept the little hotel opposite mine, had come out onto the pavement to address a lodger on the third floor. Her bare feet were stuck into sabots and her grey hair was streaming down.

Madame Monce: "*Salope! Salope!* How many times have I told you not to squash bugs on the wallpaper? Do you think you've bought the hotel, eh? Why can't you throw them out of the window like everyone else? *Putaine! Salope!*"

Thereupon a whole variegated chorus of yells, as windows were flung open on every side and half the street joined in the quarrel. They shut up abruptly ten minutes later, when a squadron of cavalry rode past and people stopped shouting to look at them.

The ending of Orwell's opening is what a journalist might call a "natural close": All action in the scene stops when the people stop to watch the cavalry ride past. This gives the writer a perfect natural opportunity to step back and launch into a summary section that tells the reader more about life on that cobblestone street.

Writers of good nonfiction know the value of conversation throughout a piece. They are particularly aware of its power to grab the reader right from the beginning. Nonfiction that doesn't let us hear the human interaction tends to lose readers.

In his justly well-known book on paleontology, *In Patagonia,* Bruce Chatwin opened Chapter 20, "An Old Log Cabin," with some very simple but vivid conversation. Although we don't hear his side of the conversation, we feel his presence, partly by the way he sticks his hand into the scene in line 2:

"Feel it," she said. "Feel the wind coming through."

I put my hand to the wall. The draught blew through the chinks where the mortar had fallen out. The log cabin was the North American kind. In Patagonia they made cabins differently and did not chink them with mortar.

The owner of the cabin was a Chilean Indian woman called Sepulveda.

"In winter it's terrible," she said. "I covered the wall with *materia plastica* but it blew away. The house is rotten, Señor, old and rotten. I would sell it tomorrow. I would have a concrete house which the wind cannot enter.

Señor Sepulveda was grogged out of his mind, half-sitting, half-lying by the kitchen stove.

"Would you buy the house?" she asked.

"No," I said, "but don't sell it for nothing. There are North American gentlemen who would pay good money to take it away piece by piece."

Chatwin shows the cabin partly by letting us hear the inhabitant (the way Orwell did earlier), and he uses those parts of the conversation that tell (show) us something about the subject (cabin), not just something about the old woman. A valuable part of this technique is that the writer (and his or her reader) get two-for-one. Through the person's words we learn something of the person while simultaneously learning something of the subject.

Chatwin uses an interesting device when he has the woman speak in Spanish, referring to *materia plastica.* The author could have had any other words in Spanish to give us the flavor of the Spanish conversation, but he chose *materia plastica,* presumably because he felt that most Norte Americanos could hardly miss the point. Again, we get a two-for-one: We learn that she's tried in vain to use some plastic stuff to keep out the wind; that the Patagonian winds of winter could lead to one's discontent; and we're reminded that the entire conversation is probably in Spanish.

Hunter S. Thompson is particularly adept at capturing the nuances of conversation and often uses them to establish the overall tone in the opening, as he did in the following piece about the Kentucky Derby, "The Kentucky Derby Is Decadent and Depraved," published in *Scanlan's Monthly* (June 1970). Whether these conversations are verbatim reports or not is moot. We do know right away that the conversations sound reasonably true to what we would expect to hear in that situation with those particular types of people. Notice how easily, efficiently, and effectively conversation gets us into a scene, taking us deeper and deeper into the article—the purpose, after all, of a dramatic, scenic, involving opening.

I got off the plane around midnight and no one spoke as I crossed the dark runway to the terminal. The air was thick and hot, like wandering into a steam bath. Inside, people hugged each other and shook hands...big grins and a whoop here and there: "By God! You old bastard! Good to see you, boy! *Damn* good...and I *mean* it!"

In the air-conditioned lounge I met a man from Houston who said his name was something or other—"But just call me Jimbo"—and he was here to get it on. "I'm ready for *anything,* by God! Anything at all. Yeah, what are you drinking?" I ordered a Margarita with ice, but he wouldn't hear of it: "Naw, naw...what the hell kind of drink is that for Kentucky Derby Time? What's *wrong* with you, boy?" He grinned and winked at the bartender. "Goddam, we gotta educate this boy. Get him some good *whiskey....*"

I shrugged. "Okay, a double Old Fitz on ice." Jimbo nodded his approval.

"Look." He tapped me on the arm to make sure I was listening. "I know this Derby crowd, I come here every year, and let me tell you one thing I've learned—this is no town to be giving people the impression you're some kind of faggot. Not in public, anyway. Shit, they'll roll you in a minute, knock you in the head and take every goddam cent you have."

I thanked him and fitted a Marlboro into my cigarette holder....

Nothing need be said about his use of conversation to open this article. It sounds to me absolutely, totally, right-on-the-money true to life. Note how Thompson has also appealed to our senses: visual (how dark it was); tactile (that the air was thick and hot like steam baths; people hugged and shook hands); and aural (his use of "whoop"); and our sense of taste (his reference to several iced drinks). He appealed to our tactile sense again when the man tapped him on the arm, and he engaged both my sense of vision and my tactile sense when he said that he "fitted" the cigarette into the holder—I could feel that fitting action. It's worth noting, too, that he did not "tell" us all about these matters in one descriptive paragraph. Each sense was tapped in context—when it came up in the story. That's the way to do it—weave, weave, weave.

In *This Boy's Life: A Memoir,* Tobias Wolff describes a scene in which he and his mother are on their way to the Northwest to escape the boy's father in Florida. This simple scene snares our attention on the first page.

> Our car boiled over again just after my mother and I crossed the Continental Divide. While we were waiting for it to cool we heard, from somewhere above us, the bawling of an airhorn. The sound got louder and then a big truck came around the corner and shot past us into the next curve, its trailer shimmying wildly. We stared after it. "Oh, Toby," my mother said, "he's lost his brakes."
>
> The sound of the horn grew distant, then faded in the wind that sighed in the trees all around us.

Richard Selzer's nonfiction piece "The Discus Thrower" collected in *The Rituals of Surgery*, begins the way a short story might. We see a person immediately, the author describing the man physically in very vivid language, language that gives us unexpected images, unexpected metaphors.

> I spy on my patients. Ought not a doctor to observe his patients by any means and from any stance, that he might the more fully assemble evidence? So I stand in the doorways of hospital rooms and gaze. Oh, it is not all that furtive an act. Those in bed need only look up to discover me. But they never do.
>
> From the doorway of Room 542 the man in the bed seems deeply tanned. Blue eyes and close-cropped white hair give him the appearance of vigor and good health. But I know that his skin is not brown from the sun. It is rusted, rather, in the last stage of containing the vile repose within. And the blue eyes are frosted, looking inward like the windows of a snowbound cottage. This man is blind. This man is also legless—the right leg missing from midthigh down, the left from just below the knee. It gives him the look of a bonsai, roots and branches pruned into the dwarfed facsimile of a great tree.

Dr. Selzer arrests us right away by his descriptions, particularly the simile that shows us what the man's eyes look like by saying they're frosted like the windows of a snowbound cottage—they look inward. He shows us through another striking simile that this legless man looks like a bonsai tree, the dwarfed facsimile of a great tree, which shows us more about this once great man than it tells us what he looked like.

Let's look now at author George Plimpton in *Paper Lion* as he puts us on the football field when he goes out for the first time to learn (the hard way) what it feels like to face a line of professional football players. He involves us not by conversation but by vivid description of himself in action—in a scene. His use of vivid, concrete words involves us immediately.

> I came up off the bench slowly, working my fingers up into my helmet to get at my ears. As I crossed the sidelines I was conscious then only of moving into the massive attention of the crowd, but seeing ahead out of the opening of my helmet the two teams waiting. Some of the defense were already kneeling at the line of scrimmage, their heads turned so that helmeted, silver, with the cages protruding, they were made to seem animal and impersonal—wildlife of some large species disturbed at a waterhole—watching me come toward them. Close to, suddenly there was nothing familiar about them. With the arc lights high up on the standards, the interiors of their helmets were shadowed—perhaps with the shine of a cheekbone, the glint of an eye—no one was recognizable, nor a word from them. I trotted by the ball. Its trade name "Duke" was face up. The referee was waiting, astride it, a whistle at the end of a black cord dangling from his neck. The offensive team in their blue jerseys, about ten yards back, on their own twenty-yard line, moved, and collected in the huddle formation as I came up, and I slowed, and walked toward them, trying to be calm about it, almost lazying up to them to see what could be done.

For another example of an opening that does not depend on dialog for its strength, read this paragraph that opens Chapter 3, "An August Day's Sail," in *Spring Tides,* by Samuel Eliot Morison:

A light, caressing southerly breeze is blowing; just enough to heel the yawl and give her momentum. The boy and I get under way from the mooring by the usual ritual. I take in the ensign, hoist the mizzen, cast off the main sheet and slack the back-stays; he helps me hoist the mainsail, sway the halyards and neatly coil them. I take the wheel and the main sheet in hand, the boy casts off the mooring rope and hoists the jib, and she goes like a lively dog let off the leash.

Now that's what this chapter is all about—letting a lively piece of writing off the leash. The longer it's held under leash by nondramatic, nonvivid, noninvolving language, the less likely the reader will be excited to continue to read. Everyone's more excited by a dog that's unleashed and hurtling forward off the page.

SUMMARY OPENINGS

Whereas the dramatic method requires the people to live out the story right before our eyes, the summary method, essential to most creative nonfiction, requires a teller. The summary method has its values and strengths, of course, but it also has its weaknesses. The weakness of the summary method lies in the teller: No matter who tells the story, the reader experiences a story being told instead of watching it unfold. As in life, we tend to believe more what we overhear than what we're told. Therein lies the explanation of why the summary method has a weakness—we prefer to be our own witness. The dramatic method relies more on seeing, the sense we're used to relying upon. Summary, by contrast, usually lacks imagery. In the next few chapters you'll see how our best nonfiction writers make even their summary writing vivid, lively, imagistic, visual. They try to get as close to purely dramatic writing as is possible through summary alone.

The summary method, using various techniques I'll soon describe, serves extremely important ends. One of its greatest strengths is its ability to telescope time, something the dramatic method can't easily do. A scene seems closer to real time; something that in fact took a long time would take that much time in a scene, or the writer would write several scenes to show the passage of time. With summary, writers can achieve the impression of continuous flow between scenes, movement without awkward conjunctions. If scenes are the building blocks of a story, summaries are the cement that binds. Cleverly written summaries between scenes can provide smooth transitions between time, even great lengths of time.

Summaries serve another important purpose related to the handling of time. They slow the pace, allowing suspense to build. Scenes accelerate the pace, not because they're short, but because they're vivid, concrete, and active in their imagery. The clever writer will pace the piece by carefully orchestrating which information is put into fast-paced scenes and which into slower-paced summary. Most of the information in a story or article can be supplied by either method, but the pace, suspense, and emotional impact will be different, and often a good mix of the two is what's best.

Creative nonfiction writers mix both dramatic and summary methods to make nonfiction more interesting for the reader. Straight exposition—facts with no drama, no description, and no interpretation—tends to make for dull reading. Journalistic writing traditionally has tended toward that kind of writing, in the interest of "objectivity." Creative nonfiction writers believe they can add drama and interpretation without destroying objectivity. They believe they are actually more objective because they're more thorough in their reporting, going to greater depth in their research. This book does not intend to argue that point; it intends only to show how with creative nonfiction you can go about the task of creating nonfiction that reads more interestingly while still respecting the facts.

Interspersed throughout this chapter are some openings that are more summary than dramatic. Keep in mind that these openings are sometimes part one type and part the other, and remember that it is the author's intent that determines how we might classify a particular opening.

The summary method is carried out by two techniques, description and explanation. First, I'll discuss "descriptive summary." In its appeal to the imagination, it's closer to the dramatic method than is "explanatory summary."

DESCRIPTIVE VERSUS EXPLANATORY SUMMARY

Descriptive summary is distinguished from explanatory by its presentation of the quality of an action. While explanatory summary would capture the sequence, logic, and meaning of the action, moving us through *time,* descriptive summary concerns itself with giving us an overall sensory impression, moving us through *space.*

If, for example, we were writing about a battle going on, descriptive summary would give us interesting snapshots of the action, details of the uniforms, the weapons, the sounds and smells of battle. Explanatory summary, on the other hand, would likely tell us about the tactics of both sides, the progress of the battle and even of the war. Descriptive summary could never give us details about the war; it would give us pictures of specific engagements, particular ships, individual soldiers and sailors. Explanatory summary would give us national strategies, information about the movement of huge armies, about the economics of war, the results of war. Descriptive summary would have us learn about war by having us hear the scream of one shell, the whimper of one man. Depending on the writer and the work, some of this descriptive work might be shifted to the dramatic method, letting us hear two wounded men in a foxhole talking about what it'll be like if they ever get home. The usual method would combine some drama, some description, some explanation.

Descriptive summary uses two descriptive techniques: informative description and suggestive description (shortened here to informative and descriptive).

INFORMATIVE AND SUGGESTIVE DESCRIPTION

Informative description tends toward analysis, lists, numbers, categories. It intends completeness. It allows no interpretation. It presents just the facts. Informative (sometimes called technical) description tells us how the new machine works, never how marvelous an invention it is, nor anything about its probable effects on the future of humankind—certainly nothing about the beauty of the beast. Beauty lies in suggestive description.

Suggestive description prefers incompleteness, favors impressionism. It looks to our imagination for its power. Informative description builds its power upon rock-solid facts, data, logic. Suggestive does not trust facts (it says, "Don't confuse me with facts!"); it prefers the truths of metaphor. Informative distrusts the inaccuracy, the incompleteness, the vagueness of metaphor. Suggestive will not hesitate to interpret the meaning of that described; informative considers interpretation pretentious and beyond its ken. Suggestive says that nothing lies beyond its ken.

The word "suggestive" is used because this kind of description suggests (and only suggests) something to the reader's imagination, enabling the reader to bring to the description his or her own previous similar experiences in order to understand. Informative would not trust the limitations of the reader's memory; it wants understanding, comprehension—and it wants it *now*.

For an example of these two forms of descriptive summary, consider the difference between two descriptions of the same thing. One is an advertisement in the paper listing a cabin to buy:

> Cabin for sale. 20 x 20 log. 1 Bdrm.
> Sm. kitch. FP. 5 ac. Stream. Shed.

Rewriting that informative description into a suggestive description for a letter home to his parents, a young man might write something like this:

Dear Folks:

I'm thinking of buying a terrific log cabin up on the Deerkill River—you know, up near where you used to go back in the old days, Dad. It's got plenty of room downstairs with a bedroom loft up under the slanting log roof. I'll love lying there and looking up at those rough-hewn timbers, thinking about Abe Lincoln and all the other greats (like me) who lived in log cabins. I understand that logs have the highest insulation value of any materials—and they look so great, outside and in. And what a fireplace! I could fit a six-foot Yule log in there next Christmas. And it's got all the fire tools and hooks for hanging pots over the fire and everything. There's this great shed attached to the back, sort of a lean-to, that I can convert into a place for writing. Do you think you could lend me....

Not too many creative nonfiction pieces fall into the informative description category because it is ordinarily too informational, too technical to be "creative." Straight informational writing is rarely used for openings by creative nonfiction writers because it naturally lacks in details, information, and data that which is human, scenic, dramatic, vivid. In "The Best of Everything," in a collection of travel pieces entitled *Journeys,* Jan Morris has found a way, however, to provide us with information set buoyantly afloat on a sea of imagery. It is not purely informative; there's a lot about its description that's suggestive, but it's more informative than suggestive.

On Sunday evening in summer the week-end sailors of Stockholm come streaming home from their sailing grounds in the Baltic peninsula—from Vasholm and Grinda, from Gallno and Djuor and Moja, where the island-jumbled waters of the Swedish coast debouch into the open sea. The sun is glinting then on the golden baubles that ornament the towers and steeples of their city; flags fly bravely from masts and rooftops; and the small boats hasten sun-bleached and purposeful through the harbor, bronzed fathers at the helm, tousled children flat on the deck, like ships of a light flotilla returning from distant action.

Into the Slussen lock the boats jam themselves, watched by the lockkeeper in his glass cabin (TV monitor flickering in its shadows), and with a ponderous movement of steel gates, a swoosh and dripping of water, they are raised from the level of the sea to the level of the lake that lies beyond; and so they disperse into the gathering dusk, away among the myriad creeks of the city, to nose their way into unsuspected canals between apartment blocks, to tie up at private jetties among the trees, or to disappear into the numberless marinas that lie concealed, like so many little naval bases, all over the watery capital.

The technical information she's put in there about Stockholm (the locks, steel gates, TV monitor, numerous marinas) is made more interesting because she's mixed it in attractively with all the more suggestive description. She has combined her informative words with her descriptive words very artistically so that not only do we come away with an excellent image in our minds of a Sunday evening in Stockholm as the weekend sailors come streaming home to harbor, but we also learn many facts (information) about Stockholm as a watery capital. Although the opening does give us factual information, it can't be considered either informative description or technical writing.

Taking a cue from Jan Morris and her enjoyment of Stockholm, I've selected the following opening that's also about Stockholm, from Cynthia Ozick's "Enchantment at First Encounter" (*Sophisticated Traveler,* the *New York Times* supplement). Ozick is better known for her fine fiction, and we can see that influence on the way she presents Stockholm to us. With this excerpt we leave informative description and turn to suggestive description, another technique for applying the descriptive summary method.

One morning in Stockholm, after rain and just before November, a mysteriously translucent shadow began to paint itself across the top of the city. It skimmed high over people's heads, a gauzy brass net, keeping well above the streets, skirting everything fabricated by human arts—though one or two steeples were allowed to dip up into it, like pens filling their nibs with palest ink. It made a sort of watermark over Stockholm, as if a faintly luminous river ran overhead; yet with no more weight or gravity than a vapor.

Since this is an example of suggestive description, we have to accept the mysteriously translucent shadow that paints itself high above Stockholm's streets. We may not be sure just what it is, but we're reasonably sure it's a cloud formation of some kind. We allow the creative nonfiction writer, as we would a poet, to bathe us in beauty. If the intent of the piece were to educate us about meteorological phenomena that visit Stockholm, of course, the writer would be obliged to tell us in no uncertain terms what this mysterious overhead stream is and what its implications are for public health, aircraft safety, etc.

Had Michael Herr written the following excerpt from *Dispatches* about just one night in a single Vietnam battle or about just one location, it could have been called a "dramatic opening," but since it deals with Vietnam scenes in general, it falls into what I've labeled the summary method, using the technique of suggestive description.

> You could watch mortar bursts, orange and gray-smoking, over the tops of trees three and four kilometers away, and the heavier shelling from support bases further east along the DMZ, from Camp Carrol and the Rockpile, directed against suspect troop movements or NVA rocket and mortar positions. Once in a while—I guess I saw it happen three or four times in all—there would be a secondary explosion, a direct hit on a supply of NVA ammunition. And at night it was beautiful. Even the incoming was beautiful at night, beautiful and deeply dreadful.
>
> I remembered the way a Phantom pilot had talked about how beautiful the surface-to-air missiles looked as they drifted up toward his plane to kill him, and remembered myself how lovely .50-calibre tracers could be, coming at you as you flew at night in a helicopter, how slow and graceful, arching up easily, a dream so remote from anything that could harm you. It could make you feel a total serenity, an elevation that put you above death, but that never lasted very long. One hit anywhere in the chopper would bring you back, bitten lips, white knuckles and all, and then you knew where you were.

Certain words and phrases give away the fact that a piece of writing is summary rather than dramatic in form. In the example from

Dispatches, we see phrases like these: "you *could watch*"; "*once in a while—I guess I saw*"; "there *would be* a secondary explosion"; "*I remembered* the way a Phantom pilot"; "coming at you *as you flew*"; "one hit... *would bring* you back".

Although many of these expressions are in past tense, that's not what makes the form summary rather than dramatic. Herr could have written something very dramatic in form and yet have had all the verbs in past tense. The difference is that the dramatic form requires that all the action be in a scene that occurs once and once only—as life's scenes naturally occur. As soon as the writer begins using phrases like "there *would be,*" and "*as you flew,*" we see that the action was actually a series of actions spread over time. The way to write dramatically is to write about one continuous action in essentially one place by essentially the same people. (For more on how to write dramatically, or scene by scene, see Chapter 3.)

The following exemplary writing opens Joan Didion's "Los Angeles Notebook" from her collection of essays, *Slouching Towards Bethlehem.* Of all the better-known creative nonfiction writers, Didion writes some of the best suggestive description (summary method). This essay about the Santa Ana wind of southern California does more than leave us with an image, it creates deep within us a mood.

> There is something uneasy in the Los Angeles air this after-noon, some unnatural stillness, some tension. What it means is that tonight a Santa Ana will begin to blow, a hot wind from the northeast whining down though the Cajon Pass, blowing up sandstorms out along Route 66, drying the hills and the nerves to the flash point. For a few days now we will see smoke back in the canyons, and hear sirens in the night. I have neither heard nor read that a Santa Ana is due, but I know it, and almost everyone I have seen today knows it too. We know it because we feel it. The baby frets. The maid sulks. I rekindle a waning argument with the telephone company, then cut my losses and lie down, given over to whatever is in the air. To live with the Santa Ana is to accept, consciously or unconsciously, a deeply mechanistic view of human behavior.

To further illustrate the distinction between the dramatic and summary methods, I've taken Joan Didion's excellent summary opening to "Los Angeles Notebook" and written it as though she had instead used the dramatic method. The following are my words, not hers. I hesitate to think how beautifully she would have handled the same task. (I should probably slouch off toward Bethlehem.)

"Juanita," she screamed over the machine, "would you please not run the vacuum in the room where I am. I've told you a thousand times—a hundred times today already. It's hot enough outside without that machine blasting hot air on my feet to remind me."

"Si, señora...about the baby."

"What *about* him?"

"He cries in his crib all the time, señora."

"Well, make him stop crying by the time I get back from the airport. That kind of stupid screaming drives his father crazy...and stop sulking. It's bad enough to have one cry-baby around here...."

She helped him tie down the wings and chock the three wheels, working hurriedly to get off the blazing concrete and into the cooler car.

"So, did your writing go well?"

"Are you kidding? What with Juanita sulking around the house, and the baby fretting—and that damned Los Angeles phone company."

"You're still fighting it out with them over that bill? Christ, it was only off by five bucks. You're driving yourself and everybody else nuts over a measly five bucks. Jesus."

"Almost six."

As soon as he got in the car, he turned on *All News Radio*.

"Good afternoon folks. Well, this afternoon is livable, but it'll be a different story later today and for the next few days. Yes, folks, that ol' devil Santa Ana is back. She's blowing in from the northeast following her usual track. So, if you can possibly do so, stay off Route 66, and especially out of Cajon Pass. A listener up that way just called in to warn us that sandstorms are already blasting across the highway—visibility zero. And there's no telling what that'll do to your nice new paint job, or your windshield."

"You know, John, even before I heard the sirens, I knew the Santa Ana was coming. I could feel it deep inside—know what I mean? And then I started behaving stupidly. God, I was so nasty to Juanita—and you know how much I love her. Come on, let's get on home. All I want to do is lie down until dinner's ready. I feel all woolly inside."

I suppose I could have written that better had I used even more words, but I wrote it only to illustrate the difference between approaching the same situation as scene rather than as summary, the method Didion used. The two methods are there for you to use—depending on the particular piece and its purpose—and your relative strengths as a writer. In hands less clever than Joan Didion's, the summary method might not have worked out here as well as it did. In her writing, you can see that the same content can be put across very efficiently and effectively in far fewer words than in descriptive writing. Still, you can see the possibilities of the dramatic method to make the writing involving. Perhaps if "Los Angeles Notebook" had been the opening chapter of a longer book, she would have used the dramatic method. As it was, she was writing a short essay and would never have squandered so many words (as I did) just to begin establishing character and to set a mood.

Didion's summary method (through suggestive description) works so well because of her excellent choice of words, details, and images. Her writing is concrete and suggestive enough that we can form our own scenes on our internal screens. That's the goal—you want to make a passage visual without using a lot of adjectives and without all of the words usually required by the dramatic method.

Nonfiction and fiction writers alike must plan in advance which things might be presented best by scene and which by summary. Since creative nonfiction is typically written scene by scene (dramatically) and since scenes are usually joined (or separated) by passages that use one or more techniques of summary, you need to study and perfect both techniques.

For another look at how various professional writers use suggestive description in their openings, let's read "New York: A

Serendipiter's Journey," an excellent piece by Gay Talese collected in *Fame and Obscurity*. Although you'll find much information about the city, the emphasis is on describing New York City. The summary opening suggests things to our imagination more than it explains what's happening in the city.

> New York City is a city of things unnoticed. It is a city with cats sleeping under parked cars, two stone armadillos crawling up St. Patrick's Cathedral, and thousands of ants creeping on top of the Empire State Building. The ants probably were carried there by winds or birds, but nobody is sure; nobody in New York knows any more about the ants than they do about the panhandler who takes taxis to the Bowery; or the dapper man who picks trash out of Sixth Avenue trash cans; or the medium in the West Seventies who claims, "I am clairvoyant, clairaudient and clairsensuous."
>
> New York is a city for eccentrics and a center for odd bits of information. New Yorkers blink twenty-eight times a minute, but forty when tense. Most popcorn chewers at Yankee Stadium stop chewing momentarily just before the pitch. Gum chewers on Macy's escalators stop chewing momentarily before they get off—to concentrate on the last step. Coins, paper clips, ballpoint pens, and little girls' pocketbooks are found by workmen when they clean the sea lion's pool at the Bronx Zoo.

The explanatory summary type of opening is well used in "Marrakech" by George Orwell. He begins his story with a great amount of descriptive detail that appeals to our imaginative powers. If he had let us hear some of the conversations going on, this excerpt might have been put under what we've called "dramatic openings," but it stands instead as an example of suggestive description summary. Certainly we learn something (informative) about the culture in Marrakech, but Orwell has woven those pieces of information so well into the description itself that we can't call it informative description. The intent of this opening is not to "inform" us, but to coax us into reading on into the third and subsequent paragraphs where he does inform us about the terrible conditions the local people endure.

As the corpse went past, the flies left the restaurant table in a cloud and rushed after it, but they came back a few minutes later.

The little crowd of mourners—all men and boys, no women—threaded their way across the market-place between the piles of pomegranates and the taxis and the camels, wailing a short chant over and over again. What really appeals to the flies is that the corpses here are never put into coffins, they are merely wrapped in a piece of rag and carried on a rough wooden bier on the shoulders of four friends. When the friends get to the burying-ground they hack an oblong hole a foot or two deep, dump the body in it and fling over it a little of the dried-up lumpy earth, which is like broken brick. No gravestone, no name, no identifying mark of any kind. The burying-ground is merely a huge waste of hummocky earth, like a derelict building-lot. After a month or two no one can ever be certain where his own relatives are buried.

As Orwell now goes into paragraph three, he provides us a good example of how a writer will switch from one basic form (suggestive description) to another basic form (general explanation) when he or she considers the opening over.

When you walk through a town like this—two hundred thousand inhabitants, of whom at least twenty thousand own literally nothing except the rags they stand up in—when you see how the people live, and still more how easily they die, it is always difficult to believe that you are walking among human beings. All colonial empires are in reality founded upon that fact....

I've included the beginning of the third paragraph to show that after using suggestive descriptive summary to lure us in, he shifts here into general explanatory summary. Orwell could have started right off with the third paragraph as his opening, but he knew that he could not draw us into the article with these rather dry words of straight explanation. He knew he could make us follow the flies straight into the story, where he wanted us. He had an important message to get across to us readers, and he used flies and corpses as bait. Homely? Yes. Ugly? Effective? Definitely.

GENERAL AND EXPOSITORY EXPLANATION

Two techniques are primarily used in applying the explanatory summary method: general explanation and expository explanation. Expository explanation is at the very end of the dramatic/summary continuum, the least dramatic of all writing. (The relationship between general explanatory and expository writing is analogous to that between suggestive and informative descriptions.)

If you were to write a book on how to write short stories, you'd have to give broad, *general* instructions that would apply to any short story a reader might someday write—this would be *general explanatory* writing. If, on the other hand, you were writing an article about how you wrote your own award-winning short story, you'd not write in a general way; you'd write in a highly specific way about that one particular story—this would be *expository* writing. (You'd be "exposing" for everyone just how you went about writing that terrifically successful story.) Now, if your article went beyond telling how you wrote that story and drew general advice out of it to show just how the reader might go about writing short stories in general, you'd have crossed back over the line into general explanatory writing. General explanation concerns itself with presenting an action. It does so by appealing largely to our imagination.

In "Golden Prague: Travels through a Police State," (*Wall Street Journal,* October 15, 1982) Manuela Hoelterhoff gets our attention by a descriptive first paragraph, and then moves into a general explanatory summary second paragraph. Recall that I make all these labels and categorizations just to give us a way of talking about the variations that exist with what I've labeled overall as "summary." You're not expected to sit down and say to yourself, "I think this calls for an opening that's three-quarters of the way along the summary part of the continuum, somewhere between informative description and general explanatory summary...."

> We still had a kilometer or so to go, but all the welcoming signs were already there...the watchtowers; the closely trimmed meadows that couldn't hide a squadron of relapsed field mice.

We pulled up the car in front of a roadblock manned by glum, baby-faced guards carrying machine guns.

As we now enter the second paragraph in Hoelterhoff's piece, we can see easily that the story has begun. Some might argue that only the first paragraph qualifies as the opening, but my feeling is that the first two paragraphs work indivisibly together to "open" the article for us:

> We'd driven here from Vienna—less than an hour from the border and some 200 miles from Prague, our destination. Straight ahead was what Neville Chamberlain described as "a faraway little land that few of us know anything about." Chamberlain, to be sure, didn't, and as a result, Czechoslovakia became for a few bloody years part of the Nazi empire. Now, of course, thanks to people with similarly informed geopolitical views, the Czechs are tied with cement overshoes to their socialist comrades in the Soviet Union.

The opening to *Landfalls in History,* by Hammond Innes, lives comfortably, and unambiguously, within the labeled walls of general explanatory summary. In these first three paragraphs we find almost no description and little exposition. Almost all of the words "tell" us what the article will be about and how it came to be written. Innes does an extremely fine job of luring us into the article by explanatory writing alone, and this requires writing of high caliber. Many nonfiction writers avoid the straight explanatory opening, fearing that it lacks the power to engage us immediately.

> Some travelers collect country houses; others ecclesiastical buildings, gardens, restaurants. I seem to collect fortresses. And since I have spent quite a slice of my life at sea, mostly with my wife and sailing our own boat, many of these have been sea fortresses on the shores of Europe, vast landmarks that have produced in me a sense of excitement. It is difficult to explain what this means to those who are not sailors. You come across the sea—the Channel, the Mediterranean, even an inland sea like the Marmara—and there is the land. But where is the shelter you are seeking? For many hours perhaps you have been

voyaging on the wind, navigating by the speed at which your sails have driven you through the water, by how the wind and tide and breaking seas have moved you, and you are searching, searching through the glasses, hoping to God you have got it right, that the port you have been aiming for will emerge over the bows.

Then, suddenly, there it is, that huge medieval fortress described as "conspic" in the pilot book, standing there solid and reassuring. Then I feel like Cook or Magellan or those distant Vikings who first sighted Vinland, the sense of discovery as strong as if I had crossed an ocean. I have made it, and there to prove it is the fort guarding the entrance to the port.

As we've seen with some of the other openings, other writers might have had Innes and his wife conversing on deck as they approach a new fort to add to their collection of landfalls made. These writers might also have described the state of the sea, the towering of the clouds, and the blowing of the whales as the form looms on the horizon so pink in the false dawn. If Innes had written his opening like that, depending on the relative amounts of description and explanation used, we might have had to classify it as a suggestive descriptive form of summary opening. As he did write it, this piece perfectly exemplifies the general explanatory form.

It is mostly the dramatic method that distinguishes what this book calls "creative" nonfiction from "traditional" nonfiction. This is not to say that all traditional nonfiction writing is undramatic. The point is that traditional nonfiction writers, journalists in particular, try not to write dramatically, fearing it plays too much on the reader's emotions and tends to distort the facts, or at least a reader's perception of the facts. The creative nonfiction writer does not want to distort the facts either, but tries, through drama and vivid writing, to get the facts across to readers, especially to readers who might otherwise not even read about the subject. Many readers avoid reading for fear of being bored to death by exposition or explanation that lacks the breath of life, that, despite the numerous facts, lacks realism.

3 AUTHORITY THROUGH REALISTIC DETAILS

Thinking back a few pages to Joan Didion's essay about the Santa Ana winds, recall how she brought the scene alive partly by including some specifics, some details about the phenomenon. When, for example, she wrote that the Santa Ana is "a hot wind from the northeast whining down through the Cajon Pass," we begin already to understand it. Just telling us that it's a northeast wind helps us imagine it. When it comes "whining down," we can hear it. When we learn then that it's whining through Cajon Pass, we're there in the pass—whether or not we have any knowledge of that pass. I imagine she could have chosen any number of passes or other ways to tell us where it comes whining down from, but she chose a specific pass—and by selecting Cajon Pass, she did one more bit of "involving" us in the situation. That Spanish-sounding word, Cajon, put me right there in southern California, or into southwest deserts, where I'm sure the winds are hot and whining. Being the excellent writer she is, she couldn't stop putting us even deeper into the picture. She has us experience the wind "blowing up sandstorms out along Route 66...."

From the beginnings of writing, authors have known the value of including details in stories and articles, but today's writers go far beyond what used to be done. Charles Dickens was particularly aware of the value of including concrete details about London's layers of social life, more, perhaps, than anyone before him. His realistic writing affected novelists for many years, but after a while they forgot the importance of realistic detail and turned to writing that was more intellectual, more abstract. With some exceptions, novelists for many years after Dickens wrote primarily from the imagination—almost neglecting the way life really was.

In a sometimes futile attempt to be objective, nonfiction writers and journalists of the past did not include much concrete detail. They most likely were aware that the mere listing of real-life details raised emotions in the reader, emotions they felt would keep the reader from reading objectively. Creative nonfiction writers also realize that the mere listing of concrete details, realistic details, and details of real life, will conjure emotions in the reader—and they include the details for that very reason. They feel that the whole truth has not been told unless the emotional context is there. Both traditional and creative nonfiction writers aim for the same thing—truth, or the accurate portrayal of life. They differ, however, on what truth means and what such accuracy involves: Is a camera lens a more accurate reporter of people, things, and events, or is the human eye, which sees in an emotional context, the best observer of the large and small truths of human existence?

TELLING THE "WHOLE TRUTH"

Emotions inform our understanding all the time. So, to tell the whole truth about most situations that involve people (and most situations do), in the words of Tom Wolfe, we need to "excite the reader both intellectually and emotionally."

The best nonfiction writers do not tell us how we should think about something, how we should feel about it, nor what emotions should be aroused. They simply present the concrete details. The reader's brain, to the extent it has experienced or known something about an exact or similar situation, will be "excited" and the old emotion reexperienced. This squares with what cognitive scientists believe happens in the brain when an experience is about to be stored in the memory. Apparently, various details about the experience are stored along with details of similar, associated, past experiences. When any detail is experienced in the future, the potential for the entire past experience (or experiences) to be recalled is there, including the emotions surrounding the earlier experience. Even the most conscientious and intelligent reader may soon forget the factual content of a piece if the material entered the brain with little emotion wrapped around it. Cognitive research indicates that humans remember best what enters the brain in an envelope of "emotion." If it is true that facts and details are stored along with attendant emotions in a system of cross-files throughout the brain, we writers must recognize it and use it to our advantage.

By "emotion," cognitive scientists mean those feelings we might normally think of as emotions, but they also mean expressions that *imply* emotion—expressions like "terrifyingly hot," rather than "200 degrees Celsius." Unless the precise figure of 200 degrees Celsius (as distinct from 199 degrees Celsius) is significant for the intended reader, "terrifyingly hot" will have more emotional meaning and thus remain longer in the mind.

Too much academic writing ignores this fact, the fact that we humans have not evolved very far from our lower animal predecessors, and thus learn (remember) best any emotion-laden images. In their attempts at objectivity and precision, some of these nonfiction writers think they must avoid interpretive words like "terrifyingly." After all, they reason, to whom is it terrifyingly hot? Not to the scientist, certainly. He or she doesn't think of being terrified by the heat of the autoclave or the molten metal, but is concerned only with recording precisely the temperature observed. If the scientist then writes an article for people unfamiliar with the heat of molten metals, or a nonscientific audience, "terrifyingly hot" will make the point more quickly and even more memorably—the twin goals of such nonfiction writing.

Conversation also provides emotion (in the sense I'm using it here) for an article, making the content more human, more understandable, more memorable. George Will, the Pulitzer Prize–winning columnist, knows how to use conversation to put us right into a situation, conversation that pulls us into "On Her Own in the

City," a *Washington Post* column written in the 1980s about some of the problems growing out of our then present welfare system.

> When police, responding to her call, arrived at her East Harlem tenement, she was hysterical: "The dog ate my baby." The baby girl had been four days old, twelve hours "home" from the hospital. Home was two rooms and a kitchen on the sixth floor, furnished with a rug, a folding chair, and nothing else, no bed, no crib.
> "Is the baby dead?" asked an officer. "Yes," the mother said, "I saw the baby's insides." Her dog, a German Shepherd, had not been fed for five days. She explained: "I left the baby on the floor with the dog to protect it." She had bought the dog in July for protection from human menaces.

The writer grabs our attention immediately with the woman's hysterical, barely articulate words: "The dog ate my baby." And later, "I saw the baby's insides." It would require an almost inhuman reader not to read on, even though it's obviously a grisly story unfolding. Will hopes that by repeating her actual words for us, he'll make us remember this article for some time to come—perhaps long enough to do something about the problems of poverty.

To help a reader fully understand an experience we're writing about, it's necessary to stimulate as many associated memories as possible. Details not only conjure up old memories, they enable us to understand the new idea. We've all experienced the difficulty of communicating a new idea to someone of limited experience. By contrast, it's easy to talk with someone with related past experiences, regardless of their possibly indirect relevance to the one now under discussion. Such a person can take a little something from each of a number of experiences and make them relevant to the present one. This also explains the strength of the metaphor. Of a metaphor, the reader says, in effect, "Oh, I understand…this is the same thing I saw (heard/felt/smelled/experienced) back then. It's not exactly the same, but I can understand better now that I've been reminded of what this is like."

As with so much in writing, caution and good sense are called for. In an attempt to provide an article with realism, a writer may load it up with so much detail that the reader is weighed down under the pressure of so many images. The secret is to use just enough detail to do the trick. But how do you know when enough's enough?

Since no rules exist, you can best get a feel for how much detail is enough by reading the authors quoted in these chapters. The main task is to be selective. Select from all of the details you may have collected, in your mind or in a field notebook, those that either singly or in their cumulative strength present what you consider the essence of the place, person, or whatever you're trying to capture. Sometimes a litany of details will be effective in their cumulative power; sometimes a single detail will suffice; other times, the best method is to weave the details into the description or the narratives as they come up, logically.

Another point to consider in the use of concrete details is in choosing time-sensitive references. In your attempt to make your subject come alive for readers, you might be tempted to use ephemeral details that will have gone out of favor in a few years (or even months) from now, and future readers won't get the point. For example, a certain TV actor and his foibles may be widely known today, but people in the future may not be familiar with the actor. The main piece of advice is to keep your wits about you as you select the details you'll use. If some seem so ephemeral that few people may know about them a year from now, look for other details that seem more long-lasting in their relevance. Even if your reader misses the significance of one or two details, he or she will have enough to work with to figure out your meaning.

Readers of all types and levels seem to need and appreciate concrete details. One difficult problem for nonfiction writers is that of writing for ill-informed readers. All I can say is that if they're poorly informed people, they're going to miss much of what you write anyway, so which concrete details you select seems unimportant. Of course, it is possible that an ill-informed, marginally literate person would be assisted in his or her understanding by the very concreteness of the details we're discussing here.

That last point raises a question difficult to answer: Who will read the creative nonfiction you'll write? The American Society of Journalists and Authors conducted some demographic studies to get a handle on just who were their readers, especially their magazine readers. The study reported that the typical reader of nonfiction magazines, among other characteristics, is about thirty years old; has about a high school education; is probably middle class and holding a blue- or a white-collar job; is most likely married; and has at least one child.

General readers, like those described by the study, are interested in many subjects if they are clearly and vividly expressed, but they're very quick to stop reading an article or ignore writing that doesn't relate directly to their personal concerns or past experiences. If the writing is on a hot topic or is so lively and well written that it captures their attention, general readers will follow even complex topics outside their usual range of interests.

Most journalists would not include the types of details this young reporter did when he wrote this account of an interview he and a female reporter conducted soon after a young Japanese woman and her mother survived an earthquake. Ernest Hemingway was in his early twenties when he wrote this very modern-sounding nonfiction piece for the *Toronto Daily Star* in 1923 (collected in *By-Line: Ernest Hemingway*).

> The door opened one narrow crack. The crack ran from the top of the door to the bottom, and about halfway up it was a very dark, very beautiful face, the hair soft and parted in the middle.
>
> "She is beautiful, after all," thought the reporter. He had been sent on so many assignments in which beautiful girls figured, and so few of the girls had ever turned out to be beautiful.
>
> "Who do you want?" said the girl at the door.
>
> "We're from *The Star*," the reporter said. "This is Miss So and So."
>
> "We don't want to have anything to do with you. You can't come in," the girl said.
>
> "But—" said the reporter and commenced to talk. He had a very strong feeling that if he stopped talking at any time, the

door would slam. So he kept on talking. Finally the girl opened the door.

"Well, I'll let you in," she said. "I'll go upstairs and ask my mother."

By putting us right up close to that crack in the door, Hemingway has involved us. We are no longer newspaper readers, we're on-the-spot observers, even participants, at the interview. He lures us deeper into the story by giving us a tantalizing glimpse of the girl we expect soon to interview. Not only does he break all journalism rules when he tells us what he thought, he tells us a bit, a small bit to be sure, but a bit about his life as a reporter going on other assignments that had promised beautiful girls. Journalists do not usually talk about their lives (particularly not back in 1923). Creative nonfiction writers may, because there are no rules about what the writer may write. Hemingway even quoted himself being interrupted by himself: "But—." This is a very small detail, but we see in it that's just the way life is. We start out with some sentence, and then shift into something different. In other words, by accurately reporting what happened instead of following some journalistic rule, the writer has involved our brains in the scene there on the doorstep. It sounds real.

Here is Hemingway again, this time giving us concrete, realistic details of life in wartime Italy. Nowhere does he tell us what to feel about all this business. He simply lays out all these details—he *shows* us.

> Sometimes in the dark we heard the troops marching under the windows and guns going past pulled by motor tractors. There was much traffic at night and many mules on the roads with boxes of ammunition on each side of their pack-saddles, and gray motor trucks that carried men, and other trucks with loads covered with canvas that moved slower in the traffic. There were big guns too that passed in the day drawn by tractors, the long barrels of the guns covered with green branches and green leafy branches and vines laid over the tractors. To the north we could look across the valley and see a forest of chestnut trees and behind it another mountain on this side of the river.

Although it sounds like nonfiction, this quote is from Hemingway's novel *A Farewell to Arms*. Most of this passage's strength comes from the simple listing of details. Some other writer might not have specified, for example, that the forest across the valley was of chestnut trees, but Hemingway knew the value of the realistic detail. Even though we might not know a chestnut tree forest when we look at one from across a valley, we feel confident that the author knows, and we feel that we're in good hands. That's it. The passage sounds authoritative.

The nonfiction writer also wants to sound authoritative. A sense of authority about a piece gives it credence. (Interesting, isn't it, that the word "author" is embedded in that word "authority.") Anyone with authority has the power to persuade. One way to convey the sense of authority is to use words that not only *are* accurate and real, but that *sound* accurate and real. Given enough of them, we believe the message within. Because realism has an inherent air of authority, writers would be wise to include realistic details, as Hemingway did in the fiction excerpt and in the nonfiction piece about the interview. I enjoy the irony that Hemingway took this technique of realism from his nonfiction writing and used it when he moved into fiction—and here we are now taking this technique from fiction and applying it to nonfiction to gain realism when writing about the real.

We can take a leaf, too, from author Budd Schulberg, as he writes about the famous Stillman's Gym in New York City.

> Americans are still an independent and rebellious people—at least in their reactions to signs. Stillman's Gym, up the street from the Garden, offers no exception to our national habit of shrugging off prohibitions. Hung prominently on the gray, nondescript walls facing the two training rings, a poster reads: "No rubbish or spitting on the floor under penalty of the law." If you want to see how the boys handle this one, stick around until everybody has left the joint and see what's left for the janitor to do. The floor is strewn with cigarettes smoked down to their stained ends, cigar butts chewed to soggy pulp, dried spittle, empty match cases, thumbed and trampled copies of the *News,*

Mirror, and *Journal,* open to the latest crime of passion or the race results, wadded gum, stubs of last night's fight at St. Nick's (manager's comps), a torn-off cover of an Eighth Avenue restaurant menu with the name of a new matchmaker in Cleveland scrawled next to a girl's phone number. Here on the dirty floor of Stillman's is the telltale debris of a world as sufficient unto itself as a walled city of the Middle Ages.

That is Budd Schulberg at work writing not nonfiction, but his novel *The Harder They Fall.* Creative nonfiction writers use this novelistic technique of including realistic, pertinent details all the time. It is a technique that enlivens nonfiction literature. Even though I've never been in such a professional gym, I know from the details Schulberg used just what it must be like. My brain informs my emotional reaction by adding to his details bits of my experience in high school gyms and U.S. Navy locker rooms aboard crowded ships. All of those details piled on details add an air of authority, but none so directly as one detail in particular—"manager's comps." That has to be *truth.* Every reader will find one or more details in there that would persuade him or her that this passage has authority. For me, my belief in that one phrase lent authority to all the other details—I know I'm inside Stillman's Gym— I'm right there and involved in the activities. I'm not looking through the window at the scene inside; I'm at ringside, hearing the leathery thuds and smelling the smells. "Manager's comps" did it for me; "cigar butts chewed to soggy pulp" may do it for someone else.

That business of manager's comps raises some interesting thoughts about the entire matter of details, authority, and realism. Should Budd Schulberg have interrupted his flow by explaining that these are manager's complimentary tickets? How much explanation about jargon or other specialized language is a writer obliged to provide? I admit that I didn't know what manager's comps are, yet here I am claiming that the phrase "did it" for me. How can that be? A writer should give enough details of various kinds that most readers will pick up on one or more, and live with the fact that no matter how much he or she explains, someone out there is not going to understand one point or another.

It comes down to intent. What is the writer's intention? If it's an educational book or article, he or she must be reasonably certain that nothing important or significant goes unexplained. If the purpose is to both inform and entertain, as is most often the case with creative nonfiction, the writer should presume a certain amount of intelligence and experience on the reader's part. The writer wants to make points clearly, yet to make them with flair, and doesn't want to be forever explaining.

All I've said about how I was persuaded by manager's comps, even though I didn't understand what they are, should not be interpreted to mean that it doesn't matter whether the writer's words are accurate, provided that the words "sound" real. Don't invent terms to "sound" authoritative. Use specialists' jargon to lend authority, but don't feel obliged to explain it. When you're uncertain about whether to explain, ask yourself this key question: Does the reader really need to know this to understand my piece? If not, consider keeping the jargon or special language (for example, the occasional foreign phrase). After all, your purpose may be to develop mood or to give the essence of a place or a person, and explanation could detract or reduce impact.

Before moving on to examples of how nonfiction writers use concrete details to lend authority to their articles and books, I want to point out an interesting parallelism that went on within the writing world. Many short story writers, like Raymond Carver, were producing what they call "realistic" writing. Their method is to write in a minimal way, largely providing the facts of a situation and accurate reporting on what people do. What it all means is left up to the reader to figure out. The writer does not tell us the meaning, nor what emotions to feel, nor what emotions the characters are feeling. All of this is left to the reader's brain, to add its details from personal experience to what's happening in the story, thereby bringing to the story the emotions the reader felt in the original experience. Like a haiku, this kind of writing requires an intelligent, experienced reader for it to achieve in the reader's brain an emotion as close as possible to what the writer experienced originally.

Carver wrote with great attention to realistic details, down to a person's smallest moves. I've included this short discussion of Raymond Carver's fiction writing because his use of so many realistic details is similar to creative nonfiction writing. Carver took realistic details to the ultimate level, one that nonfiction writers should probably not emulate. But creative nonfiction writers could study Carver's use of details to create a feeling of being there. The following section is from "Furious Seasons," a short story from the collection by the same name.

> He fumbled in the closet for his insulated boots, his hands tracing the sleeves of each coat until he found the rubber slick waterproof. He went to the drawer for socks and long underwear, then picked up his shirt and pants and carried the armload through the hallway into the kitchen before turning on the light. He dressed and pulled on his boots before starting the coffee. He would have liked to turn on the porch light for Frank but somehow it didn't seem good with Iris out there in bed. While the coffee perked he made sandwiches and when it had finished he filled a thermos, took a cup down from the cupboard, filled it, and sat down near a window where he could watch the street. He smoked and drank the coffee and listened to the clock on the stove, squeaking. The coffee slopped over the cup and the brown drops ran slowly down the side onto the table. He rubbed his fingers through the wet circle across the rough table top.

Hunter S. Thompson is another master of the telling detail. In his book *Hell's Angels* he recalls this scene about when the gang he's riding with (for his research work) was confronted by a man working for the local sheriff:

> Luckily, my garb was too bastard for definition. I was wearing Levi's, Wellington boots from L.L. Bean in Maine, and a Montana sheepherder's jacket over a white tennis shirt. The burr-haired honcho asked me who I was. I gave him my card and asked why he had that big pistol on his belt. "You know why," he said. "The first one of these sonsabitches that gives me

any lip I'm gonna shoot right in the belly. That's the only language they understand." He nodded toward Mohr in the phone booth, and there was nothing in his tone to make me think I was exempted. I could see that his pistol was a short-barreled Smith & Wesson .357 Magnum—powerful enough to blow holes in Mohr's BSA cylinder head, if necessary—but at arm's length it hardly mattered.

Details like Levi's and Wellingtons from L.L. Bean help lend authority to the scene, but I could have invented those even though I have no knowledge whatsoever about motorcycle gangs. When the honcho spoke, I didn't just hear him, I saw him. Those were the words I'd expect him to say, but I might have invented those words, too. When Thompson mentioned the .357 Magnum (which I might have come up with, too) he went on to describe it as short barreled and furthermore that it was made by Smith & Wesson. That did it. I was in his power. Now, I'm just reasoning *ex post facto* about what my unconscious was doing, but I know I ended up seeing that scene, hearing that burr-haired lummox, and seeing the hugeness of the opening in the barrel of that Smith & Wesson. I note, too, that he's absolutely correct—Smith & Wesson *does* have an ampersand in it. It's not Smith "and" Wesson. Had the author not done his research (in this case, field research), he would not have had that little ampersand in there, and that would have lessened his credibility in the mind of anyone knowledgeable about pistols. (Someone out there always knows more than the writer about something.) As if he didn't already have me, Thompson threw in that business about a cylinder head—a BSA cylinder head yet. *That's* writing.

MASTERING THE TELLING DETAIL

Richard Rhodes, author of *Looking for America* and *Ultimate Powers,* wrote the following in his first book, *The Inland Ground.* In the midst of a section entitled "Death All Day," he wrote this description of one of the men going with him on a hunt for coyotes with his other friend's dogs.

The other third of our party is Ron Nolan, an Ohio boy who overcame New York a few years back to homestead a two-room cabin in the woods outside Kansas City. His cabin contains an Italian racing motorcycle, a KLH-20, plus Stereo, a wall of books, tennis rackets, board games, a hookah, rifles, pistols, a Beretta Golden Snipe .12-gauge over-and-under shotgun, a Pacific shotshell reloader, and outside a golden sand Jaguar XKE convertible and for short hauls an aging Morris Oxford station wagon, likely the only one in the Midwest. Ron is a bachelor.

The quality of these objects that fill Ron's cabin certainly paints a picture for me of a probably young man with more money that anybody needs—and I'd rather learn it this way than have the author tell me this was Ron's economic condition. All of the details did their job, but I was pulled in solidly by that hookah, a Pacific shotshell reloader, and by his specifying that the Jaguar was a golden sand color—especially after hearing earlier about a Golden Snipe. I don't know that the author intended to have these golden references add to the generally affluent scene. (I am sure, however, the advertising executives knew of it when they named the Jaguar and the Beretta.) Over- and undertones of gold never hurt a shotgun sale. As a married man with no hope of a golden sand Jag, I appreciated particularly that short, emphatic sentence—"Ron is a bachelor."

John McPhee wrote in the November 26, 1985 issue of the *New Yorker* about the workaday world of a Maine warden-pilot with the unlikely name of John McPhee. As one of the acknowledged masters of the telling detail, the writer McPhee described a flying trip he took with the warden McPhee to check on men ice fishing within the warden's jurisdiction.

Brown's Point is actually the delta of a small stream that enters the lake beside the hangar and spews nutrients to crowds of waiting fish. Boats collect in the summer; and as soon as the lake is hard, fishing shacks arrive and remain through the winter. Fishing shacks tend to be heated, furnished, closer to civilization, close to paved and numbered roads—shantytowns platted on ice, and clustered where fish are likely to be. In architectural style, at Brown's Point, they range from late-middle Outhaus to the Taj Pelletier, a ten-piece portable cabin with nearly a hundred square feet of floor space, red-curtained windows, cushioned benches, a Coleman stove, a card table, a hi-fi spilling country music, and hinged floorboards that swing upward to reveal eight perfect circles in the ice through which lines can be dangled from cup hooks in the ceiling. If the air outside is twenty below zero, the air inside will be a hundred degrees warmer, while the men in shirtsleeves interrupt their cribbage to lift into the room a wriggling salmon.

McPhee, the author, had me in his thrall, as usual, after only a few sentences, largely by his creative use of telling details. As I looked back at my experience of reading this paragraph, I found that the details were orchestrated to involve me more and more as I went. I may have been slightly involved when I read that the shack came in ten pieces and that it was nearly a hundred square feet, but when I got to the red curtains, I was suddenly there. When I read about those curtains, I had the feeling of seeing the lamp come on in the shack and some rose-colored light coming through those curtains. The cushioned benches (not chairs) made sense to me and added to the realism of my vicarious experience, but when those hinged floorboards swung up, making me step to one side, I was right there in that strange environment. I was truly hooked, though, by those cup hooks. *Cup hooks.* Never in a million years would I have been able to invent that detail. This had the ring of truth—no, this *was* truth. This was real(ism).

Similarly, Thomas H. Rawles in his *Small Places: In Search of a Vanishing America* included many concrete details, such as names of equipment, to lend authority to his writing and to provide an up-close look at his subject's life.

Parker pulls the Power Wagon in next to the barn and parks beside the new logging winch that he will be using in future timber harvests. He will hook it up to a recently acquired 57-horsepower, four-wheel-drive Belarus tractor. New, the Soviet workhorse cost him less than $7,000, probably a third of what it would have cost him to buy green or blue or red—John Deere,

Ford, Case/International. Parker admits to having a conservative nature; he dislikes debt. His wife says, "I'm frequently the risk taker. He is so practical, so down to earth. I jostle his steadiness." She urged him to get the tractor.

Greta Tilley demonstrates further the versatility of using concrete details as technique in her February 7, 1982 piece, "A Suicide at Age 16." A feature writer for the *Greensboro News and Record,* she took on what has to be one of the most challenging subjects to write about—teenage suicide. With such an emotion-laden subject, the writer does not want to make an obvious attempt to evoke the reader's emotions, or it becomes a sob story.

> Seven weeks have passed, yet the dim lavender room with the striped window curtains has been kept as Tonja kept it. Haphazardly positioned on top of the white French Provincial-style dresser are staples of teen-age life: Sure deodorant, Enjoli cologne, an electric curling wand.
>
> A white jewelry box opens to a ballerina dancing before a mirror. Inside, among watches and bracelets, is a gold Dudley High School ring with a softball player etched into one side and a Panther on the other. Also inside was a mimeographed reminder that a $9 balance must be paid in Mrs. Johnson's room for the 1982 yearbook. The deadline was Jan. 15.

There's no need to analyze this, item by pathetic item. It's enough to say that we would all recognize from the listing a teenage girl's dresser, and more important, the interests, the excitements, the life of a teenage person. Even if a reader's experience has been only with a teenage boy's dresser top, there's enough carryover to evoke appropriate emotion.

Leaving this sad story, let's leap across the world to mainland China to note how Annie Dillard, in *Encounters with Chinese Writers,* uses concrete details to put us right beside her on the outskirts of a city. She had made the point earlier on the page that China must depend for most of its food on millions of square miles of terrible soil, soil so dense with clay that China's labor-intensive agricultural system is reflected by actual fingerprints in the soil.

Driving to this meeting we saw fields on the outskirts of the city, and patches of agriculture. There was a field of eggplant. Separating the rows of eggplants were long stripes of dried mud, five inches high, like thick planks set on edge. These low walls shield shoots and stems from drying winds. We stopped to look. The walls were patted mud; there were fingerprints. There were fingerprints dried into the loess wall around every building in the western city of Xian. There were fingerprints in the cones of drying mud around every tree's roots in large afforestation plots near Hangzhou, and along the Yangtze River. There is good soil in China, too, on which peasants raise three and even four crops a year, and there are 2,000-acre fields, and John Deere tractors—but there is not enough.

In addition to many examples of good writing here, like the alliteration of "walls shield shoots and stems" and the strikingly accurate simile of thick planks set on edge, we find author Dillard pulling down close to the good earth for some close-up views of five-inch-high walls—all in preparation for us to see those peasant fingerprints. I could see a master writer at work when she deliberately chose the verb "patted" to prepare our minds to readily accept the image of fingerprints. I find, too, within that accurate verb, the immediate understanding that this is indeed labor-intensive agriculture, and that the peasant may pat this mud with some care—though perhaps I'm too romantic. In any event, the verb "pat" did what its author probably intended: It prepared the way for the fingerprints.

The cones of mud around every tree's roots gave some authority to this paragraph, because that's not agriculture the way we experience it here, but what clinched it for me was the surprising arrival on the scene of that symbol of American agribusiness, the John Deere tractor. Now I knew I was in the hands of not only a capable writer but one with the authority that comes with knowledge, knowledge of the details. John Deere, indeed—wow.

To wrap up for the moment this discussion of realism (although the entire book could be said to deal with it), let's hear a description of the Great Depression written by the man who helped bring this economic phenomenon to the nation's conscience with his novel *The Grapes of Wrath*. Nothing could have been more real for the people who experienced it, but for those who came later, its description needs words that recapture that reality. John Steinbeck did a great service in that regard with his various fictional writings of that era, but what follows comes from a nonfiction article he wrote in the October 1973 *Esquire* entitled, "A Primer on the Thirties."

> The Depression was no financial shock for me. I didn't have any money to lose, but in common with millions I did dislike hunger and cold. I had two assets. My father owned a tiny three-room cottage in Pacific Grove in California, and he let me live in it without rent. That was the first safety. Pacific Grove is on the sea. That was the second. People in inland cities in the closed and shuttered industrial cemeteries had greater problems than I. Given the sea a man must be very stupid to starve. That great reservoir of food is always available. I took a large part of my protein food from the ocean. Firewood to keep warm floated on the beach daily, needing only handsaw and ax. A small garden of black soil came with the cottage. In northern California you can raise vegetables of some kind all year long. I never peeled a potato without planting the skins. Kale, lettuce, chard, turnips, carrots and onions rotated in the little garden. In the tide pools of the bay mussels were available and crabs and abalones and that shiny kelp called sea lettuce. With a line and pole, blue cod, rock cod, perch, sea trout, sculpin could be caught.

I've read other articles about life in the Depression that purported to tell what it was like, but they would typically say something like "People lived wherever they could find a roof; they'd grow some food if they could; and those near the sea would fish." Somehow, Steinbeck knew it was not enough to say simply that they would burn driftwood to keep warm. He added that all you needed was a handsaw and ax. These two simple, homely words added reality for me. I could see Steinbeck wandering the beach near Pacific Grove, saw in hand, ax on shoulder. I liked, too, the specificity of the *black* soil. It sounded like rich soil that could grow all those vegetables, with several crops a year. I was very young during the Depression, but I do remember chard—and I seem to recall that only near-starvation would make me turn to chard. It was the mention of chard here, however, that lent authority to everything else. As a man from Milton, Massachusetts, my brain couldn't make direct contact with those abalones, but it knew chard—oh, it knew chard.

Some creative nonfiction writers bend over backward not to tell readers what meaning they should take from their words, but they do it anyway through the realistic details they select to tell the story. All writing involves selection, as everything can't be said. Whether the writing is an essay, an article, or a book, some things rather than others are singled out for mention. That which is singled out is considered more important to the author than what was left out. The overall impression created by this selection constitutes the writer's style, meaning, or individual truth.

As a writer, you cannot avoid giving yourself away in this fashion, and you shouldn't try. Rather, you should try to reveal only true things which you feel are important, and to arrange them in relationships that reflect what you believe to be the meaning, the truth, of whatever subject you're considering. A laundry list of landmarks and dates is no less a true picture of New York than a representative slice-of-life description of what one might see at Broadway and 42nd between 1:00 and 6:00 in the morning. But they're not the same truth, the same vision. The key word here is "representative."

What is representative is what the author presents as representative. The writer's reliability rests in how able he or she is to persuade us that the representation is fair—that it is accurate and illuminating to the whole, not distorted or fabricated, but honest in the impression it creates.

If the selection of event and detail is good, it won't need much commentary from the author to show what it means. The process of selection and arrangement should do that. Excessive commentary is intrusive overkill. It's like a comic telling the audience how funny a joke is going to be. You don't want to be told—if it's funny, you'll laugh. If it's not, being told how funny the comic thought it would be isn't any help at all. The writer should show, rather than tell, as much as he or she can, and let the selection and combination of details speak for themselves as much as possible. Describing his final preparations to rediscover America by hiking along the Appalachian Trail, Bill Bryson wrote in *A Walk in the Woods*:

> I ended up with enough equipment to bring full employment to a vale of sherpas—a three-season tent, self-inflating sleeping pad, nested pots and pans, collapsible eating utensils, plastic dish and cup, complicated pump-action water purifier, stuff sacks in a rainbow of colors, seam sealer, patching kit, sleeping bag, bungee cords, water bottles, waterproof poncho, waterproof matches, pack cover, a rather nifty compass/thermometer keyring, a little collapsible stove that looked frankly like trouble, gas bottle and spare gas bottles, a hands-free flashlight that you wore on your head like a miner's lamp (this I liked very much), a big knife for killing bears and hillbillies, insulated long johns and undershirts, four bandannas, and lots of other stuff, for some of which I had to go back again and ask what it was for exactly. I drew the line at buying a designer groundcloth at $59.95, knowing I could acquire a lawn tarp at Kmart for $5. I also said no to a first-aid kit, sewing kit, anti-snake-bite kit, $12 emergency whistle, and small orange plastic shovel for burying one's poop, on the grounds that these were unnecessary, too expensive or invited ridicule. The orange spade in particular seemed to shout, "Greenhorn! Sissy! Make way for Mr. Buttercup!"

WRITING SCENE BY SCENE

In addition to all of the other methods creative nonfiction writers use to achieve a high level of realism, they tend also to walk readers through a story scene by scene. In traditional journalism, the basic building block was the fact. Reporters rushed around collecting facts from dusty records at City Hall, interviewing experts, and talking with the people involved. Facts piled on facts, interview quotes stacked on interview quotes. All of this took place in the name of accuracy, completeness, and objectivity—certainly not in the name of readability or memorability. Creative nonfiction writers, by contrast, remain as respectful of facts. They usually have the time to dig up far more facts about a story than do deadline-haunted reporters, but they don't think of them as the basic building blocks for their stories; they "think scenes" instead.

The scene is the dramatic element in fiction and creative nonfiction. The scene is the fundamental block around which the writer forms the story. A story usually has a number of scenes, and the method best used in creative nonfiction is to develop the story scene by scene. A scene reproduces the movement of life; life is motion, action.

In creative nonfiction you almost always have the choice of writing the summary (narrative) form, the dramatic (scenic) form, or some combination of the two. Because the dramatic method of writing provides the reader with a closer imitation of life than summary ever could, creative nonfiction writers frequently choose to write scenically. The writer wants vivid images to transfer into the mind of the reader; after all, the strength of scenic writing lies in its ability to evoke sensual images. A scene is not some anonymous narrator's report about what happened some time in the past; instead, it gives the feeling that the action is unfolding before the reader. A scene makes the past present. The reader sees the characters in action, sees their gestures, hears their voices in conversation. Their participation (involvement) in the story is greater. The reader can't take part in a summary narrative; as readers of narrative, we're just students in a room listening to a lecture. As soon as we see the scene, we feel it, smell it, hear it, and believe, for the moment, that we're in it.

The main point behind writing scene by scene is that since the brain is "involved" in the scenes, it more readily accepts the narrative information. As in fiction, in creative nonfiction you can use scenes to do certain narrative work. A lot of characterization, for example, can be smuggled into a scene through captured conversation.

By little bits of narrative prose stealthily slipped in around conversation, you can reveal, for example, some of the characters' physical characteristics—hairstyles, beards, kinds of eyes. If the bits remain short and scattered, the reader doesn't hear the narrator's voice intruding and remains involved in the scene. Where narrative summary must be used, try to have a main character, or some character, provide the summary statement through a quote, direct or indirect. The reader more readily accepts the words of a character than those of the narrator. Even an indirect quote can retain the voice of the character, and give the reader a continued sense of participation in the scene—or at least give the reader the feeling of observing the scene firsthand, instead of through the eyes of the narrator.

As you plan a story, consider the events, incidents, or happenings with the most dramatic potential. Which scenes have the best visual, imagistic potential? These become your inventory of possible scenes—all else must be handled through narrative summary.

As in fiction, certain events typically have great dramatic potential. Watch for:

turning points	*showdowns*	*arguments*
flashbacks	*disasters*	*hardships*
successes	*failures*	*life reversals*
beginnings	*births*	*deaths*

However, don't overlook the potential of small, seemingly insignificant incidents that you can work up into a scene to use for your narrative purposes. There is a place for content and a place for method. The content of a scene may be simple (not very dramatic), but the scenic method makes it come alive for us. The following passage from Russell Baker's memoir, *Growing Up,* is an "insignificant" scene that serves as a wonderful example of the scenic method. Note that this scene has none of the typical captured conversation, but the concrete details make it form tactile, visual, and auditory images in our brains.

Before this passage, Russell Baker has pointed out that when he was a child, the outermost edge of his universe was Brunswick, Virginia, "as distant and romantic a place as I ever expected to see." When his father took him on a trip to Brunswick to see three of Russell's uncles, he discovered that the city had electric lightbulbs, telephones, radios. "Rich people lived there. Masons, for heaven's sake. Not just Red Men and Odd Fellows and Moose such as we had around Morrisonville, but Masons. And not just Masons, but Baptists, too...." When they visited his Uncle Tom, the blacksmith, young Russell fell in love with a miracle in a small room.

> At the top of the stairs lay the miracle of plumbing. Shutting the door to be absolutely alone with it, I ran my fingers along the smooth enamel of the bathtub and glistening faucet handles of the sink. The white majesty of the toilet bowl, through which gallons of water could be sent rushing by the slightest touch of a silvery lever, filled me with envy. A roll of delicate paper was placed beside it. Here was luxury almost too rich to be borne by anyone whose idea of fancy toiletry was Uncle Irvey's two-hole privy and a Montgomery Ward catalog.
>
> After gazing upon it as long as I dared without risking interruption by a search party, I pushed the lever and savored the supreme moment when thundering waves emptied into the bowl and vanished with a mighty gurgle. It was the perfect conclusion to a trip to Brunswick.

Imagine that written as narrative summary by someone other than Russell Baker, someone who didn't appreciate the dramatic potential of a boy seeing his first indoor bathroom: *He was impressed to discover that unlike Uncle Irvey's, Uncle Tom's bathroom had running water. He enjoyed listening to the water rushing down into the toilet bowl. The delicate paper next to the bowl was a far cry from the Montgomery Ward catalog in the two-hole privy he was used to at home.* The words accomplish essentially the same narrative work but miss the potential to involve us in the experience and see it through the boy's eyes—no drama. Since no conversation went on in either passage, the difference lies in the concreteness of the details and the sensory content of Baker's. His writing is vivid; it has the stuff of life in it. Mine was merely reporting the facts; his was drawing a scene, reporting the drama inherent in a minor incident.

THE SCENE AND ITS VALUE

J. Anthony Lukas writes with a clear understanding of the value of writing scene by scene. In his book *Common Ground,* most of the chapters center on one of the three families (Diver, Twymon, or McGoff). Lukas introduces the families in three short opening chapters, beginning each chapter with the scene when a member of the family first hears about the assassination of the Reverend Martin Luther King, Jr.

Chapter 1/Diver

Sunlight struck the gnarled limbs outside his windows, casting a thicket of light and shadow on the white clapboards. From his desk high under the eaves, Colin Diver could watch students strolling the paths of Cambridge Common or playing softball on the neatly trimmed diamond. It was one of those brisk afternoons in early spring, the kind of day which in years past had lured him into the dappled light, rejoicing in his good fortune. But here he lurked in his study, walled in by books, overcome by doubt.

Chapter 2/Twymon

An hour after the transistor radio in the project had blared the news of King's death, Snake and Sly (Twymon) were out on Eustis Street slinging rocks at the police. Around the corner on Dearborn Street, someone had thrown a brick through a grocery store window and every few minutes a kid would scamper across, grab a juicy grapefruit or a handful of plums, then dash to safety in the jiving black crowd.

Chapter 3/McGoff

It was the moment she liked best, the vegetables spread out before her in voluptuous profusion: squeaky stalks of celery, damp lettuce, succulent tomatoes, chilled radishes. From the sink rose the earthy smells of wet roots and peels, and from all about her the clamor and fracas of a busy kitchen, gearing up for dinner only minutes away.

Mark Patinkin, writing under deadline pressures for the *Providence Journal-Bulletin* in 1985, sent back from Africa some of the most touching stories about life in the drought-stricken areas. His articles captured the pathos through dramatic, often scene-by-scene writing. In "They Flee from Hunger but Keep Their Humanity," he writes of life within a refugee camp containing 55,000 men, women, and children at the point of terminal starvation.

> We walked on, into one of the hospital units. I paused by a father and son. The son lay in the father's arms. The father called softly to the son.
>
> I turned to the doctor. "That child looks bad," I said.
>
> The doctor bent over for a closer look. "He died during the night," he said.
>
> Back outside, the sun hit the mountains with a beauty that made me stop and stare. We moved toward the more hopeful side of the camp. A hundred fires were going. The day's cooking had begun, with the last of the wood. This was not a secret place. The whole camp knew this was where the limited food supply was prepared. And no one bothered it.
>
> "I still find it hard to understand," said the doctor.
>
> He had long since been able to pull the curtain down on the tragedies of this place. The one thing he could not get used to was the decency.

Patinkin saw in this small incident (small in terms of all he was witnessing throughout Africa) the potential for drama, drama small enough for the reader to comprehend and become involved in. The overall scene happening to 55,000 people cannot get to our emotions the way a father holding his dead son can. That scene stands, in a sense, for the thousands of similar "minor" incidents happening to these starving refugees. It's meaningful...representative, and therefore, realistic.

4 🌿 THE REALITIES OF GROUP LIFE

Creative nonfiction writers invest their articles and books with the feeling of real life, life as it's lived, not as we think it might be, or should be, but as close as possible to the various realities that exist simultaneously in this world. One of the most effective techniques for accomplishing this is the inclusion of details. Since most creative nonfiction deals with men and women, writers pay particular attention to how people live, not in the abstract, but in the everyday world. Now, you may be thinking, "Don't all nonfiction writers write the truth about the people they're discussing? Do journalists lie?" No, they don't lie; they all believe they're talking about real people and would never agree that they speak in the abstract about people—but many do. They've been trained that way in college and on the job.

Until fairly recently, for example, most newspaper and magazine writers would never quote someone swearing or blaspheming—their words would either be shown with censoring dashes or dots, and only the more "civilized" words would be quoted. If the writer wanted, nevertheless, to write truthfully, he or she would be limited to saying that the man swore and blasphemed outrageously (now, that's writing in the abstract!). If a prisoner on his way to the cell raised his middle finger at the reporters, it would likely have been reported that he gestured obscenely. This is not being realistic. We know that every person from grammar school on probably knows this obscene gesture and may even have used it. The creative nonfiction writer should report the concrete details, *les petits vrais* (the little truths), of the realities of group life. Concrete details include gestures and curses; sports and games; fashion and food fads; religious activities; the trappings of professions; where and how the people live; and bits of their captured conversations.

In the October 1983 *Sophisticated Traveler* section of the Sunday *New York Times,* William F. Buckley, Jr. wrote about the advantages of cruising the Caribbean in a chartered yacht rather than traveling commercially. All you have to do to make the weekly charter costs is to share the yacht with two other couples.

> I confess I have not been aboard a commercial cruising boat during the conventional one or two weeks in the Caribbean. Probably there is much to be said for this way of seeing the islands, in preference to hotel life. But your very own boat is really the way to go, and one might as well quickly confront the proposition, "Isn't this out of the question for the average pocketbook?" The answer is: Yes. But so is a week aboard any of the more luxurious liners or a week at any of the fancier hotels. In round figures—if you include meals, drinks, tips, taxis—you are talking about something over $400 per couple a day, times seven comes to—well, close to $3,000 a week. Last Christmas we chartered a boat that cost $1,000 a day, including food but not drinks, tips or taxies. Throw these in even profusely, and you are still short of $9,000 a week. But there are three couples sharing the boat, so that the cost, for each couple—less than $3,000—is comparable to the hotels.

These matter-of-fact words about the costs of yachts, taxis, and tips give us an immediate, realistic impression of life as lived by the wealthy. It's the straightforwardness of the discussion that makes it real for us. Buckley doesn't apologize for, or seem embarrassed by, these high figures. He doesn't compare or contrast that lifestyle with how the rest of us live on vacation. He just says what he wants to say to his audience through accurate and precise details.

When Annie Dillard traveled with the Chinese writers she recorded in *Encounters with Chinese Writers,* some vignettes of life in China that stay with the readers, first because of her accuracy of observation, and second because of her willingness and ability to put them down just as experienced—not after first putting the thoughts through some kind of ideological pasta machine. My impression is that she writes of the real.

> In the cities, where incomes are five times those in the country, families are saving industrial coupons for years on end to buy a bicycle, or to buy a sewing machine with which to fashion both clothes and bedding from their cotton allotment of six yards per person per year. The family lives in its one or two cement rooms. The wife washes the twigs and stones from the rationed rice and cooks some cabbage on a shared stove. Six days a week the husband and wife put in long hours in their production units; the wife spends two hours a day buying food. On Sundays they bring the baby home from the nursery school, where one-third of Beijing's babies live. They all dress up and go to the park, which has several plots of flowers.

The writer impressed me by how much I learned about China in so short a paragraph. I can imagine some other writer faced with giving basically the same amount of information, but being unable to put it down simply. Such compression (while retaining some gracefulness of expression) could only be accomplished through such conscientious attention to those details that said something directly about life at that place at that time. She didn't, for example, contrast that twig- and stone-laced rice with Americans' snow-white, pure rice; there was no discussion about the comparative nutrient value of the two rices and no long political explanation of "rationed rice"—just the plain, clearly expressed images of what she saw and heard. She took me with her when she ended on the quiet irony that this park for which everyone dressed up has but several plots of flowers.

Novelist Sara Davidson has also published articles in many of the magazines that appreciate creative nonfiction writing: *Harper's, Esquire, Rolling Stone,* and *Ms.* In *Real Property,* a book that presents many of these articles, she includes the following piece about group life in Venice, California, the closest place to downtown L.A. where you can live on the beach—and the only place in that giant, spread-out city where there's real life in the street. As she says in that book, "You are guaranteed to see people outside their cars." Here's part of her presentation of life in Venice.

> Living in Venice is like living in a camp for semi-demented adults. At every hour, day and night, there are people playing volleyball, running, rolling on skates, riding bikes, skateboards, surf boards, flying kites, drinking milk, eating quiche lorraine. Old people sit under umbrellas playing checkers. Body builders work out in a sandy pen, and crowds line up three deep to perform on the paddle tennis courts. When do these people work? I used to wonder.
>
> The residents of Venice fall into two groups. Those who work, and those who don't. The latter includes senior citizens, drifters, drug addicts, hopeful moviemakers and aging hippies and surfers who have made a cult of idleness and pleasure. The other groups includes lawyers, dentists, real estate brokers, accountants. Many are workaholics, attached to their jobs as they are to nothing else. They work nights and weekends, eat fast food while driving to and from their work and live alone, longing, in the silence before falling asleep, for connection.
>
> Everyone comes together on the boardwalk. The natives own their own skates, and the tourists rent them from places like "Cheapskates" and "United Skates of America."

I like the way Sara Davidson lured me into the paragraph by saying that Venice is "a camp for semi-demented adults." I couldn't resist reading on to learn what she meant (or half-meant). She didn't *tell* me in some sociological fashion, she *showed* me these adults riding their skateboards, flying their kites, and drinking their milk (what a delightful surprise). As I read that paragraph, I began to wonder how all these adults could be out playing around, seemingly all the time—and then she answered me. A sociologist would never do it, but a creative nonfiction writer can do it—divide the population into just two groups, those who work and those who don't. I found it particularly good writing to then bring these divided groups together again—on the famous boardwalk where girls in sequined tube tops skate gracefully in and out of the slower pedestrian traffic. My memory even served up a commercial that showed a young woman on skates delivering soft drinks to customers along that boardwalk—another example of how, when concrete details are used, the reader's memory will supply bits and pieces of relevant information to make more understandable the new information it is receiving. Someone else will not dredge up that same commercial; they'll dredge up the handsome man who graced a roller rink in Fort Wayne at a church outing ten years ago. Such is the combined power of concrete details and the brain for achieving realism.

FILLING IN THE BLANKS

Dr. Loren Eiseley wrote about anthropology and other sciences so that the well-educated nonspecialists could understand him. Like Dr. Lewis Thomas, the medical researcher, Eiseley wrote clearly and persuasively about sophisticated topics. These eminent scholars were able to go beyond so-called sophistication and come back to what I consider true sophistication—writing that's clear, interesting, witty, and graceful. They usually wrote on serious topics which, in other hands, might put the reader to sleep. In the following excerpt from his book *The Night Country*, Eiseley writes about the elderly poor and ill who live in the railroad terminals of many major cities. He compares them to dying old brown wasps he's observed in midwinter. Like them, these old folks prefer to die in the center of things, not somewhere in lonely isolation.

Now and then they sleep, their old gray heads resting with painful awkwardness on the backs of the benches.

Also they are not at rest. For an hour they may sleep in the gasping exhaustion of the ill-nourished and aged who have to walk in the night. Then a policeman comes by on his rounds and nudges them upright.

"You can't sleep here," he growls.

A strange ritual then begins. An old man is difficult to waken. After a muttered conversation the policeman presses a coin in his hand and passes fiercely along the benches prodding and gesturing toward the door. In his wake, like birds rising and settling behind the passage of a farmer through a cornfield, the men totter up, move a few paces and subside once more upon the benches.

One man, after a slight, apologetic lurch, does not move at all. Tubercularly thin, he sleeps on steadily. The policeman does not look back. To him, too, this has become a ritual. He will not have to notice it again officially for another hour.

Once in a while one of the sleepers will not awake. Like the brown wasps, he will have had his wish to die in the great droning center of the hive rather than in some lonely room....

Perhaps the most important point to take from this particular image of group life is that Eiseley does not lecture us about the plight of these poor, feeble old folks. He simply paints for us a realistic (though impressionistic) picture of the policeman making his round, and the responses (and nonresponses) of those who huddle on those hard benches. Because he doesn't clutter up his writing with excess words, we can see the gray old heads tilted back against the hard benches, mouths forced open. Not that he supplied those open mouths—I did. As a reader, I brought to his simple, clear image something from my memories of seeing folks just like these in Grand Central Station. Had he put in many descriptive words, as some writers are prone to do, I wonder whether I'd have supplied that associated memory.

When too much description is presented the reader, he or she thinks, subconsciously, that it's all there—no other details are needed. Our brains enjoy filling in details—it's a primitive form of problem solving. Our brains are made to solve problems, and they'll do it when given the least encouragement. We can give that encouragement by providing a minimum of (carefully selected) information. Have you ever noticed how attractive a photograph can be of a person's face seen through a rain-streaked, misty window? We like it because we get to create—we fill in the missing information about the face and experience joy in doing so.

Jane Howard, in *Esquire*'s June 1985 issue, writes about a group not often described in so interesting and straightforward a way, "The Mormons of Salt Lake City." Naturally, it takes more than one paragraph to give us a comprehensive picture, but this one does give us a thumbnail sketch. She told about awakening in her hotel at 3:00 A.M. to a disturbing series of beeping sounds.

> The beeping sounds turned out to be traffic signals telling the blind when to cross the streets. Nobody jaywalks. Shoppers, emerging from malls that smell of fudge, wait patiently for lights to change, clutching parcels. What is in them? Maybe Jots and Tittles: The Trivia Game for Latterday Saints (Mormons), from the Deseret Bookstore. (*Deseret* is the Mormon word for "honeybee," which is what Utahans in general and Mormons in particular are supposed to be as busy as.) Maybe something from ZCMI, Zion Cooperative Mercantile Institution, where you get a discount on a new coat if you bring your old one in to donate to the needy. Maybe embroidery supplies; as the Mormon Handicrafts Center behind the hotel suggests, this is a very big town for sewing.

Jane Howard manages to tell us in this short paragraph, mainly by showing us, a fair amount about the lives lived by Mormons—and by others who live among them in Salt Lake City, where their influence prevails. Perhaps because of their influence, the city has installed beepers for the few blind folks in the city; the people are described indirectly as law abiding, through that powerful, short statement—"nobody jaywalks"—she implies that the people are wholesome. Their malls smell of fudge; they lead a life similar to other Americans, yet distinct—they have their own brand of trivia game; they are practical and compassionate—you can get a discount if you bring in clothing for the needy; and they lean toward austerity, or at least away from flamboyance—the citizens are big on home sewing. All of this information came across not by formal lecturing, but by the inclusion of telling details from everyday life.

Warren Hoge wrote about Rio de Janeiro's better-off citizens in an article for the *Sophisticated Traveler* (the *New York Times* supplement) in October 1983:

> Don't be bothered by the way Brazilians litter their beaches with paper wrappers, soft-drink cans, and other disposables. In the early evening, when the veil of mist from the surf and the fog off the mountains meet and soften the edges of vision, platoons of sanitation men in bright orange uniforms rake the beach of the day's debris. Aside from leaving things clean for the next morning, their gentle march across the sands is also a reminder that in Rio the most commonplace things can borrow grace from natural splendor....
>
> Ricardo Amaral, owner of Rio's hottest nightspot, the Hippopotamus discotheque, rolls his eyes to the heavens at mention of the 4:00 A.M. closing time in New York (he is also proprietor of Club A in midtown Manhattan). Walk out of Hippopotamus at an hour when runners are already in the street, calisthenics classes have commenced on the beach and vendors are setting up their stalls in the farmers' markets, and, if you glance behind, you'll see that the frolic inside is still pulsating as if there weren't already a tomorrow.

The first paragraph gives us a quick look at two groups of people living in Rio, the *cariocas* who seem to always live on the beach, and the army of sanitation men who clean up after them. The image of mist and fog merging to soften the edges of vision was inspired, but I was put onto the beach by his men in orange uniforms, which captured the red rays of the setting sun, all softened by the misty air. Yes, I supplied that part about how the red rays of a setting sun move anything orange closer toward red. I don't think I've ever seen orange uniforms in the sunset, but I do see almost every night how the setting sun turns the hairy bark of my red cedars nearly flame red. Truly inspired was Hoge's metaphor of a gentle march across the sands. In all the millions of words I've read over a lifetime, I'm sure I've never seen the words "gentle" and "march" paired up. They belonged together here. Perfect. Evocative. *Accurate.*

Beach swimmers in another part of the world live a different life. In fashionable Newport, Rhode Island, the wealthy belong to the Spouting Rock Beach Association and swim at its Bailey's Beach. Until you've managed to get a cabana at Bailey's Beach, you haven't arrived, according to Cleveland Amory, who writes so well about the wealthy and their strange group behavior patterns. In *Newport: There She Sits,* he writes:

> Like other Newport clubs Bailey's is run on a double-membership basis; in other words, one must become first a seasonal subscriber, then a stockholder and a full-fledged member. Supporting a cabana at Bailey's often runs as high as $1,500 a year, because they are owned outright and the upkeep and all improvements are in the hands of the owner, not the Beach Association. All cabanas have locks, but not to keep outsiders out; they are to keep the owners out. The superintendent of the beach keeps all keys and every night at seven locks all cabanas; then, all night long every hour, a watchman makes the rounds to see that no owners have tried to get in. Bailey's wants no part of after-dark bathing or cabana courtships, and the fact that the younger generation does not like the beach's blue laws bothers *éclat*-minded Newporters not at all. "Young people have a good time at Bailey's," declares Mrs. George Tyson, a sister of Mrs. (Perle) Mesta and a woman whose cottage overlooks the beach, "but it is a good time in an awfully nice way."

The main point a writer can learn from this paragraph is that Amory does not tell us how to feel about these strange goings-on at Bailey's Beach. He simply lays out the facts accurately and interestingly, leaving the figuring out to us readers.

One group that needs its balloons punctured more often is the high-brow intellectuals, and especially academics. As a professor I know what a long, weak branch I'm crawling out on, but I loved the way Russell Lynes, former managing editor at *Harper's,* stuck needles into our puffed-up egos. The following is from an article he wrote for *Harper's* in 1949, "Highbrow, Lowbrow, Middlebrow."

There is a certain air of omniscience about the highbrow, though the air is in many cases the thin variety encountered on the tops of high mountains from which the view is extensive but the details are lost.

You cannot tell a man that he is a lowbrow any more than you can tell a woman her clothes are in bad taste, but a highbrow doesn't mind being called a highbrow. He has worked hard, read widely, traveled far, and listened attentively in order to satisfy his curiosity and establish his squatters' rights in this little corner of intellectualism, and he does not care who knows it. And this is true of both kinds of highbrow—the militant, or crusader, type and the passive, or dilettante, type. These types in general live happily together; the militant highbrow carries the torch of culture, the passive highbrow reads by its light. The carrier of the torch makes a profession of being a highbrow and lives by his calling. He is most frequently found in university and college towns, a member of the liberal-arts faculty, teaching languages (ancient or modern), the fine arts, or literature. His spare time is often devoted to editing a magazine which is read mainly by other highbrows, ambitious undergraduates, and the editors of middlebrow publications in search of talent. When he writes for the magazine himself (or for another "little" magazine) it is usually criticism or criticism of criticism. He leaves the writing of fiction and poetry to others more bent on creation than on what has been created, for the highbrow is primarily a critic and not an artist—a taster, not a cook. He is often more interested in where the arts have been, and where they are going, than in the objects themselves. He is devoted to the proposition that the arts must be pigeon-holed, and that their trends should be plotted, or as W. H. Auden puts it—

> Our intellectual marines,
> Landing in Little Magazines,
> Capture a trend.

In my opening comments to this excerpt, I said that Lynes stuck needles in our puffed-up egos. Actually, of course, he didn't do it—I (the reader) did. He pointed to the behavior patterns of this group and I provided the needles from my own prejudices. As Cleveland Amory did in describing the behaviors of the wealthy at Bailey's

Beach, so did Lynes put forth only some observations, interestingly and accurately, leaving the reader to interpret their meaning. Perhaps a true highbrow would not feel the needles at all. As Lynes said, the highbrow doesn't care who knows what he or she is.

ENTERTAINING THOUGHTS

In creative nonfiction writing you can sometimes get at the realities of group life by looking at what people do for entertainment. William Least Heat-Moon, for example, wrote in *Blue Highways* about his drive toward New Orleans and "Cajun Country."

> I switched on the radio and turned the dial. Somewhere between a shill for a drive-up savings bank and loan and one for salvation, I found a raucous music, part bluegrass fiddle, part Texas guitar, part Highland concertina. Cajun voices sang an old, flattened French, part English, part undecipherable.
>
> Looking for live Cajun music, I stopped in Opelousas at The Plantation Lounge. Somebody sat on every barstool; but a small man, seeing a stranger, jumped down, shook my hand, and insisted I take his seat. In the fast roll of Cajun English, he said it was the guest stool and by right belonged to me. The barmaid, a woman with coiled eyes, brought a Jax. "Is there Cajun music here tonight?" I asked.
>
> "Jukebox is our music tonight," she snapped.

Heat-Moon not only succeeded in telling (showing) us something about the musical entertainment of some rural Cajun people in Louisiana, he also informed us about their unusual speech patterns. A few paragraphs later, he managed to slip in several more bits about their "entertainment" in a listing of references to Evangeline, who had come down from Nova Scotia (Acadia) in 1755.

> If you've read Longfellow, you can't miss Cajunland once you get to the heart of it: Evangeline Downs (horses), Evangeline Speedway (autos), Evangeline Thruway (trucks), Evangeline Drive-In, and, someone just said, the Sweet Evangeline Whorehouse.

In an article David Halberstam wrote for *Esquire* in June 1985, "The Basket-Case State," he described at length the love affair Indiana has with basketball—its chief entertainment. By concentrating on even one form of entertainment, he manages to tell us something about life in Indiana (at least in his view):

> It was a sport for the lonely. A kid did not need five or six other friends; he did not even need one. There was nothing else to do, and because this was Indiana, there was nothing else anyone even wanted to do. Their fathers nailed backboards and rims to the sides of garages or to nearby trees. The nets were waxed to make them last longer, and the kids spent their days shooting baskets in all kinds of weather. This was the land of great pure shooters, and the true mark of an Indiana high school basketball player was hitting the open shot.

A few paragraphs later, Halberstam claims that basketball game-going is a custom of the state:

> Basketball worked in Indiana not just because kids wanted to play it but because adults needed to see it, needed to get into a car at night and drive to another place and hear other voices. So it began, and so it was ingrained in the customs of the state. What helped fan the flame was the instant sense of rivalry, the desire to beat the next village, particularly if it was a little larger. The town of five hundred longed to beat the metropolis of one thousand, and that metropolis ached to beat the city of three thousand, and the city of three thousand dreamed of beating the big city of six thousand. If it happened once every twenty years, said Hammel, that was good enough. The memory lasted, and the photograph of the team members, their hair all slicked down, stayed in the local barbershop a very long time.

Just after reading that fine article in 1985, I took a vacation trip through the Midwest (including Indiana) and found that the memory lasted not only because of the barbershops but because of the very large highway signs just outside town. There, we tourists with our lamentable lack of knowledge about basketball history are informed that this town's high school basketball team won the Regionals in 1980.

Halberstam gave us considerable insight when he told us that the people "needed to see it," *needed* to get out of the house "and hear other voices." I appreciated also the carefully selected verbs by which he described the emotional states of the various sized towns—the smallest "longed," the next "ached," and the next to largest merely "dreamed." Not simply an attempt to vary the verbs, this was writing (and thinking) at its best. I found this progression of emotion accurate. Such subtle accuracy must be strived for. A progression like that does not simply arrive on the page; it's sought. When finally found, it's a thrill only a writer can fully appreciate. Such are the rewards of writing.

Many creative nonfiction writers (including Norman Mailer) seem to enjoy writing about the celebrities of this world. In this final section about how writers frequently describe a group's entertainment as a way to understand the group, Norman Mailer tells us about the dangers of celebrity in an *Esquire* (December 1983) article, "The Prisoner of Celebrity," about Jackie Kennedy Onassis.

> For celebrities are idiots more often than you would expect. Few of one's own remarks should still offer pleasure, but I do like, "Fame? Fame is a microphone in your mouth." To celebrities, the wages of success are those flashbulbs in the eye. If one were hit with no more than ten good jabs every day, the brain would soon reflect its damage; the flashbulbs are worse than jabs and sear one's delicacy. They even jar the last remains of your sensibility. So celebrities are surprisingly flat, bland, even disappointing when you talk to them. Their manner has something in common with the dull stuffed-glove feel in the handshake of a professional boxer. His hands are his instruments, so a fighter will guard his hands. Personality is the failing currency of overexposed celebrities, so over the years they know they must offer less and less to strangers. Those flashbulbs cauterize our souls.

DRESS AS A BADGE OF GROUP LIFE

In addition to looking at a group's methods of entertaining itself, writers frequently look at the way people dress. Only an individual, not a group, can dress, of course, but if the individual is a member of some more-or-less identifiable group, he or she will likely dress like others in that group. In *Zen and the Art of Motorcycle Maintenance,* for example, its author, Robert M. Pirsig, and his son Bill are sitting at lunch in Miles City, Montana, when Bill says: "This is a great town, really great. Surprised there were any like this left. I was looking all over this morning. They've got Stockman's bars, high-top boots, sil-ver-dollar belt buckles, Levis, Stetsons, the whole thing...and it's *real.* It isn't just Chamber of Commerce stuff.... In the bar down the block this morning they just started talking to me like I'd lived here all my life." The author (or Bill) mentions only several articles of clothing, but we are already forming a mental picture of how men dress in Miles City, and we think we know something about their character—a dangerous presumption, of course, but we know enough to await further indications of their true character(s).

In *La Place de la Concorde Suisse,* John McPhee's book about the important role(s) played by the army and its reserves in Switzerland, he focuses on the realistic, accurate details:

> Each wears boots, gaiters, a mountain jacket, and a woolly-earflap Finnish hat, and carries a *fusil d'assaut,* which can fire twenty-four bullets in eight seconds and, with added ono-matopoeia, is also known as a Sturmgewehr. Massy wears hob-nailed boots. Most of the other soldiers are younger, and when they came into the army were issued boots with rubber soles—Swiss crosses protruding from the soles in lieu of hobnails.

A group forever changing its mind about how to dress is teenagers. According to Charles Haas in *Esquire* (June 1985), when any new way to achieve a treat is discovered, its technology is rushed to Westwood, California, which he calls the Silicon Valley of silly delight. In the article. "Tinsel Teens," he describes the teenagers and their latest clothing fad(s):

On a Saturday afternoon the kids start drifting in from all over the city to kick things off with some serious clothes shopping. Boys who can name you every designer in their outfit, from Generra all-cotton jacket down, are heard to swear undying love for the shoes at Leather Bound. The Limited Express, with technopop on the PA, offers Day-Glo sweat-fleece cardigans and other punch-line looks; a few doors down, at the other Limited store, the emphasis is on foreign designs—Firenza, Kenzo. But what is key for the Westwood girl of the moment— even more key than Esprit—is Guess?, a line of sportswear heavy on soft-shaped whites, pastels, and denims. "They'll buy anything Guess?—the *label* sells," says a seventeen-year-old salesgirl at MGA. "They spend a lot of money, but then, *clothes* are a lot of money now." The biggest hit garment with the girls is a hugely oversized white jacket with overlapping seams, a jacket so shapeless and enveloping that its wearers look like a sculpture waiting to be unveiled at adulthood.

In addition to Haas's interesting description of the clothes the Westwood teens were into, he uses irony in reporting that boys are heard to swear undying love for certain shoes. He also uses a typographical device to help us hear the teenager's exaggerated voice by italicizing the fact that "the *label* sells" and "*clothes* are a lot of money now." Since the writer is now leaving his discussion of clothing fads and going into a discussion of food fads, he winds it up with a piece of humorous irony: They look like sculptures "waiting to be unveiled at adulthood." A perfect metaphor in that we get the image of a teenager's typical posing, as a sculptor's model might, but we also see, through his use of "unveiling," an image of a sculpture hidden until the ceremony in a great, shapeless drape of material, reminding us of how he's just described the shapeless and enveloping white jackets the girls of the moment are probably swearing undying love for—and then he winds up the metaphoric image for us by reminding us quietly that there's hope. These young people will someday shed these cocoons and take wing as full-fledged adults. All of those thoughts are (or may be) triggered in the minds of intelligent, imaginative readers. The metaphor, well done, is a powerful device for the creative nonfiction writer.

We tend to think that the form of creative nonfiction we're talking about is a fairly new phenomenon, but here is an excerpt from an article written for the twenty-fifth anniversary issue of *Esquire,* an article about the then-recent (1959) death of the teenage idol of the moment, movie actor James Dean. He was killed when his white Porsche Spyder hit head-on a car driven by Donald Turnupseed, devastating America's teenagers.

In the article "The Death of James Dean," the writer used several interesting techniques possibly never used before. He alternated actual newspaper headlines, small sections of the newspaper's text, narrative full of realistic details, and long sections of prose poetry.

TEEN-AGE DANCES SEEN THREATENED
BY PARENTS' FAILURE TO COOPERATE
MOST OFFENDERS EMULATE ADULTS

James Dean is three years dead but the sinister adolescent
still holds the headlines.
James Dean is three years dead;
But when they file out of the close darkness and the
breathed-out air of the second-run motion picture theatres
where they've been seeing James Dean's old films
they still line up;
the boys in the jackboots and the leather jackets the boys in
the skintight jeans, the boys in broad motorbike belts,
before the mirrors in the restroom
to look at themselves
and see
James Dean;
the resentful hair,
the deep eyes floating in lonesomeness,
the bitter beat look,
the scorn on the lip
Their pocket combs are out; they tousle up their hair and
pat it down just so;
make big eyes at their eyes in the mirror pout their lips in a
sneer;

the lost cats in love with themselves,
just like James Dean.
   The girls flock out dizzy with wanting to run their fingers
through his hair, to feel that thwarted maleness; girl-boy
almost, but he needs a shave... "Just him and me in the back
seat of a car..." Their fathers snort,
   but sometimes they remember, "Nobody understood me
either. I might have amounted to something if the folks had
understood."
   The older women struggle from their seats wet-eyed with
wanting
   to cuddle,
   to mother (it's lack of mother love
   makes delinquents), to smother with little attentions
   the poor orphan youngster,
   the motherless, brotherless, sisterless, lone-wolf brat strayed
from the pack, the poor mixed-up kid.

   LACK OF PARENTAL LOVE IS
   BLAMED IN SLAYING

The writer of that modern-sounding and most creative nonfiction
article? John Dos Passos. We can see his creative turn-of-mind at
work here, not to mention his poetic side. The details he singles out,
and even the way he breaks up his lines and thoughts, make clear
that the writer was fully aware of how the younger generation (not
to mention the mothers and fathers) were reacting to this young phenomenon of the moment. As far as I can determine, no one heralded
this article at the time as some kind of breakthrough into a new kind
of reporting. Perhaps they expected the unusual from this unusually
gifted author—we accept creative efforts by men and women already
seen as "creative." Had he been a "regular" journalist, I wonder
whether more might have been made of this remarkable approach
and format. Even today, over forty years later, it seems avant-garde.
Esquire thought enough of it to run the article again in its fortieth
anniversary issue, in October 1973.

FURTHER DIMENSIONS OF GROUP LIFE

We've seen how creative nonfiction writers get at the heart of groups by writing about their typical daily lives, their entertainments, their dress, and their fads. Let's look now at other dimensions frequently written about: their ornaments, decorations, adornments, architecture, and arts.

As you'll see here and elsewhere, these dimensions include all kinds of things, from furniture to pets. Rex Reed has for many years written interestingly of life in and around Hollywood, succeeding in getting to the heart of the individuals and their society more accurately than many who have attempted the same. In the following paragraph, he opens a piece about Ava Gardner: "Ava: Life in the Afternoon," from his book, *Do You Sleep in the Nude?*

> She stands there, without benefit of filter lens against a room melting under the heat of lemony sofas and lavender walls and cream-and-peppermint-striped movie-star chairs, lost in the middle of that gilt-edge birthday-cake hotel of cupids and cupolas called the Regency. There is no script. No Minelli to adjust the CinemaScope lens. Ice-blue rain beats against the windows and peppers Park Avenue below as Ava Gardner stalks her pink malted-milk cage like an elegant cheetah. She wears a baby-blue cashmere turtleneck sweater pushed up to her Ava elbows and a little plaid mini-skirt and enormous horn-rimmed glasses and she is gloriously, divinely barefoot.

Reed manages, in this one paragraph, to work in details about her ornaments, decorations, adornments, architecture, and, perhaps subliminally, something of her artistic taste. From a technical standpoint, we writers should notice how much he accomplished with his hyphened noun coinages. What an excellent shorthand description of the Regency's architecture: "gilt-edge birthday-cake hotel of cupids and cupolas called the Regency." We enjoy the words not only for the visual image they combine to create, we love the alliteration he's achieved through "cake," "cupids," "cupolas," and "called." He could easily have chosen other images, other words, but his ear heard the aural potential in these visual words. The author's creative touch also shows up when he refers to the turtleneck sweater pushed up to her "Ava elbows." He uses that idea as a recurrent note throughout the article: "'Hell, I've been here ten years and I still can't speak the goddam language,' says Ava, dismissing him with a wave of the long porcelain Ava arms...." "The Ava legs dangle limply from the arm of a lavender chair while the Ava neck, pale and tall as a milkwood vase, rises above the room like a Southern landowner inspecting a cotton field...." "'You're looking at me again!' she says shyly, pulling short girlish wisps of hair behind the lobes of her Ava ears." "The Ava eyes brighten to a soft clubhouse green." "She laughs her Ava laugh and the head rolls back and the little blue vein bulges on her neck like a delicate pencil mark."

Seen pulled together like that, the device sounds overly used, but distributed through the article, it surprises us with delight as it pops up unexpectedly. We should take this as a good reminder, nevertheless, that a device like this can easily be overdone, and must be reserved for the appropriate article and audience.

William Least Heat-Moon, in *Blue Highways,* shows us a completely different segment of society when he describes some of the ornaments and adornments of people living near Danville, Kentucky:

> The highway took me through Danville, where I saw a pillared antebellum mansion with a trailer court on the front lawn. Route 127 ran down a long valley of pastures and fields edged by low, rocky bluffs and split by a stream the color of muskmelon. In the distance rose the foothills of the Appalachians, old mountains that once separated the Atlantic from the shallow inland sea now the middle of America. The licks came out of the hills, the fields got smaller, and there were little sawmills cutting hardwoods into pallets, crates, and fenceposts. The houses shrank, and their colors changed to white to pastels to iridescents to no paint at all. The lawns went from Vertagreen bluegrass to thin fescue to hard-packed dirt glinting with fragments of glass, and the lawn ornaments changed from birdbaths to plastic flamingoes and donkeys to broken-down automobiles with raised hoods like tombstones. On the porch stood one-legged wringer washers and ruined sofas, and, by the front doors, washtubs hung like coats of arms.

Let's take a look at Tom Wolfe, the master of describing what he calls "status life," as he shows us how people in certain strata of society have given up the worship of a spiritual god to take up, instead, the worship of art. The following paragraph comes from an essay Wolfe adapted from the 1983 T. S. Eliot Lectures he delivered at England's University of Kent. This is an excerpt of the adaptation as published in *Harper's* (October 1984), "The Worship of Art: Notes on the New God."

> There was a time when well-to-do educated people in America adorned their parlors with crosses, crucifixes, or Stars of David. These were marks not only of faith but of cultivation. Think of the great homes, built before 1940, with chapels. This was a fashionable as well as devout use of space. Today those chapels are used as picture galleries, libraries, copper kitchens, saunas, or high-tech centers. It is perfectly acceptable to use them for the VCR and the Advent. But it would be in bad taste to use them for prayer. Practically no one who cares about appearing cultivated today would display a cross or Star of David in the living room. It would be...in bad taste. Today the conventional symbol of devoutness is—but of course!—the Holy Rectangle: the painting. The painting is the religious object we see today in the parlors of the educated classes.

When Tom Wolfe writes about culture, irony drips from the cross and the star alike, but he does paint here a partial picture of one segment of society, one that used to merely collect but now worships works of art. Wolfe goes on in this delightful vein to call the Lincoln Centers and Kennedy Centers of the world the cathedrals of the late twentieth century. When the wealthy of old were in trouble with God, they gave money to support the great cathedrals. When the giant corporations develop an odor today, Wolfe went on to say, they support the arts and Public Broadcasting.

These examples from the extremes of the social spectrum illustrate how a creative nonfiction writer can tell us a great deal about the realities of a group's life simply by selecting details about the things with which people surround themselves. In the following chapter, "The Realities of Individual Lives," we'll explore how so much can be learned about the realities of group life when the writer vividly describes the day-to-day life of one person.

5 🌿 THE REALITIES
OF INDIVIDUAL LIVES

Individuals form the more complex fabric of a group. Sometimes the best way to "show" the realities of a group is to focus on showcasing an individual who typifies the group. This can be done by a more comprehensive personality profile, by a sparser sketch, or even by a bare glimpse, such as that from a bus window; vivid initial impressions and judgments can be made with very little information provided by the source.

Richard Goldstein wrote a character sketch, "Gear," for the *Village Voice* in 1966 that tells us much about the type of person or a group of them (older teenagers).

> He sits on his bed and turns the radio on. From under the phonograph he lifts a worn fan magazine—*Pop,* in bright fuchsia lettering—with Zal Yanovsky hunched over one P, Paul McCartney contorted over the other, and Nancy Sinatra touching her toes around the O. He turns to the spread on The Stones and flips the pages until he sees The Picture. Mick Jagger and Marianne Faithful. Mick scowling, waving his fingers in the air. Marianne watching the camera. Marianne waiting for the photographer to shoot. Marianne, Marianne, eyes fading brown circles, lips slightly parted in flashbulb surprise, miniskirt spread apart, tits like two perfect cones under her sweater. He had to stop looking at Marianne Faithful a full week ago.
>
> He turns the page and glances at the shots of Brian Jones and then his eyes open wide because a picture in the corner shows

Brian in Ronnie's pants. The same check. The same rise and flair. Brian leaning against a wall, his hands on the top of his magic hiphuggers. Wick-ked!

A newspaper writer who made his reputation partly on his insights into the man in the street, Jimmy Breslin, wrote in 1982, in New York's *Daily News,* about a woman police officer, Cibella Borges, who had posed for nude photographs back before she became a cop. At the time of this article, it looked certain that she'd lose her job. In a few short sentences he gives us only a snapshot of her—not enough for us to make any kind of informed judgment about her but enough for us to begin to see some of the realities of her life.

> When she had been asked to pose, back in 1980, Cibella, who had been operated on once for a cyst, had just been informed that she needed another operation and this one probably would end her ability to have children. "What's the difference. I can't have any kids, so who's going to marry me?" Cibella said. She went to a studio on the West Side, posed for the pictures, put on her clothes, and went home to Orchard Street, where her front door is between two stores, one selling baby clothes and the other men's suits. Clothes hung outside the stores and blew in the wind over Cibella's head as she came home. Her apartment was two floors up.

In this short paragraph, Jimmy Breslin has given us several glimpses of this woman much in New York City's papers at the time— glimpses certainly different, more human, than the usual news reports about her and her problems. He used a number of small, realistic details to focus this glimpse, but I saw her as she hurried into her building greeted by those clothes that blew over her head. I can't explain the workings of my mind; I can only report them. I saw a sunny day with cumulus clouds piling up and gusts of wind snapping those clothes above her head. Now, the writer didn't say any of that, except for the wind and clothes. I supplied the rest of the image. Perhaps no clouds rose on that day, but my imagination saw them. A writer can't keep readers' minds from doing what they will, but he or she can stimulate them by provoking a few concrete details. Naturally, if the writer had thought it significant that it was not a sunny day with gusts but a day of low and ominous clouds with hurricane-force winds, he would have told me that. Otherwise, it didn't matter too much how I filled in the image. Had he given me no details about the weather, I wouldn't have formed that image (or any image at all) of this woman coming home to her apartment two floors up. As it is, he "involved" me and I turned from the sidewalk with her and climbed behind her up those two flights.

V. S. Pritchett frequently writes travel pieces, and, as we might expect, does it with creative flair. In "Pritchett's London," a piece for the *Sophisticated Traveler* (the *New York Times* supplement, March 1983), he maintains that Londoners are compulsively eccentric and describes several individuals as proof of this assertion.

> We have a fair number of that London specialty, the eccentric. Most of us are reserved and dissimilate in the London way, but the eccentric publicly dramatizes his inner life. Why does that man suddenly open his jacket and display a naked chest tattooed with a nest of serpents? Why does that respectable woman with the dog stamp and shout her ways into shops denouncing "the technological, scientific, communistic-capitalist society" and scream out that "the blacks, Chinese, Indians, are taking your jobs"? No one takes any notice of her diatribes. We shrug our shoulders; the blacks and Asians politely smile. Who is that tall, ghostly, rather distinguished lady in the long evening dress and satin slippers who once asked me whether I would "adopt" her because she happened to be "temporarily short of funds"? Or that man who steers his way through the crowd, arm outstretched, his finger pointing accusingly at all of us? These people are martyrs to compulsion. They are carrying to extremes something present in most Londoners: a suppressed histrionic gift. London, as Dickens observed in his street prowling, is a theater populated by actors asserting a private extravagance. The desire to be a "well-known character," to enlarge modestly a hidden importance, is endemic.

In *Encounters with Chinese Writers,* Annie Dillard gives us an unusual (and unexpected) glimpse of a Chinese woman writer attending a conference of American writers and the leading members of the Beijing Writers Association in China.

> Today the usual tea-serving maids do not seem available, so the woman writer pours the tea. There is always one woman. She may have the second-highest rank in the room, or she may have written the novel most admired all over China. It takes her fifteen minutes to pour tea, and she will do this three or four times in the course of the morning. After she serves, she takes an inconspicuous seat, sometimes on the one little hard chair stuck behind the real chairs.

A short, one-paragraph glimpse of one woman writer doing one simple act, but Annie Dillard has said a great deal about China, at least about its attitude toward women writers (and, we might infer, women in general). The technique to note here is that the author did not tell us about life in China; she showed us one woman writer at a conference of Chinese and American writers—and we inferred a message about life for women in today's "egalitarian" China.

SLICE-OF-LIFE WRITING

The Last Cowboy, Jane Kramer's study of Henry Blanton's life, stands as a classic of creative nonfiction. Through this profile of one modern cowboy, Kramer provides us insights into the lives of many cowboys of today's American West. She gives us in her extended profile a good many glimpses of Henry Blanton, like the one that follows. Glimpses like this accumulate over many pages to give us the man in all his dimensions.

> Henry valued his authority. He hurried through breakfast so that he could always greet his men with the day's orders looking relaxed and confident. He liked to sit on the wagon, waiting, with his scratch pad in his hand and a pencil behind his ear, and

he made it a point to be properly dressed for the morning's work in his black boots, a pair of clean black jeans, and his old black hat and jacket. Henry liked wearing black. The Virginian, he had heard, wore black and so had Gary Cooper in the movie *High Noon,* and now Henry wore it with a kind of innocent pride, as if the color carried respect and a hero's stern, elegant qualities. Once, Betsy discovered him in the bathroom mirror dressed in his black gear, his eyes narrowed and his right hand poised over an imaginary holster.

In *The Pine Barrens,* John McPhee describes how he went up to a house in the midst of New Jersey's Pine Barrens to ask for water and met one of Hog Wallow's residents, Frederick Chambers Brown. "I called out to ask if anyone was home, and a voice called back, 'Come in. Come in. Come on the hell in.'"

> I walked through a vestibule that had a dirt floor, stepped up into a kitchen, and went into another room that had several over-stuffed chairs in it and a porcelain-topped table, where Fred Brown was seated, eating a pork chop. He was dressed in a white sleeveless shirt, ankle-top shoes, and undershorts. He gave me a cheerful greeting and, without asking why I had come or what I wanted, picked up a pair of khaki trousers that had been tossed onto one of the overstuffed chairs and asked me to sit down. He set the trousers on another chair, and he apologized for being in the middle of his breakfast, explaining that he seldom drank much but the night before he had had a few drinks and this had caused his day to start slowly. "I don't know what's the matter with me, but there's got to be something the matter with me, because drink don't agree with me anymore," he said. He had a raw onion in one hand, and while he talked he shaved slices from the onion and ate them between bites of the chop....

Almost like a cinematographer, McPhee walks with his *cinema verité* camera on his shoulder through the vestibule, the kitchen, and into another room where the camera pans across the overstuffed chairs, one strewn with a pair of trousers, and finally reveals the source of the orig-inally shouted invitation to come on the hell in—Fred Chambers

Brown in his undershorts. While Fred redistributes the trousers, he gives a friendly greeting and invites the unexpected visitor to sit down.

A fiction writer could not have written a better line than what Fred Brown says about drink no longer agreeing with him. Would a fiction writer have made up such a scene—a man in his undershorts happily slicing and eating onions in between bites of a pork chop? Yes, some fiction writer might, but this scene appeals to us because we know it's not made up. John McPhee, whom we have learned to trust, simply reports what the man says and each of his actions, as simple as they might be. This is realism because it is real. The fiction writer would have to work hard to create the same feeling of realism; McPhee is observing and reporting the real. His creativity comes in with his selection of the details to be brought before the camera from all the many he had in his mind and notebook, the sequence with which he brings them on stage, the selection of which captured conversational bits to report, and the word choices he makes.

It's worth noting here how simple and straightforward McPhee's words are and how simple and clear his sentences. No fancy footwork, no attempt to show what a clever writer he is and what a "power vocabulary" he commands. We have here, instead, a careful professional thinking only about the scene at hand and the clarity with which he can transmit that through words alone.

BECOMING A "PEOPLE WATCHER"

To achieve a fully dimensional character, fictional or real, a writer must watch people closely, much more closely than the average person would. He or she looks especially for anything unusual or distinct about the person or persons involved, but does not ignore what is ordinary and typical. The writer then reports, in as interesting a way as possible, these poses, posturings, habitual gestures, mannerisms, appearances, glances. Not that the writer limits observations to these, but these frequently appear in creative nonfiction writing. Here are some examples of acute observation at work in the writings of McPhee, Faulkner, Steinem, Talese, Pritchett, and Rhodes.

In a straight-backed chair near the doorway to the kitchen sat a young man with long black hair, who wore a visored red leather cap that had darkened with age. His shirt was coarse woven and had eyelets down a V neck that was laced with a thong. His trousers were made of canvas, and he was wearing gum boots. His arms were folded, his legs were stretched out, he had one ankle over the other, and as he sat there he appeared to be sighting carefully past his feet, as if his toes were the outer frame of a gunsight and he could see some sort of target in the floor. When I entered, I had said hello to him, and he had nodded without looking up. He had a long, straight nose and high cheekbones in a deeply tanned face that was, somehow, gaunt. I had no idea whether he was shy or hostile.

John McPhee
The Pine Barrens

The Geisha's mass of blue-black lacquered hair encloses the painted face like a helmet, surmounts, crowns the slender body's ordered and ritual posturing like a grenadier's bearskin busby, too heavy in appearance for that slender throat to bear, the painted fixed expressionless face immobile and immune also above the studied posturing; yet behind that painted and lifeless mask is something quick and alive and elfin; or more than elfin: puckish; or more than puckish even: sardonic and quizzical, a gift for comedy and more: for burlesque and caricature for a sly and vicious revenge on the race of men.

William Faulkner
"Impressions of Japan,"
Esquire (October 1973)

She had shared all the vilification and praise without ever emerging in public as an individual. I was eager to meet her, but all her other interviewers said Mrs. Nixon had put them straight to sleep.

She was sitting in the front of the plane, freckled hands neatly folded, ankles neatly crossed, and smiling a public smile as a sleek young staff man sat me next to her. I didn't want to ask the questions she had answered so blandly and often about her husband ("I just think he'd make a wonderful president") or politics ("You'll have to ask Dick about that"), but to ask about herself.

Gloria Steinem
"Patricia Nixon Flying"
Outrageous Acts and Everyday Rebellions

The two blondes, who seemed to be in their middle thirties, were preened and polished, their matured bodies softly molded within tight dark suits.

They sat, legs crossed, perched on the high bar stools. They listened to the music. Then one of them pulled out a Kent and Sinatra quickly placed his gold lighter under it and she held his hand, looked at his fingers: they were nubby and raw, and the pinkies protruded, being so stiff from arthritis that he could barely bend them. He was, as usual, immaculately dressed. He wore an oxford-grey suit with a vest, a suit conservatively cut on the outside but trimmed with flamboyant silk within; his shoes, British, seemed to be shined even on the bottom of the soles. He also wore, as everybody seemed to know, a remarkably convincing black hairpiece, one of sixty that he owns, most of them under the care of an inconspicuous little grey-haired lady who, holding his hair in a tiny satchel, follows him around whenever he performs. She earns $400 a week.

Gay Talese
"Frank Sinatra Has a Cold,"
Esquire (April 1966)

But, that social life. Where do we all meet? At shops and pubs, of course, but mainly in the street market, the melting-pot of all inner London districts. It is mostly run by the Cockneys, whose aim in life is to shout and play-act at stalls everywhere between Shoreditch and Soho and beyond. "You're in England. Stick to language, carntcher? Speak up! What is it, love?" That final phrase is imposed to heal all wounds. For the market we are not Mr. or Mrs., Sir or Madam, or even Mum and Dad, but, in the thick wash of sentiment, "love," "ducks," "dear," and "darling" for the women and "guv" for the men. We are people who are used to being rained on and jeered at;

the street market is the heart of any London village—and town planners dare not do away with it or impose a cross-channel elegance.

V. S. Pritchett
"Pritchett's London" *Sophisticated Traveler,*
New York Times (March 1983)

And all the while we listen to the cowboy come on over the radio like Red Barber announcing the Yankees as the other hunters rack up their coyotes for the afternoon: "THERE HE COMES, LES, OUT THAT SOUTH FENCE—GO SOUTH, LES! GO SOUTH, GO SOUTH, HE'S CROSSED THE ROAD, HE'S IN THAT SOIL BANK IN THE NEXT SECTION, BETTER GO WEST AND HEAD HIM OFF, LES, JOHNNY WAGONBLAST, WHERE ARE YOU? YOU OUT ON THE WEST ROAD? COME NORTH, JOHNNY, HE'S IN THE NORTHWEST QUARTER, COME NORTH," and Harold nudging me, Harold in love with his radio, "See, I told you he was a real good boy, regular sportscaster," and then the sound, sweet jealous sound now, of the dogs dropped from Johnny's truck, and cowboy's back on the horn, "HE'S GOT HIM, JOHNNY WAGONBLAST'S GOT HIM, THEY GOT THE COYOTE!"

Richard Rhodes
Death All Day

Another dimension a creative nonfiction writer will not neglect is a person's dialect, accent, or colloquial speech patterns. Such detail doesn't really get to the heart of a person, but it does involve the reader more closely. Jimmy Breslin readily captures the various dialects, accents, and colloquialisms of people on his beat for the *Daily News.* To understand fully the next quote from one of his columns, "Give a Beggar a Horse...," all the reader needs to remember is that he always referred to his wife in his columns as The Former Rosemary Dattolico. In this portion of the column, we're with his mother-in-law, the former Rose Dattolico's mother, as she wanders through one of many supermarkets seeking out the best deals.

She stopped and began scolding a young woman from the neighborhood who came along with boxes of eighty-nine-cent paper napkins atop her shopping cart. The former Rosemary Dattolico's mother tapped the paper napkins.

"Somebody on an income of twelve thousand dollars can't afford paper napkins that cost eighty-nine cents."

The young woman said, "You're broke, a little fancy you need."

"Nonsense," the former Rosemary Dattolico's mother said. She sent the young woman back to the shelves to change the paper napkins and her ultimate advice followed the young woman. "You're cheaper off."

Creative nonfiction writers pay close and appreciative attention not only to regional and local variations on the mother tongue, they also listen and write to capture the specialized languages and jargons of the specialists among us. The writer listens carefully to the specialist's language, partly to learn enough to be able to use some of it in the narrative portions of the article or book, and partly to select quotes and partial quotes from all those the specialist may have used, in order to simulate a fuller conversation with the specialist. Up to a point, the reader doesn't mind not fully understanding the jargon or specialized language—in fact, as we've said earlier, its very obscurity lends credibility to what's being read by the nonspecialist. The writer must be careful, however, not to go beyond that point because the reader may become totally lost—perhaps never to be found again. The writer needs to give just enough to intrigue and provide credibility. It isn't necessary to explain all the jargon for the nonspecialist reader, if its purpose is to establish mood, setting, or character. Naturally, if the meaning of the specialized language is essential to understanding what follows, the meaning must somehow be conveyed as succinctly as possible, or else the piece becomes a textbook or specialist's manual.

John McPhee wrote a fascinating profile of an ecologist as she went about her field work. In this excerpt from *Travels in Georgia* we hear them working a swamp at night:

Silent ourselves, we pushed on into the black. Carol moved a flashlight beam among the roots of trees. She held the flashlight to her nose, because the eye can see much more if the line of sight is closely parallel to the beam. She inspected minutely the knobby waterline of the trees. Something like a sonic boom cracked in our ears. "Jesus, what was that?"

"Beaver."

The next two slaps were even louder than the first. Carol ignored the beaver, and continued to move the light. It stopped. Out there in the obsidian was a single blue eye.

"A blue single eye is a spider," she said. "Two eyes is a frog. Two eyes almost touching is a snake. An alligator's eyes are bloody red."

Two tiny coins now came into her light.

"Move in there," she said. "I want that one."

With a throw of her hands, she snatched up a frog. It was a leopard frog, and she let him go. He was much within his range. Carol was looking for river frogs, pig frogs, carpenter frogs, whose range peripheries we were stalking. She saw another pair of eyes. The canoe moved in. Her hand swept out unseen and made a perfect tackle, thighs to knees. This was a bronze frog, home on the range....

McPhee knows that his writing gains authority not only through his use of specialist's jargon but through evidence of specialized knowledge. When we read that Carol held her flashlight up to her nose in the middle of that swamp at night, we see we're with a woman who knows her job. This evidence is reinforced when we hear the conversation about eyes in the dark, and later, the list of frogs most of us have not met.

Notice that McPhee does not tell us that the way to catch a frog is to grab it just above the knees; he shows us Carol sweeping her hand out, unseen, and tackling the frog. He can't resist describing that perfect tackle in football terms. Perhaps he should have resisted this next one, but he tells us that the frog she's tackled so nicely can be thrown back because he's not beyond the peripheries of acceptable frog wanderings; he's home on the range. Little sparks of wit like this keep people reading John McPhee. We learn all kinds of specialized knowledge in his books and articles, but it's not like the learning in a classroom—it's leavened with wit, not heavy-handed humor, but wit.

Specialized knowledge and its concomitant jargon has probably reached an all-time high in the space exploration business. Everyone has been infected by its way of shorthanding and acronymizing everything. Norman Mailer gained authority in his *Of a Fire on the Moon* by capturing faithfully this specialized knowledge and language. In writing about the first moon walk, he reported part of the effort this way:

> ...Star checks were taken. Meanwhile, Armstrong was readying the cameras and snapping photographs through the window. Now Aldrin aligned the Abort Guidance Section. Armstrong laid in the data for Program 12, the Powered Ascent Guidance. The Command Module came around again. The simulated countdown was over. They had another Stay. They powered down their systems.
>
> In the transcript the work continues minute after minute, familiar talks of stars and Nouns, acronyms, E-memory dumps, and returns to POO where Pings may idle. They are at rest on the moon, but the dialogue is not unencumbered of pads, updata link switches and noise suppression devices on the Manned Space Flight Network relay.

Specialists are not necessarily scientific or other high-flying people; they can be specialists of any stripe. For example, William W. Warner's Pulitzer Prize–winning, *Beautiful Swimmers,* takes us into the far reaches of Chesapeake Bay to learn how the watermen and their crabs live. In the following excerpt, Warner works in specialized knowledge, fishing jargon, and local dialect.

> "Some people are plain feared of crabs, though Lord knows they can't hurt you much."
>
> Mike grins from one jug ear to another. "Sometimes they get to you," he says.
>
> Indeed they do. Maine lobstermen can safely remove the much smaller numbers of lobsters found in their pots with

bare hands, seizing them from the rear. Chesapeake crabbers cannot do this. Unlike the lobster, the blue crab has excellent rear vision. There are too many crabs in each pot in any case for such individual seizure. You simply plunge in with both hands and separate the tangling masses as best you can, suffering an occasional bite from a big Jimmy (male) that will make even the most hardened crabber wince. Between such bites and the constant handling of pot wire the fabric-lined "Best" rubber gloves last no more than two weeks during periods of heavy catches. "You get a hole in them," Grant adds, "the crabs will find it."

We pull up a shiny new pot set down a few days ago. It is absolutely jammed. Maybe fifty sooks (females). "New pots seem to attract females this time of year," Grant observes. "Don't know why. Ain't nobody really knows about crabs."

William Warner describes vividly for us a Chesapeake crabber's life. He accomplishes that partly through the concrete details of how a crab behaves and how the crabber works with the captured crabs; partly through sensory details like the bite; and partly through letting us hear Mike's voice through bits of captured dialog. I'm discussing these elements of language use as though the writers use them one by one. In practice, however, all these elements (and many others discussed in this book) work together, even within one paragraph. The next chapter explores captured conversations; short snatches of conversation (as in the Warner quote); quotes from letters, memoirs, journals, and the like; and words heard over the phone, radio, and television, and the powerful role they play in your writing.

6 DIALOGS, MONOLOGS, AND OTHER LOGS

Whether you're writing fiction or creative nonfiction, the most effective technique for involving readers—making them feel as though they are right there—is well-written dialog. I've decided not to use the word "dialog" for this book because I don't want to mislead and have the reader think that I'm talking about "created" dialog when I discuss creative nonfiction. "Captured conversation"—conversation overheard (or taken from a formal interview) while conducting research for an article or book—is the term I use for creative nonfiction dialog.

A creative nonfiction writer does not use all the conversations captured during research. Similar to the use of character detail, only those bits that seem most illustrative of the subject matter under consideration or revelatory of one or more of the persons involved in the conversation are used. To avoid distortion, the writer exercises great care in selecting those bits. Anyone can seem stupid, brilliant, humorous, humorless, obfuscatory, vague, or otherwise unusual in any single conversation. Do not let the desire to write interestingly and dramatically make you select those conversations that serve drama over truth.

People reveal themselves and shed light on situations through other devices besides conversation, providing the writer many opportunities to collect information and making his or her work more varied, more vivid, more dramatic, more involving, more interesting. People reveal something directly, or indirectly, through historic letters, court records, memoirs, journals, diaries, reminiscences, official letters, newspapers, and the use of telephones. We believe we understand a people or a region a bit better by the signs and symbols we read along the road or in a hotel room—not to mention graffiti we read on their walls. People reveal themselves not only through regular conversations but through monologs, conversation where one participant speaks at such length that his or her parts in the conversation resemble more a series of monologs. All of these devices of revelation provide grist for the word mills of creative nonfiction writers. Let's look at some examples of how our better writers have used these devices, beginning with the main one—captured conversation.

CAPTURED CONVERSATION

In his bestselling book, *The Selling of the President,* Joe McGinniss captured many conversations that seemed to reveal President Richard M. Nixon. In the following excerpt, Mr. Nixon has come to the Green Room of the White House to make a political (commercial) videotape.

> He took his position on the front of the heavy brown desk. He liked to lean against a desk, or sit on the edge of one, while he taped commercials, because he felt this made him seem informal. There were about twenty people, technicians and advisors, gathered in a semi-circle around the cameras. Richard Nixon looked at them and frowned.
> "Now when we start," he said, "don't have anybody who is not directly involved in this in my range of vision. So I don't go shifting my eyes."
> "Yes, sir. All right, clear the stage. Everybody who's not actually doing something get off the stage, please. Get off the stage."
> There was one man in the corner, taking pictures. His flash blinked several times in succession. Richard Nixon looked his direction. The man had been hired by the Nixon staff to take informal pictures throughout the campaign for historical purposes.

"Are they stills?" Richard Nixon said. "Are they our own stills? Well then, knock them off." He motioned with his arm. "Can them. We've already got so goddamned many stills already." Richard Nixon turned back toward the cameras.

"Now, when you give me the fifteen-second cue, give it to me right under the camera so I don't shift my eyes."

"Right, sir."

The entire chapter about the taping or filming of commercials showed the president trying to look his best, but McGinniss has included this captured conversation to illustrate Nixon's concern about his famously shifting eyeballs. Many advisers told him he must control those inadvertent shiftings because close-up camera shots magnify their shiftiness—and people tend to associate shifty eyeballs with "shifty" character. Note that McGinniss didn't write all this that I just wrote about shiftiness; he simply quoted Nixon. McGinniss did, however, select this particular conversation to report on, so apparently he did hope that his readers would pick up on that concern of the president.

"Nixon's Neighborhood," one of Paul Theroux's articles collected in *Sunrise with Seamonsters,* tells of Theroux's interviews with men and women in the streets of San Clemente, where Nixon resided when not at the White House. He asked them, among other things, about the book Mr. Nixon was writing.

> The book was mentioned by many people I met in San Clemente. In southern California, a book is considered a mysterious thing, even by college students who gather on Nixon's beach to turn on. One of these, Martin Nelson ("I think Nixon's a real neat guy. If you could see his house you'd know it was a prime place"), majors in Ornamental Horticulture at Pasadena. He hopes to get an M.A. and possibly a Ph.D. in Ornamental Horticulture and become America's answer to Capability Brown. He spoke with awe about Nixon's book, so did Mr. Phillips, the security guard, and Brian Sardoz, the scuba diver, and Mrs. Dorothy Symms of San Clemente Secretarial Services, publisher of *Fishcarts to Fiestas, the Story of San Clemente.*

"I met the man who's writing Mr. Nixon's book," said Mrs. Symms.

I said, "Isn't Mr. Nixon writing the book?"

"No. There's a man doing it for him. He writes all the movie stars' books. He's a very famous writer. You say you're from England? Oh, this man wrote Winston Churchill's memoirs, too."

I imagine that Churchill's heirs would be surprised to learn from the author of *Fishcarts to Fiestas* that Winston had to rely on a ghost writer for his memoirs.

Gay Talese wrote "The Silent Season of a Hero" about the great baseball player, Joe DiMaggio. This excerpt comes from *Fame and Obscurity,* the book that presents many of Talese's excellent pieces about people who've come and gone. DiMaggio and several old pals are leaving a golf course to go to a banquet when Talese captures the following conversation:

Later, showered and dressed, DiMaggio and the others drove to a banquet about ten miles from the golf course. Somebody had said it was going to be an elegant dinner, but when they arrived they could see it was more like a country fair; farmers were gathered outside a big barn-like building, a candidate for sheriff was distributing leaflets at the front door, and a chorus of homely ladies were inside singing "You Are My Sunshine."

"How did we get sucked into this?" DiMaggio asked, talking out of the side of his mouth, as they approached the building.

"O'Doul," one of the men said. "It's his fault. Damned O'Doul can't turn *anything* down."

"Go to hell," O'Doul said.

Soon DiMaggio and O'Doul and Ernie Nevers were surrounded by the crowd, and the woman who had been leading the chorus came rushing over and said, "Oh, Mr. DiMaggio, it certainly is a pleasure having you."

"It's a pleasure being here, ma'am," he said, forcing a smile.

"It's too bad you didn't arrive a moment sooner, or you'd have heard our singing."

"Oh, I heard it," he said, "and I enjoyed it very much."

"Good, good," she said. "And how are your brothers Dom and Vic?"

"Fine. Dom lives near Boston. Vince is in Pittsburgh."

"Why, hello there, Joe," interrupted a man with wine on his breath, patting DiMaggio on the back, feeling his arm.

"Who's gonna take it this year, Joe?"

Talese does a fine job setting the scene for us and then simply records what he heard of several conversations, all of which add up to banality, but he does not tell us that this is all banal. His simple, straightforward description put me right in step with this small group approaching the barn. Until he told me that Joe had said something out of the side of his mouth, I was up in a tree watching the scene of the men approaching, but as soon as he told me how it was said, I was right down there close—involved. Although Talese slipped out of the objective gear and into the subjective when he told me that Joe smiled and claimed he'd enjoyed the ladies' rendition of "You Are My Sunshine," I loved it. When he added that Joe was forcing a smile, of course, he stopped objective reporting and began subjective reporting. A subtle example of the fine line that sometimes divides the two.

Michael Herr's "Khesanh," as collected in Tom Wolfe's *The New Journalism,* gives us some of the most involving writing ever done about the Vietnam War. He's writing this excerpt about a U.S. Marine nicknamed Day Tripper (because of his hatred for the night hours and his desire to get everything done during the safer daylight hours) who keeps excellent mental records of the days, hours, minutes, and seconds he has left to serve.

> [Day Tripper] had assumed that correspondents in Vietnam *had* to be there. When he learned that I had asked to come here he almost let the peaches drop on the ground. "Lemmee... lemmee jus' hang on that a minute," he said. "You mean you doan' *have* to be here? An' you're *here?*" I nodded.
>
> "Well, they gotta be paying you some tough bread."
>
> "You'd be depressed if I told you."
>
> He shook his head.

"I mean, they ain' got the bread that'd get me here if I didn't have t'be here."

"Horse crap," Mayhew said. "Day Tripper loves it. He's short now, but he's comin' back, ain't you Day Tripper?"

"Shit, my momma'll come over here and pull a tour before I fuckin' come back."

Four more marines dropped into the pit.

"Where's Evans?" Mayhew demanded.

"Any of you guys know Evans?"

One of the mortarmen came over.

"Evans is over in Danang," he said. "He caught a little shit the other night."

"That right?" Mayhew said. "Evans get wounded?"

"He hurt bad?" Day Tripper said.

"Took some stuff in the legs. Nothing busted. He'll be back in ten days."

"That ain't bad enough, then," Day Tripper said.

"No," Mayhew said. "But ten days, sheeit, that's better'n nothin'."

As a writer, try to imagine getting across through straight explanatory reporting all the attitudes and feelings that come across so vividly in that conversation among men at the front. Try writing, for example, a summary explanatory paragraph that gets across what's expressed in the final three lines of that captured conversation. It could be done, but it would lack the vividness, the believability that those three lines possess. This is captured conversation. These are not abstract thoughts; these ring of the real.

Back across the Pacific, we read of the horrors of fighting the battles of Hollywood filmmaking. Gay Talese wrote a chapter called "The Soft Psyche of Joshua Logan" in his book *The Overreachers*. It's a scene that couldn't be more different from the scene in Vietnam, yet the same technique of letting straight captured conversation tell the story works just as well here.

Now he was back in the dark theatre, the lights of the stage beaming on the actors going through a scene in the garden of their Louisiana shack; Claudia McNeil's voice was now softer because she had had a touch of laryngitis a few days before. But at the end of the scene, she raised her voice to its full power, and Logan, in a pleasant tone, said, "Don't strain your voice, Claudia."

She did not respond, only whispered to another actor on stage.

"Don't raise your voice, Claudia," Logan repeated.

She again ignored him.

"Claudia!" Logan yelled, "don't you give me that actor's revenge, Claudia."

"Yes, Mr. Logan," she said with a soft sarcastic edge.

"I've had enough of this today, Claudia."

"Yes, Mr. Logan."

"And stop Yes-Mr. Logan-ing me."

"Yes, Mr. Logan."

"You're a shocking, rude woman!"

"Yes, Mr. Logan."

"You're being a beast."

"Yes, Mr. Logan."

"Yes, Miss Beast."

"Yes, Mr. Logan."

"Yes, Miss Beast! "

Suddenly, Claudia McNeil stopped. It dawned on her that he was calling her a beast; now her face was grey and her eyes were cold, and her voice almost solemn as she said, "You...called...me...out...of...my...name!"

"Oh, God!" Logan smacked his forehead with his hand.

It would be difficult to invent for a fictional story such a petulant conversation. We enjoy it particularly here because we know that it was not "created" by this creative writer of nonfiction but was simply captured at the moment it occurred.

One of the best ways to show the inefficiency, the stupidity, or the absurdity of an institution is to accurately quote its staff as it deals with its public. James Michener does this extremely effectively in the following excerpt from *Iberia,* his study of Portugal and Spain. Merely describing in narrative form the situation shown here could not begin to achieve the reality we feel as we listen to this captured conversation. We have all faced such Catch-22 situations in our lives. Michener jogs our memories and we bring them to bear on our reading of this passage.

> In Badajoz I also learned something about the government of Spain. At the post office I purchased ten air-letter forms and paid six pesetas (ten cents) each for them. I went back to the cathedral plaza and spent most of one morning writing ten letters, a job I find difficult, for words do not come easily to me. The next day I took the ten letters to the post office to mail but a clerk refused them, saying, "The price of air-letters went up this morning from six pesetas to ten."
>
> "All right. Give me ten four-peseta stamps and I'll stick them on the letters."
>
> "We can't do that, sir, because it states very clearly on the form that if anything whatever is enclosed in the form or added to it, it will be sent by regular post."
>
> "Then let me give you the difference, and you can stamp them as having ten pesetas."
>
> "There is no provision for that, sir."
>
> "Then what can I do? Mail them as they are and let them go regular mail?"
>
> "No, because they're no longer legal. They've been declassified."
>
> "It took me a long time to write these letters. How can I mail them?"
>
> "Take each one. Place it inside an airmail envelope. Readdress the envelope and place twelve pesetas' worth of stamp in the corner and mail it as a regular air-mail letter."
>
> This I did, and the letters were delivered in various countries, but I was so astounded by the procedure that I called upon a high government official to ask how such a thing could happen. His answer was revealing. "The clerk did right. The forms you bought were valid yesterday. Today they're not. Each form states clearly that nothing may be added, so there was no way to mail the old forms."

Note that Michener simply reported the conversation. He did not tell us in between the pieces of dialog just how the clerk said the words, nor how Michener could feel his blood pressure rising. He left all that to the reader's memory of similar, frustrating experiences to fill in the physical and other feelings probably going on at the time. The only direct clues we get about his feelings on the matter are that he did then ✗ go a higher-up government official—and he uses the simple word "astounded"—which gives us a clue to the tenor of that second conversation.

C. D. B. Bryan's book *Friendly Fire,* about the Vietnam War and the effect of a son's death upon a family, quotes many people, sometimes to great dramatic effect. Chapter 6 of that book ends with a captured conversation that leaves an impression on the reader more lasting than any summary statement about the awful nature of war and the loss of sons. Peg and Gene Mullen have recently lost their son, Michael, in Vietnam and are shown here visiting a woman who has lost a son in Vietnam on the same day that Michael was killed. They hope to comfort her by sharing their thoughts with her, as they have with other distraught mothers and fathers who have suffered the loss of sons in Vietnam.

> The Mullens followed the man along the dirt section roads, zigged and zagged until they finally reached a dilapidated and paint-peeled farmhouse and a broken-down farm. When Peg and Gene came up to the door, the woman invited them in right away. The Mullens explained why they had come, that Michael had died on the same day as their son, and Peg noticed that here, too, no one had visited or brought food. The mother thanked and thanked them for coming, explained that she was on welfare, and it had been very hard on them lately, but she hoped things would be better. "You know, Mrs. Mullen"—the woman sighed—"this was the third of my sons to go to Vietnam."
>
> "Your *third?*" Peg asked.
>
> "I have seven sons," she explained, "and I prayed the first two out of the war, but when they drafted my third son, I was so discouraged…. He was my best son, mentally, physically, in every way, and when they drafted him, too, well I kind of lost faith in God. I guess I couldn't pray hard enough to pray him

back home. But," she said, smiling bravely," the draft board is so kind. When I went to visit with them, they told me they would only draft five of my sons for Vietnam."

MONOLOGS

"Monolog" may not be the technically accurate word to cover what I have in mind here, but I refer to a speech given by one person. It may be a formal speech, or an excerpt from it, or it may simply be a lengthy speech by one person within a lengthier conversation between two or more people. It could also be a lecture, or part of one, given by a professor, minister, or drill sergeant. They come in many variations and disguises, but what follows here are three that illustrate how the writer can say a great deal about a person simply by recording accurately what he or she says, especially when speaking at length.

In the "Delhi" chapter of her book *Destinations,* Jan Morris captures the flavor of India through a monolog given by a government spokesman.

> "Certainly," said the government spokesman, perusing my list of questions, "by all means, these are all very simple matters. We can attend to them for you at once. As I told you, it is our duty! It is what we are paid for! I myself have to attend an important meeting this afternoon—you will excuse me I hope?—but I will leave all these little matters with our good Mrs. Gupta and all will be taken care of. I will telephone you with answers myself without fail—or if not I myself, then Mrs. Gupta will be sure to telephone you either today or tomorrow morning. Did you sign our register? A duplicate signature if you would not mind, and the requisite application form for a pass—it will make everything easier for you, you see. Have no fear, Mrs. Gupta will take care of everything. But mark my words, you will find the spiritual aspects of our city the most rewarding. Remember the River Ganges! As a student of history you will find that I am right! Ha ha! Another cup of tea? You have time?"

We come away from this monolog with some understanding of the government official, especially his feeling of self-importance, but we also come away with a feeling about how it must be to deal with the government of India. I came away wanting to meet our good Mrs. Gupta. Surely she and many other Mrs. Guptas provide the government whatever efficiency and effectiveness it has. Had the author chosen to interrupt this monolog with little summary bits about what the official looked like, what his office smelled like, or to give a glimpse of Mrs. Gupta in the outer office, much more would have been lost than gained.

The following excerpt from "The General Goes Zapping Charlie Cong" by Nicholas Tomalin, as collected in Tom Wolfe's *The New Journalism,* is a good example of specialists' language, and it also makes an important point about how effective the direct quotation of a monolog can be.

> The General has a big, real American face, reminiscent of every movie general you have ever seen. He comes from Texas, and he's 48. His present rank is Brigadier General, Assistant Division Commander, United States Army (which is what the big red figure on his shoulder flash means).
>
> "Our mission today," says the General, "is to push those goddam VCs right off Routes 13 and 16. Now you see Routes 13 and 16 running north from Saigon toward the town of Phuac Vinh, where we keep our artillery. When we got here first we prettied up those roads, and cleared Charlie Cong right out so we could run supplies up."
>
> "I guess we've been hither and thither with all our operations since, an' the ol' VC he's reckoned he could creep back. He's been puttin' out propaganda he's going to interdict our right of passage along those routes. So this day we aim to zapp him, and zapp him, and zapp him again till we've zapped him right back to where he came from. Yes, sir. Let's go."

Creative nonfiction writer Joe McGinniss, in his book about the Alaska of today, *Going to Extremes,* does not use many conversations or monologs, but he does quote one short monolog captured aboard one of Alaska's state ferries. A small group of Alaskans are sitting around the ferry's bar as they prepare to leave Seattle for the north.

> Eddie the Basque moved quickly to a corner table, where he had spotted two heavy young women with teased hair. I sat at the bar and ordered an Olympia beer. Duane Archer was telling the high state official about his new truck, a Ford, and about the way he had bought it. He had two cigarettes going at once.
>
> "So I said to that son of a bitch, 'Listen, you son of a bitch, I want that heavy-duty bumper on there and I want them studded snow tires on there and I want that extra layer of undercoating on there and I want that auxiliary heater hooked up and I want this taken care of by four o'clock tomorrow when I come back here to pick this baby up and I don't want any more shit about it."
>
> The high state official was nodding. Duane Archer took a swallow of his drink. V.O. and water was what he drank.

OTHER LOGS

Since the Greek root word "logos" means such varied things ("word," "saying," "speech," "discourse," "thought"), I feel safe referring to the following as other kinds of "logs": journals, diaries, memoirs, court records, personal letters, official letters, telegrams, memoranda, messages, headlines, and news reports. These written records of people communicating with each other are useful in nonfiction articles and books. A fiction writer may invent such communications to lend verisimilitude, to make his or her story sound real. In nonfiction, the writer uses these sources to help communicate the fact that what he or she is writing is the truth, not fiction. These sources also add variety and can help the creative nonfiction writer reinforce a point he or she is making in the more straightforward summary parts. Because the writer frequently sets these special forms of communication in their original format, sometimes including photographic reproductions of handwritten diary entries, for example, they serve also to "add light" to the page. The reader can appreciate these visual breathers in the midst of an otherwise dense page of type.

In a historical study, such as Evan S. Connell's *Son of the Morning Star,* about General Custer and his last stand, the author uses historical letters, memoirs, soldiers' reminiscences, and Court of Inquiry records. In the following excerpt, we learn something about Generals Custer, Sheridan, and Sherman. The first short quote is from historian Stephen Ambrose; the major quote is from a communication sent by General Sherman to General Sheridan.

> Historian Stephen Ambrose characterized him [Custer] as an obstinate little man, given to intense rages, made with battle lust during an engagement, quick to censure and slow to forgive, bursting with energy, forever demanding the most of his men…. Women found him exciting, and unlike Sheridan, he seldom cherished a grudge; otherwise, they must have been much alike. Custer might erupt at any instant, he loved to fight and was quick to blame. He could be sarcastic and impossibly demanding. They understood each other, these two. Sheridan perceived in the audacious young cavalryman a sympathetic spirit, one who was not reluctant to discipline troops and who thought the best way to handle dangerous redskins was to crush them. Little Phil [Sheridan] was supported by his boss, William Tecumseh Sherman—himself no shrinking violet. He wrote to Sherman on October 15 that it was up to the Indians themselves to decide whether or not they would be exterminated….
>
> "As brave men and soldiers of a government which has exhausted its peace efforts, we, in the performance of a most unpleasant duty, accept the war begun by our enemies, and hereby resolve to make its end final. If it results in the utter annihilation of these Indians, it is but the result of what they have been warned again and again, and for which they seem fully prepared. I will say nothing and do nothing to restrain our troops from doing what they deem proper on the spot, and will allow no more vague general charges of cruelty and inhumanity to tie their hands, but will use all the powers confided in me to the end that these Indians, the enemies of our race and our civilization, shall not again be able to begin and carry on their barbarous warfare on any kind of a pretext that they may

choose to allege.... You may now go ahead in your own way and I will back you with my whole authority, and stand between you and any efforts that may be attempted in your rear to restrain your purpose or check your troops."

Historians make heavy use of historic letters in their research, and frequently quote all or parts of letters that help them make a point. Readers immediately get more involved when they hear people speaking out of the past than they do when reading the historian's words alone. In the following paragraphs from the chapter "The Quarrel with America" in his monumental series *A History of the English-Speaking Peoples,* Winston Churchill quotes from an "anonymous" letter by "Junius," and then from a newspaper, the *North Briton.* We do not usually see Britain's former prime minister, Winston Churchill, described as a creative nonfiction writer. I've included him here to show how a writer of history works in quotes from letters and newspapers of the historic period but also to show that he is creative in his writing of history—he doesn't "create" history; he's creative in his use of language to tell history.

> The first decade of his [George III's] reign passed in continual and confused manoeuvering between different Parliamentary groups, some of them accepting the new situation, some making passive resistance to the new motion of the Crown. George was angry and puzzled at the wrangling of the political leaders. Pitt sat moodily in Parliament, "unconnected and unconsulted." Many people shared Dr. Johnson's opinion of the Scots, and Bute, who was much disliked, fell from power early in 1763. His successor, George Grenville, was a mulish lawyer, backed by the enormous electoral power of the Duke of Bedford, of whom "Junius" wrote in his anonymous letters, "I daresay he has bought and sold more than half of the representative integrity of the nation." Grenville refused to play the part of "The Minister behind the curtain"; but for two years he clung to office, and must bear a heavy share of responsibility for the alienation of the American colonies.
> There were other conflicts. On April 23, 1763, a newspaper called *The North Briton* attacked Ministers as "tools of despotism

and corruption....They have sent the spirit of discord through the land, and I will prophesy it will never be extinguished but by the extinction of their power."

One of the best sources of historical information comes from court records, where the words of men and women are recorded verbatim and preserved. For *Son of the Morning Star,* Evan S. Connell went back to the records of a Court of Inquiry convened by President Rutherford Hayes to investigate the matter of U.S. Army Major Reno's behavior in the battle now known as "Custer's Last Stand," or the Battle of Little Big Horn. Reno testified at length, partly about the battle itself, partly about General Custer, as we listen in on the following excerpt from his testimony:

> Reno was asked about his relationship with Custer. He replied that he felt no animosity, he and the General got on well enough. But the implication of this was unmistakable, so he added that even if his own brothers had been riding with Custer he could not have done any more than he did.
> His response did not satisfy Lt. Lee. "The question is, did you go into that fight with feelings of confidence or distrust?"
> Reno again responded that he and General got along all right. "My feelings toward Gen. Custer were friendly."
> "I insist that the question shall be answered," said Lee.
> "Well, sir, I had known General Custer a long time," Reno said, "and I had no confidence in his ability as a soldier."

Author Connell, with all those records in front of him, could have simply said something to the effect (taken from the end of that piece of testimony) that Major Reno had no confidence in General Custer's ability as a soldier, but he elected to quote the testimony ahead of that point. I'm speculating, of course, but I imagine that as a creative nonfiction writer (and as a first-rate fiction writer, too) he saw the dramatic possibilities inherent in the way Lt. Lee kept at Major Reno until he said something damaging. Connell let the suspense build, using only the Court of Inquiry's words. He did not invent a sequence of questioning the way a fiction writer would be allowed to. Nonfiction writers also know the value of suspense in involving and holding the reader.

Joseph Wambaugh reported to good effect the verbatim transcript of a criminal's statement to detectives in his nonfiction novel *The Onion Field*. In his foreword, he wrote, "The courtroom dialogue was not re-created." Wambaugh could have told his readers what he thought was the state of Jimmy Smith's mind as he talked to detectives, but he made the point much more effectively by letting us hear the wanderings of this tortured mind.

> The statement was difficult to follow, at times incoherent, and Pierce Brooks looked at Jimmy Smith and imagined the absolute fear that was on him that night when he huddled there, handcuffed, a blanket over his naked shoulders, his feet bloody and painful, while he was interrogated, not for his usual five-dollar shoplift, but for the *murder* of a cop. He could easily imagine Jimmy babbling incoherently, and he could understand how a man like Jimmy Smith could have survived his wretched life by *never* giving anything *but* an indirect, evasive reply to anything anyone ever asked of him.
>
> Brooks could *understand,* but that was all. He despised the lying coward too much for a quantum leap into pity. Jimmy had blurted things to the Bakersfield detectives: "When I hit the county jail, I'm gonna make them give…give me…I know that I…you know,…that I, you know…that I'm not mental, that I couldn't do it, you know, do *that.* I *hope* I didn't do it. I might do it, you know, in a pinch, or maybe if I was shoved into it, or something, but I mean, as far as just outright, you know, just kill a man, you know. Was there anything else you wanna know?"

Presidents, members of Congress, generals, and other notable people tend to write memoirs about their experiences, and writer/historians turn to these written records as research sources. When sections from memoirs are pulled out and quoted in articles and books, they give readers more than facts—they give them human beings. For this reason, creative nonfiction writers frequently quote from memoirs, as in the following excerpt from the Pulitzer Prize–winning historical study of the final year of America's Civil War, *A Stillness at Appomattox*, where Bruce Catton quotes from Ulysses S. Grant's *Personal Memoirs*.

> The pursuit of [Confederate General] Early had been ineffective because too many men were in position to give orders to soldiers like Wright and Emory. All lines of authority were crossed, and the War Department was buzzing and fretting and issuing innumerable orders, taking time along the way to modify, alter, or countermand the orders other people were issuing. Looking back long after the war [General] Grant wrote his verdict: "It seemed to be the policy of General Halleck and Secretary Stanton to keep any force sent there in pursuit of the invading army moving right or left so as to keep between the enemy and our capital; and generally speaking they pursued this policy until all knowledge of the whereabouts of the enemy was lost."

Author Catton wisely mixes quotes from senior military officers like Grant with letters and reminiscences from the lower-ranking officers and enlisted men. In this passage about an ill-fated charge, he draws from Charles H. Banes's *History of the Philadelphia Brigade*.

> Down to the right were the troops which had made the unsuccessful attack earlier in the day, and it was resolved to send them back in again. The men had just succeeded in re-forming their lines after the repulse when a staff officer came galloping up, riding from brigade to brigade with orders for a new attack. One of the men who had to make this charge wrote afterward that "there was an approach to the ridiculous" in the way in which these orders were given. He specified:
> "No officer of higher rank than a brigade commander had examined the approaches to the enemy's works on our front, and the whole expression of the person who brought the message seemed to say, 'The general commanding is doubtful of your success.' The moment the order was given the messenger put spurs to his horse and rode off, lest by some misunderstanding the assault should begin before he was safe and out of range of the enemy's responsive fire."

The soldier who wrote so bitterly about the way the charge was directed confessed that some of the best men in the army "not only retired without any real attempt to carry the enemy's works, but actually retreated in confusion to a point far in the rear of the original line and remained there until nearly night." Staff officers sent to recall them found the men quietly grouped around their regimental flags, making coffee.

Official letters and telegrams are sometimes of such dramatic content that the writer includes one—even reproducing its actual format. C. D. B. Bryan, in *Friendly Fire,* did just that with the type of letter no one wants to receive.

DEPARTMENT OF THE ARMY
OFFICE OF THE ADJUTANT GENERAL
WASHINGTON, D.C. 20315

20 Apr 1970

I have the honor to inform you that your son has been awarded posthumously the Bronze Star Medal and the Good Conduct Medal.

Prior to his death, Michael had been awarded the National Defense Service Medal, Vietnam Service Medal, Vietnam Campaign Medal, Combat Infantryman Badge, and the Marksman Badge with rifle, automatic rifle, and machine gun bars.

Arrangements are being made to have these awards presented to you in the near future by a representative of the Commanding General, Fifth United States Army.

The representative selected will communicate with you in the next few weeks to arrange for presentation. Any inquiry or correspondence concerning presentation should be addressed to the Commanding General, Fifth United States Army, Fort Sheridan, Illinois, 60038.

My continued sympathy is with you.

Sincerely,
S/Kenneth G. Wickham
Major General, USA
The Adjutant General

People also expose bits of themselves when they talk on the telephone, the radio, or television, so creative nonfiction writers are well advised to keep their ears alert. Sometimes the writer can hear both sides of a telephone conversation; other times he or she may have to re-create one side from what's heard on the other end or from what one person recalls about the other side of the conversation. Reporting only one side of a conversation, however, can lend drama and verisimilitude to a report of an incident. Gay Talese, in his extended article about bridge building "The Stage in the Sky" (collected in his book *Fame and Obscurity*), captured this telephone conversation between Chris Reisman and someone named Willy:

> The day after Reisman had been hired by the American Bridge Company and sent to Murphy's shack on the Staten Island shore, Murphy's welcoming words were, "Well, I see we got another ass to sit around here." But soon even Murphy was impressed with twenty-three-year-old Reisman's efficiency as a secretary and his cool manner over the telephone dealing with people Murphy was trying to avoid.
> "Good *morning*, American Bridge…"
> "Yeah, say is Murphy in?"
> "May I ask who's calling?"
> "Wha?"
> "May I ask who's calling?"
> "Yeah, dis is an old friend, Willy…just tell 'im Willy…"
> "May I have your last name?"
> "Wha?"
> "Your *last* name?"
> "Just tell Murphy, well, maybe you can help me. Ya see, I worked on the Pan Am job with Murphy, and…"
> "Just a minute, please," Chris cut in, then switched to Murphy on the intercom and said, "I have a Willy on the phone that worked for you…"
> "*I don't want to talk to that bastard,*" Murphy snapped back.
> Then, back on the phone, Reisman said, "I'm sorry, sir, but Mr. Murphy is not in."
> "Wha?"
> "I said I do not expect Mr. Murphy to be in today."

"Well, okay, I'll try tomorrow."

"Fine," said Chris Reisman, clicking him off, picking up another call with, "Good *morning,* American Bridge...."

Not much need be said about that phone conversation except that we learn a fair amount about Murphy and Chris Reisman, and about the general caliber of operation going on. To get so much background information to the reader through straight exposition would have lacked much and would not have put us right there in that construction workers' shack. People seem to enjoy overhearing phone conversations—and we tend to believe what we learn about something in this manner.

In Jan Morris's lengthy study of the inner and outer workings of New York's Port Authority and its ports, *The Great Port: A Passage through New York,* she captures this end of a phone conversation in a union hiring hall somewhere down near New York's piers:

> I felt rather like a hoodlum boss myself, as we swept around the docks in the recesses of an immense Cadillac, which if not actually bullet-proof (it was only rented) smelt authentically, I thought, of bourbon and cigars. The hiring hall we visited certainly seemed innocent enough. The hiring bosses looked genteel, and the longshoremen, told there was work at Hoboken or Brooklyn, stepped into their waiting cars rather as though they were off to the office (though, in fact, since they are paid for the time they take in travelling to the piers, they often stop off for unnaturally long coffee breaks). It reminded me of Sotheby's, and was conducted, like that other earthy institution, with a certain ritual urgency. In the office a man was on the telephone, collating the needs of the port for labor that morning.
>
> "Okay, Jersey City wants twelve drivers, eight banana men ...Sure, I got a driver at Bayonne, where d'ya want him?...No, like I say, they don't want work in the hold...Yeah, yeah, send him to Berth 7, ITO...Whassat you say? Sure, category A, yeah..."

In remote parts of places like Africa, northern Canada, and Alaska, transportation is expensive and difficult, and telephone service nonexistent, so many people must depend on radio messages. Joe McGinniss wrote about this in his *Going to Extremes* and captured for his readers some typical messages going out over the open airwaves. Sometimes people without a radio themselves have to depend on someone else's hearing and recording the message—and getting it to them somehow, sometime, somewhere.

> Bush Pipeline on the radio: a way to make contact when you are out in the backcountry without a telephone, or when you were trying to reach someone who was.
> "For Mom at Shell Lake. I had my physical yesterday and it was all right, except it cost fifty-one dollars. Gordon."
> "To Julie at Chase. Ellen will be at Talkeetna Saturday. Would you come down?"
> "To Mom and Sparky at Peter's Creek. Come into town as soon as possible. Might have a job lined up for Sparky."
> "For David Burns at Gakona, or on the Gulkana River. Call your attorney at 274-7522 at once. From Geri, your attorney's secretary."
> "For Boulder Creek Lodge. The transmission won't be finished until tomorrow. I'll be out with fresh supplies if the weather holds and I'm able to make it through the pass."

Sometimes a writer will find that snatches of conversation may be telling, dramatic, vivid, involving, despite their shortness of burst. Joan Didion, in her short study of El Salvador, *Salvador,* collected what professional photographers in the field sometimes call "grab shots"—photographs made on the run, shot from the hip—shots that, if properly set up, would most likely be missed because of the pace of action. With a tape recorder, or a good ear, the writer can grab snatches of conversation, as Joan Didion did here.

> There had been, they agreed, fewer dead around since the election, fewer bodies, they thought, than in the capital, but as they began reminding one another of this body or that there still seemed to have been quite a few. They spoke of these bodies in the matter-of-fact way that they might have spoken, in another kind of parish, of confirmation candidates, or cases of croup.

There had been the few up the road, the two at Yoloaiquin. Of course there had been the forty-eight near Barrios, but Barrios was in April. "A *guardia* was killed last Wednesday," one of them recalled.

"Thursday."

"Was it Thursday then, Jerry?"

"A sniper."

"That's what I thought. A sniper."

Paul Theroux's *Sunrise with Seamonsters,* in a chapter about New York City's subways, captures for us some of the straaange goings-on and straaange snatches of conversation we hear on New York's streets and subways.

> Then a Muslim flapped his prayer mat—while we were at Flushing Avenue, talking about rules—and spread it out on the platform and knelt on it, just like that, and was soon on all fours, beseeching Allah and praising the Prophet Mohammed. This is not remarkable. You see praying, or reading the Bible, or selling religion on the subway all the time. "Hallelujah, brothers and sisters," the man with the leaflets says on the BMT-RR line at Prospect Avenue in Brooklyn. "I love Jesus! I used to be a wino!" And Muslims beg and push their green plastic cups at passengers, and try to sell them copies of something called *Arabic Religious Classics*. It is December and Brooklyn, and the men are dressed for the Great Nafud Desert, or Jiddah or Medina—skull cap, gallabieh, sandals.
>
> "And don't sit next to the door," the second police officer said. We were still talking Rules. "A lot of these snatchers like to play the doors."
>
> The first officer said, "It's a good thing to keep near the conductor. He's got a telephone. So does the man in the token booth. At night, stick around the token booth until the train comes."

Jan Morris reports in her book *Destinations* that New York City's daily life is "spattered with aspects and episodes of unhinged sensibility" and lists a few items she snatched up during a two-week stay. Here are some items selected from her list:

Item: At the headquarters of the New York police, which is a functionary called the Chief of Organized Crime, I heard an administrator say to a colleague on the telephone there: *You're going sick today? Administrative sick or regular sick?*

Item: A young man talks about his experiences in a levitation group: *Nobody's hovering yet but we're lifting up and down again. We're hopping. I've seen a guy hop fifteen feet from the lotus position, and no one could do that on the level of trying.*

Item: An eminent, kind and cultivated actress, beautifully dressed, is taking a cab to an address on Second Avenue. Cabdriver: *Whereabouts is that on Second Avenue, lady?* Actress, without a flicker in her equanimity: *Don't ask me, bud. You're the fucking cabdriver.*

A special category of conversational snatches is the one-sided conversation between the pet owner and pet. Jan Morris, in the same listing of items, snatched this one as it went by on a leash:

Item: I feel a sort of furry clutch at my right leg, and peering down, find that it is being bitten by a chow. *Oh Goochy you naughty thing,* says its owner, who is following behind with a brush and shovel for clearing up its excrement, *you don't know that person.*

I suppose I could write an entire chapter on graffiti found in and around our cities and toilets as illustration of the point that we, as a people, do say something about our society through what some of us write on walls, sidewalks, and subways. I'll be content here to add simply the one bit of graffiti given by Jan Morris.

Item: Graffito in Washington Square.
YIPPIES, JESUS FREAKS AND MOONIES
ARE GOVERNMENT OPERATED

People also reveal something by the instructions they write for the public in public places, like hotel rooms, restaurants, and highways. I recall one sign in an English hotel room where my wife and I were staying. On the back of the door was a series of instructions for various things like checkout time and room rates. The instructions on what to do in the event of fire consisted of about six items. Before they instructed us about crawling close to the floor to find unused oxygen, or about not using the lift during a fire, they gave what the English must consider a priority instruction: "(1) Put on your wrapper."

Not long after returning home, I came upon an article in the *New York Times* by Donald Carroll, author of the book *The Best Excuse*. I've excerpted several examples of public instruction from his article, "Truly Inspired Gibberish":

> Consider, for example, this advice from the brochure of a car rental firm in Tokyo: *When a passenger of foot heave in sight, tootle the horn. Trumpet him melodiously at first, but if he obstacles your passage then tootle him with vigor.*
>
> Back in your hotel room, if the hotel is Japanese, you might well be confronted with a polite warning combined with an impossible request: *Is forbidden to steal the hotel towels please. If you are not person to do such thing is please not to read this.*

The final instruction says more about the Japanese people's desire never to offend guests than any amount of long, expository writing or lecturing could accomplish. At first, such items seem simply humorous, but then we see something deeper. Sometimes, of course, the mangling of English or other languages leads to something no deeper than a chuckle, such as the sign Carroll reported in the same article: "There is, for instance, a dentist in Hong Kong who advertises: TEETH EXTRACTED BY THE LATEST METHODISTS."

I guess there are one or two things to be learned from all the foregoing: (1) Non-Methodist tourists—better have that six-month checkup before leaving home, and (2) if you should be recommending this book to a friend, trumpet its praises at first melodiously; that failing, tootle with vigor.

7 ANGLES OF APPROACH AND POINTS OF VIEW

The business of point of view seems to confuse most of us when we begin getting serious about our writing. Much of the explanation in textbooks does more to confuse than clarify. Part of any confusion comes from the several different meanings of the phrase "point of view." Everyone, in casual conversation, will say something like, "Well, that's her point of view; mine's quite different!" or "Everyone has his own viewpoint on that," or, close to that phrase, "What's your view on this, John?" All these variations express the notion that where you stand affects your view—a metaphor that gives us an image of someone, say a military scout, standing atop a rocky point and saying: "From my vantage point I believe we've already lost the battle or are about to, General." The general, from his point of view down in the forest, had thought everything was going well. Now, seeing things through the eyes of his scout, he has to reconsider. These meanings of point of view are similar to the meanings used by writers, but the student of writing must set those aside and concentrate on the several meanings the phrase has within the literary world. It's hard enough to keep the following two literary distinctions clear without also carrying along the informal meanings used in casual conversation.

ANGLES OF APPROACH

A story's angle of approach does not concern itself with who tells the story (the concern of point of view) but rather with how the writer approaches it. That approach can be either objective or subjective.

OBJECTIVE

When you sit down to write a piece you must first decide whether to write from an objective or subjective angle of approach. The decision is crucial because the angle of approach determines to a great degree what kinds of facts should be included and what should be considered irrelevant and therefore left out.

If you were writing as a military strategist, for example, you would adopt an objective angle of approach and include how many bombs dropped on the city. You might well include how many civilians died as a result of the bombing. You would not, however, include descriptions of the children dying in the streets as the bombs fell. In a larger sense, such facts are important and relevant, but when the angle of approach is objective, the facts of how horribly the children died are not relevant. Given the same situation, if you were writing as a psychologist, how the children and their parents suffered would be relevant (and therefore included), but the facts about how many bombs of what kind fell that night would be viewed as irrelevant. Judgments and opinions have no place in a piece with an objective angle of approach. They belong in works using a subjective angle of approach.

SUBJECTIVE

Given the same bombing scene, a man who had been an ambulance worker might later write an article about the experience using a subjective angle of approach. If so, his descriptions would not only be vivid, they'd likely be emotional. He would write about his own emotions when he slid the injured children into the back of the

ambulance, and he might describe the emotional responses of the parents as the ambulance rushes, sirens blaring, to the hospital. Chances are that an ambulance worker would not write in the same article about the Eighth Air Force's bombing strategy against the cities of western Germany; that would be a more objective than subjective approach.

Scientists or other specialists writing an article (especially an expository one) about their specialty will usually write in an objective (impersonal) *voice*. The voice is impersonal in that the specialist will probably not introduce his or her personal feelings on the subject and won't tell readers how to feel about the subject. Sometimes we can read between the lines and sense personal feelings, but nothing is said directly—the writer using the objective approach doesn't deliberately make him or herself the focus of the article or insert personal reactions or attitudes.

Consistency of approach is important for both the reader and the writer. If a writer switches back and forth between impersonal and personal, the reader will become confused. A writer of creative nonfiction will be apt to write with a personal voice, which is all right, provided it is consistent. Given the example of the bombing raid, consider the confusion caused by the military strategist who changes his or her angle of approach in the middle of a narrative and begins describing the horrors of war (i.e., a shift to a subjective approach). Think of the confusion caused by the psychologist-writer who interrupts a cogent discussion of the mental damage suffered by the dead children's parents to go on at some length about how many tons of bombs fell, from what kind of aircraft, and at what intervals. What is relevant for one specialist is irrelevant for the other, yet their angle of approach is the same—objective.

POINTS OF VIEW

After the writer has made the key decision about angle of approach, he or she must make an equally important decision—from whose point of view shall the article or book be told? Point of view concerns through whose eyes the reader views the action. There are several points of view from which to select, and, as a general rule, only one point of view should be used in a single piece. To tell a story through more than one set of eyes tends to confuse the reader. Writers strive for unity; multiple points of view destroy unity. Sometimes a story or article can be divided into two parts, each told from a different point of view, and still be successful, but a piece that switches back and forth between viewpoints all the way through can be confusing.

In selecting a point of view, the writer has to answer several fundamental questions: Whose story is this? Who could best tell it? The story might, for example, be George Orwell's, but after some thought, the writer may decide that George's story would be more interestingly, or more effectively, told by someone other than George. If George tells it, the writer uses first person ("I"), but if someone else narrates Orwell's story, the writer must use third person.

FIRST PERSON POINT OF VIEW

In the case of George Orwell's book *Down and Out in Paris and London,* he was the writer and the main character, and he told his story in first person.

> I travelled to England third class via Dunkirk and Tillbury, which is the cheapest and not the worst way of crossing the Channel. You had to pay extra for a cabin, so I slept in the saloon, together with most of the third-class passengers. I find this entry in my diary for that day:
> "Sleeping in the saloon, twenty-seven men, sixteen women. Of the women, not a single one has washed her face this morning. The men mostly went to the bathroom; the women merely produced vanity cases and covered the dirt with powder. Q. A secondary sexual difference?"

Another question the writer must address is, What is the relationship between the one who tells the story and the story itself? In Orwell's book, the narrator is the main character, so almost everything relates to him in one way or another. If someone else observes and narrates the action that relates to the main character, the writer may also use the first person, but in a different voice. If, for example, George Orwell had had a friend, Bill, traveling with him, and Bill was now writing a book about their experiences living down and out, he would narrate the story. It might still be George Orwell's story, but told by an observer, a fellow participant. Such a passage might sound like this:

> *We* travelled to England third class via Dunkirk and Tillbury, which is the cheapest and not the worst way of crossing the Channel. You had to pay for a cabin, so *we* slept in the saloon, together with most of the third-class passengers. I found this entry in *my* diary for that day:
> "Twenty-seven men and sixteen women slept with *us* in the saloon. In the morning, *George* and I used the bathroom, as did the other men, but not a single woman did; they simply produced vanity cases and covered the dirt with powder. *George* asked whether I thought this might be a newly discovered secondary sexual difference."

My italicized words show that this hypothetical Bill, too, would use the first person, but by referring directly to "George," he makes it clear to us that George is not the narrator, not the "I" in the story. Such a short passage could not make it clear that it is still George's story his companion is narrating, but it would soon be apparent by the emphasis he would give to George rather than to himself.

One great danger in writing first person narrative is the tendency for the "I" narrator to take over, rather than keeping the focus on the main character. Nonfiction and fiction writers run this risk every time they elect to write in the first person. Naturally, when the piece is autobiographical, the central character is automatically kept in the limelight by the first person technique—just where he or she should be. The problem comes only when the narrator is an observer reporting on the main character through first person point of view.

William Zinsser likes to write in a personal voice and often in the first person, yet he keeps the limelight on the character or thing he's writing about. His presence is felt, but not intrusively. In his profile about two great jazz musicians, Willie Ruff and Dwike Mitchell (*Willie and Dwike: An American Profile*), Zinsser goes with them on concert tours, but he's not forever telling us about himself, what he did, how he reacted. We just sense that he's with them through the occasional reference to himself in first person:

> Mitchell and Ruff go to the auditorium early to look it over. It's handsome, like the rest of the building, but with the intimacy of a small concert hall. Backstage, it has a door big enough for the biggest combine to drive through—this theatre can present a full case of Deere's green and yellow tractors, works of art in themselves.
>
> The piano is an almost seven-foot grand, and Mitchell tries it out before he even takes off his coat. It hasn't been tuned. "The piano's got eight A's, all different," he tells *me*. Ruff is hailed from the highest tier by a young man who says he will be operating the lights. Ruff shouts up to him that whatever he wants to do will be fine. The hall begins to fill up with men and women who have driven out from the Quad Cities. *I* recognize quite a few who were at the Sunday afternoon concert. Lois Jecklin works the house, asking the new arrivals whether they are on the mailing list of Visiting Artists. They gladly fill out a card for her; in America the arts have one sacred text—the mailing list.

Like my hypothetical companion to George Orwell, Bill Zinsser accompanied Willie and Dwike and wrote the Willie and Dwike story as an observer, not as a deeply involved observer, but simply as observer. Zinsser has written in the personal voice without writing totally in the first person. I examined *Willie and Dwike* for several pages surrounding that passage and found that the "me" and "I" (that I've italicized above) were the only first-person references to Bill Zinsser's presence. Those two totally unintrusive references were enough to keep the personal voice and the first person point of view throughout. Many writers don't have as much control as Zinsser, and write their pieces either intrusively in first person, or in the third person where it's easier to remain unintrusive. I think the Zinsser approach works best, if you can maintain control over that limelight.

THIRD PERSON POINT OF VIEW

The choice of first person or third person centers on distance. Do you want close-up, intimate, immediate, involved writing? First person does a better job of that. Do you want to stand back for an overview, deal with more characters, more descriptions of people and settings? Third person would be a better choice.

When the New Journalists of the early 1960s were experimenting with the kind of creative nonfiction writing we're talking about here, they were criticized for putting the journalist too much in the forefront. In a sort of overreaction to all the years when journalists had to stay totally, absolutely invisible, some writers did push themselves so much stage-front that the limelight fell on them rather than on the characters or the events about which they were writing. Tom Wolfe led the way at the time, but in his more recent work, including *The Right Stuff,* he stays largely in the background, although we know he's present. We like having Tom Wolfe present. He says in his book *The New Journalism* that some of the best writing of this "new" kind has been done in third person. He mentions writers like Capote, Talese, and John Gregory Dunne as examples of people who write in a personal voice but use third person.

Third person point of view has less immediacy than first person and always has an impersonal voice. The narrator seems to stand above it all, but there are limits to how much he or she is "allowed" to observe as a nonparticipant in the action. Literary convention allows the third person narrator some latitude. In fiction, the omniscient narrator may enter any or all characters' minds. He or she may observe any action anywhere. In creative nonfiction, however, the writer has less latitude, less omniscience. He or she is limited by the facts available to a character or reasonably deducible by that character. Historical biographies, for example, use this kind of third-person narrative, a narrator whose camera has a wide-angle lens. Other writers of nonfiction carry a literary camera with interchangeable lenses, one of which is a close-up lens. The best way to make clear this distinction between third person (close-up) and third person (panoramic or wide-angle) may be through two passages from the same book, *The Right Stuff*. Both passages deal with Alan Shepard's first orbital flight. The first takes place within the tiny capsule where we not only see Shepard close up, we go inside his mind (the ultimate close-up). The second passage shows us what happens soon after Shepard arrives in New York City. Tom Wolfe takes off the close-up lens and inserts the wide-angle lens to enable the narrator to watch Alan go by on parade, and then he widens his lens to include Alan's hometown and New England—all in the same third person. These two passages show the versatility of third person point of view.

In this part of the story, Shepard had forgotten to take the filter off the capsule's periscope, so he was seeing everything on Earth in black and white—yet he knew that the folks back home wanted to hear about it in color:

> "What a beautiful view!" he said. He could hear Slayton say: "I bet it is." In fact, there was a cloud cover over most of the East Coast and much of the ocean. He was able to see the Cape. He could see the west coast of Florida...Lake Okeechobee.... He was up so high he seemed to be moving away from Florida ever so slowly.... And the inverters moaned up and the gyros moaned down and the fans whirred and the cameras hummed.... He tried to find Cuba. Was that Cuba or wasn't that Cuba? Over there, through the clouds.... Everything was black and white and there were clouds all over.... There's Bimini Island and the shoals around Bimini. He could see that. *But everything looked so small!* It had all been bigger and clear in the ALFA trainer, when they flashed the still photos on the screen.... The real thing didn't measure up. It was not *realistic*. He couldn't see anything but a medium-gray ocean and the light-gray beaches and the dark-gray vegetation....

We know Tom Wolfe has snapped on the close-up lens as soon as we hear those inverters, gyros, fans, cameras. Then he really goes in tight on Alan Shepard when we hear the astronaut thinking about Cuba and whether he's seeing it or not. The irony of his thought that the flight simulation had been more realistic than the real thing follows. He stays in close with sounds that Alan Shepard could have heard (and no sounds that he could not reasonably have heard), and then enters the man's mind as he watches the world through his periscope. We eavesdrop on a brain at work—the ultimate in personal writing—yet we do it in third person, which we tend to think of as the impersonal point of view. The scene is even more personal and up close than if Wolfe had used the first person and had Shepard telling us what he'd thought back then in the capsule. Instead, Wolfe shows us Shepard's thought processes. Naturally, Wolfe had not been inside Shepard's mind. He interviewed Alan Shepard about his thoughts and then re-created them for us in this interior monolog. The values and challenges of using this technique in creative nonfiction are addressed in Chapter 8.

Now, let's watch as Wolfe shows us the Broadway ticker-tape parade with his wide-angle lens:

> The next day New York City gave Al a ticker-tape parade up Broadway. There was Al on the back ledge of the limousine, with all that paper snow and confetti coming down just the way you used to see it in the Movietone News in the theaters. Al's hometown, Derry, New Hampshire, which was not much more than a village, gave Al a parade, and it drew the biggest crowd the state had ever seen. Army, Navy, Marine, Air Force, and National Guard troops from all over New England marched down Main Street, and acrobatic teams of jet fighters flew overhead....

MULTIPLE POINTS OF VIEW

Switching points of view back and forth in a piece tends to confuse the reader, but handled right, it's possible to switch points of view successfully. C. D. B. Bryan, author of *Friendly Fire,* wrote in the third person as he told about how the young soldier, Michael

Mullin, was killed accidentally by our own guns. As soon as the writer went to visit Michael's parents, however, Bryan switched to the first person. Because this was the first time he had come into the story himself, the switch to first person seemed totally natural. No reader could have been confused by that switch—and he didn't switch back to third person.

A similar type of single switch occurs in Joe Eszterhas's much-praised story, "Charlie Simpson's Apocalypse" (collected by Tom Wolfe in *The New Journalism*), when he tells the story in third person until the end. At that point, he does come into the story to explain to his readers how he happened to come upon the story and how he worked on it. Again, this kind of simple, single shift of point of view is allowable because there's no danger that the reader will wonder what's going on.

Jane Kramer begins her book *The Last Cowboy* in first person, telling us how she came to write about cowboy life and, particularly, why she selected Henry Blanton to write about. After she explains a bit about her method of working with Henry and his wife, she ducks out of the limelight and lets it fall almost totally on Henry for the remaining 95 percent of the book. No problem here.

Michael Herr's excellent book *Dispatches,* reporting on life for the U.S. Marines fighting in Vietnam during the Tet Offensive, uses multiple points of view as Herr switches from talking about specific marines in the third person to giving his own, noncombatant's feelings in the first person. Wisely, he kept the limelight on the fighting marines most of the time, only returning occasionally to himself. By doing it proportionately like that, he accomplished two objectives. First, we believed what he wrote partly because of the captured conversations with the marines, which kept our eyes and ears on the young fighting men. Second, by occasional references to himself he reminded us, unobtrusively, that this was not a secondhand report written in a Saigon bar; this man was sitting there in the slit trench, head down, talking with these men. So, it's a matter of proportion. Above all, keep in mind whose story you're telling, and keep the grammatical person appropriate for telling that particular story. Then, if needed (and only if needed), switch point of view.

Then there's the very deliberate, very conscious, very artistic use of multiple points of view. Tom Wolfe makes an art of switching points of view in the middle of a story, in the middle of a paragraph, in the middle of a sentence. At times the reader is confused, I imagine, but Wolfe is always going for the overall effect, tone, and feeling for the scene rather than trying to keep the reader right on track every moment. In his book *The New Journalism* Wolfe writes about an article he wrote:

> I began a story on Baby Jane Holzer, entitled "The Girl of the Year," as follows:
>
> Bangs manes bouffant beehives Beatle caps butter faces brush-on lashes decal eyes puffy sweaters French thrust bras flailing leather blue jeans stretch pants stretch jeans honeydew bottoms eclair shanks elf boots ballerinas Knight slippers, hundreds of them, these flaming little buds, bobbing and screaming, rocketing around inside the Academy of Music Theater underneath that vast old moldering cherub dome up there—aren't they super-marvelous!
>
> "Aren't they super-marvelous!" says Baby Jane, and then, "Hi, Isabel! Isabel! You want to sit backstage—with the Stones!"
>
> The show hasn't even started yet, the Rolling Stones aren't even on the stage, the place is full of a great shabby moldering dimness, and these flaming little buds.
>
> Girls are reeling this way and that way in the aisle and through their huge black decal eyes, sagging with Tiger Tongue Lick Me brush-on eyelashes and black appliques, sagging like display-window Christmas trees, they keep staring at—her—Baby Jane—on the aisle.

After Tom Wolfe's clever opening paragraph that presents the reality of the teenagers' lifestyle through a disembodied narrator in a third person point of view, he switches to Baby Jane's third person point of view. The switch occurs with the phrase, "aren't they super-marvelous!" When the text gets down to "they keep staring at-her-Baby Jane-on the aisle," Wolfe has switched the point of view again. This time, we're seeing the scene through the eyes of the young buds as they look at Baby Jane. He uses three points of view in this piece—his own, the young girls', and Baby Jane's. It's all rather subtly done, and we end up with an understanding of how it must have felt to be there in the Academy of Music surrounded by all those noises and bobbing buds.

Tom Wolfe went on to say: "Eventually a reviewer called me a 'chameleon' who constantly took on the coloration of whomever he was writing about. He meant it negatively. I took it as a great compliment. A chameleon...but exactly!"

PSEUDO POINT OF VIEW

I have coined the name for this point of view because I'm unaware of an official name for it, although I suspect it's what Tom Wolfe called the "downstage voice," not a bad label for people familiar with the stage. What I'm about to describe also has a chameleon quality to it. Tom Wolfe is one of the few writers to make artistic use of this technique, as he does in this excerpt from a piece that helped earn him a reputation for innovation back in 1965. "The Last American Hero Is Junior Johnson. Yes!" chronicles the lifestyle of Junior Johnson, the famous stock car racer and former moonshine runner. Wolfe uses the first and the third person as called for, but he periodically switches to what at first sounds like a different point of view, like someone else at the race. Reading on, we find that the narrator is still Tom Wolfe, but now he's talking just like a good ol' boy. So, it's not truly a different point of view, it's a pseudo point of view, a sort-of-but-not-quite-new point of view. We're *sort of* hearing from a new angle (maybe I should call it "point of hearing"). Wolfe accomplishes this sometimes with a single word that we realize immediately is not the sophisticated, East Coast Tom Wolfe-with-the-white-shoes voice, yet we can hear that he's still there, guiding things along. Sometimes he lets us hear long passages in the local lingo.

God! The Alcohol Tax agents used to burn over Junior Johnson. Practically every good old boy in town in Wilkesboro, the county seat, got to know the agents by sight in a very short time. They would rag them practically to their faces on the subject of Junior Johnson, so that it got to be an obsession. Finally, one night they had Junior trapped on the road up toward the bridge around Millersville, there's no way out of there, they had barricades up and they could hear this souped-up car roaring around the bend, and here it comes—but suddenly they can hear a siren and see a red light flashing in the grill, so they think it's another agent, and boy, they run out like ants and pull those barrels and boards and sawhorses out of the way, and then—Ggghzzzzhhhggggzzzzzzeeeeong!— gawdam! there he goes again, it was him, Junior Johnson!, with a gawdam agent's si-reen and a red light in his grill!

Perhaps we can't tell immediately that Wolfe has switched into a pseudo point of view, but we can certainly tell when we get down to, "Finally, one night they had Junior trapped…." From there on, the almost continuous run-on sentence of about one hundred words sounds like someone telling a tale. We hear the pseudo-narrator imitating the sound of Junior ripping through the would-be road-block. Then Wolfe hits us with a couple of "gawdams" and the sound of a "si-reen." We know it's not Wolfe, yet it's no one else identifiable. We know that the Wolfe lurks nearby.

Joe Eszterhas opened his article "Charlie Simpson's Apocalypse" with an excellent example of a pseudo point of view. It starts out sounding like a normal third person narrative in a personal voice, but it gradually becomes something else.

Right after the sun comes up, first thing folks do around Harrisonville, Missouri, is to go up to the barn and see if the mare is still there. Horse-thieves drive around the gravel roads and brushy hills in tractor-trailers looking to rustle lazyboned nags. Then they grind them up into bags of meat jelly for the dogfood people. It's getting so bad that a man can't live in peace anywhere, not even on his own plot of land.

Harrisonville is just 42 miles southeast of Kansas City along Interstate 71, just down the blacktop from the red brick farmhouse where Harry S. Truman, haberdasher and President, was born. The little town is filled with weeping willows, alfalfa, Longhorn steer, and Black Whiteface cows. Life should be staid and bucolic, a slumbering leftover of what everyone who buys the $3.00 Wednesday night Catfish Dinner at Scott's Bar B-Q calls Them Good Old Days. But it isn't like that anymore.

There's always some botheration to afflict a man these days and if it isn't the horse-thieves or the velvetleaf that plagued the soybeans last year, then it's them vagrant tornadoes.

I've arbitrarily broken his text into paragraphs that illustrate how he's used a combination of normal third-person point of view and pseudo point of view. In the final sentences of the first paragraph we can clearly hear the voice of someone local, even though the first few sentences are not too clearly third or pseudo. The second paragraph is a straight third-person point of view. We hear the voice of the outside writer/narrator. It's written in a personal voice, but it's not the voice of the local person we think we heard at the end of the first paragraph. The third paragraph sounds like a local person's point of view, yet he or she is not identified: It's the writer deliberately making the narrator sound more in touch with the place and the people—a pseudo point of view.

It takes a writer with a sensitive, well-tuned ear to simulate a local person's voice. Not very many writers attempt it, but it's an excellent technique for the creative nonfiction writer if handled cleverly and in good taste.

VOICE

In objective (impersonal) writing, the writer/narrator writes about thoughts shared by many people, ideas available in the literature, the newspapers, and in the general public opinion. The impersonal narrator never gets "personal" by voicing his or her emotions or deeply held thoughts about the topic at hand. Journalists have been told to write in this impersonal voice to maintain an "objective" tone—the reader should not know how the journalist feels about the subject, only what others say about it.

Writing done in a subjective (personal) voice does allow the writer to openly inject his or her feelings on the subject to let the reader know whose mind the ideas are filtering through. The New Journalists of the 1960s thought this was the honest way to report the world to the public. They got into trouble sometimes by injecting themselves so much into the story that they became the center of it. They wrote so personally that the attention was focused on them and their (sometimes) histrionics. Tom Wolfe, often called the father of the New Journalism, was so happy to get out from under the fetters of traditionally impersonal journalistic writing that he wrote wildly (wonderfully, but wildly in the eyes of traditional journalists). He tried out his wings, and he flew in great style to great heights. Neither of these voices is the voice I'm taking up here.

Lewis H. Lapham, editor of *Harper's* magazine, and a creative nonfiction writer of consummate skill, in 1983 wrote a piece called "On Reading" in his column, "Notebook." His opening paragraph said as well as can be said just what "voice" means:

> On first opening a book I listen for the sound of the human voice. By this device I am absolved from reading much of what is published in a given year. Most writers make use of institutional codes (academic, literary, political, bureaucratic, technical), in which they send messages already deteriorating into the half-life of yesterday's news. Their transmissions remain largely unintelligible, and unless I must decipher them for professional reasons, I am content to let them pass by. I listen, instead, for a voice in which I can hear the music of the human improvisation as performed through 5,000 years on the stage of recorded time.
>
> ...As a student, and later as an editor and occasional writer of reviews, I used to feel obliged to finish every book I began to read. This I no longer do. If within the first few pages I cannot hear the author's voice...I abandon him at the first convenient opportunity.

All creative nonfiction writers do not write in the personal voice, but the ones this book celebrates do write in a voice of their own that we can hear. One group of creative nonfiction writers believes that writers should subordinate themselves, telling the story in its own terms, not theirs. As writers, they intend to portray reality just as it is and not interpret it for the reader. This is not altogether possible, of course, but they try. Creative nonfiction writers in the other group do insert themselves and approach reporting the world as an art. They make it clear that things are being filtered (and very likely distorted) through their unique intelligence, and they try to write it in language that approaches literature. Writing of this kind calls attention to itself, and the reader enjoys it partly for the information and partly for the intellectual joy of hearing it filtered through a respected intelligence. The former group believes, like the minimalists in fiction, that writing should be transparent, not calling attention to itself by its fanciness, its beauty.

But these two groups—those that believe in presence of the writer's voice in a story and those who believe the voice has no place—share some qualities. These two groups belong under the same umbrella in creative nonfiction because they do write with the voice of a human being, not in an institutional nonvoice, or what Wolfe calls the "beige" voice. Neither group writes in beige. Their writing is vivid, writing that brings the subject alive. Traditional journalism and nonfiction writing in general avoid this. When we read a piece that lives, that has a human sound to it, we know we're reading creative nonfiction—writing with voice. By voice, I do not mean authorial intrusion, but rather the writer's unique style. While one group of creative nonfiction writers may believe that the writer should never make his or her presence known, both groups welcome the writer's voice.

I'll end this discussion of voice with words and ideas from Mark Kramer, as reported in Norman Sims' book *The Literary Journalists.* The introduction of personal voice, according to Kramer, allows the writer to play one world off another, to toy with irony. "The writer can posture, say things not meant, imply things not said. When I find the right voice for a piece, it admits play, and that's a relief, an anti-dote to being pushed around by your own words. Voice that admits of 'Self' can be a great gift to readers. It allows warmth, concern, compassion, flattery, shared imperfections—all the real stuff that, when it's missing, makes writing brittle and larger than life."

8 🌿 CHARACTER DEVELOPMENT

Traditional nonfiction, particularly journalistic nonfiction, never concerned itself with developing characters. Fiction writers worked at characterization; nonfiction writers concentrated on events. Creative nonfiction writers say that because so many events occur as the result of human interactions, the event cannot be fully understood without also understanding something of the people (characters) surrounding it. The word "character" has been so long associated with fictional characters that I hesitated to use it in this nonfiction context, but I could find no suitable substitute. Please bear in mind that the "characters" talked about here are real people, and most of the time I'll be referring to their character—that is, what makes them tick.

When I write about character development, I'm talking about how the writer goes about revealing a person's character—how the writer develops the revelation, not how the real person develops character over a lifetime. The creative nonfiction writer does not "create" characters; rather, he or she reveals them to the reader as honestly and accurately as possible. Like most contemporary fiction writers, creative nonfiction writers reveal character much as it happens in real life—bit by bit.

When we first meet a character (person) in real life, no one reads us a résumé or life story. We learn a few tidbits about that person's background and form some initial impressions about the person's character by what we talk about, what that person said in response to what we said, how it was said, what words were used, and the like; before the next meeting, we may hear what other people (friends and others) say about the person; in subsequent meetings we form more impressions and revise earlier ones. In the case of spouses, for example, we may go on learning more and more for fifty years as his or her character continues to be revealed, bit by bit.

Writers don't usually have fifty years to collect data; they must collect what they can when they can, and then, very selectively, choose those bits that seem to reveal character best. They reveal the bits in a sequence that is reasonably connected with the unfolding narrative and simulates life in its nonlinear, unpredictable revelations, spreading pieces of characterization through the article or book instead of trying to reveal all aspects of a character at once.

I've discussed a variety of techniques for revelation in previous chapters. These techniques serve several functions, making them extremely valuable to know about and use. In a single piece of captured conversation (Chapter 6), for example, we might hear references to several concrete details that resonate in our memories and stir up emotions while, at the same time, the diction and the specialist language (Chapter 5) used may give us one or more dimensions of the character. When considering what to use from captured conversations, select those pieces that serve multiple functions, when possible.

The fiction writer creates dialog that serves several narrative purposes. The creative nonfiction writer, by contrast, cannot create dialog; he or she can only select those captured conversations or comments that do some of the narrative work. Why select one conversation or comment that serves only one purpose when you could just as easily select a multipurpose one?

DIALOGS, MONOLOGS, AND OTHER LOGS

DIALOGS (CAPTURED CONVERSATIONS)

Both fiction and nonfiction writers have a basic choice to make when faced with establishing character: They can do it directly through a written summary of traits (telling) or indirectly through dialog and action (showing). Teachers of fiction writing usually tell new students that they can "characterize" best by showing a character in different situations and letting us note how he or she behaves—and what he or she says. One fundamental reason for this is that readers begin to suspect a writer who keeps tugging at our elbow and telling us, in effect, how to think about a character. This is bad enough in fiction writing; it's even more questionable in nonfiction. Fiction writers have a certain responsibility to tell readers how they should think about a character so they can draw some moral point; nonfiction writers are not in business to instruct readers in moral behavior. Nonfiction writers have a responsibility to limit themselves to showing readers how things look to them in the world, leaving the reader to interpret what it all means. Therefore, for the nonfiction writer, reporting as accurately as possible what people say is one of the best ways to establish character; we tend to reveal ourselves through our speech, even when we don't want to.

The creative nonfiction writer must stay close to the action to take down by tape recorder, handwritten notes, or memory what everyone is saying. At first, this may sound no different than the traditional reporter who is "going after quotes." But the difference is great. The traditional, hard-news reporter on deadline seeks answers to questions he or she poses to get good quotes. He or she doesn't record everything said by everyone present. The reporter looks not for quotes that characterize but for quotes that explain. The creative nonfiction writer also listens for quotes that may explain, but he or she listens to everything else as well, knowing that some unsolicited comments by "unimportant" people may explain even more than those received from the "notables." Reporters tend to quote the notables—the lawyers, the officers, the preachers, the drug pushers. The creative nonfiction writer knows that these people can give only parts of the story—in some cases, they deliberately give only certain parts of the story. Sometimes the enlisted men provide more useful quotes and better insights than the officers. They see the event through a different point of view; they may see it from a foxhole, while the general sees it from an aerial photograph.

Snatches of conversation can also reveal something of a character. Short phrases, outbursts, curses captured on the fly make interesting and possibly revelatory reading. But these pieces should be used only if the writer believes them typical for the character. (Examples of snatches of conversation are given in Chapter 6.)

We learn about characters not only through what they say, but from how they say it. The ancient Greeks said, "Speak so I may see you." Well put. Until a character (real or fictional) speaks, he or she is but an abstraction for us. From the moment the character begins speaking, we believe we're beginning to know the person. We also know through experience that we can be deceived by what a person says and how he or she says it, but we also know there's little hope of understanding someone fully until we listen to what he or she says.

The creative nonfiction writer should capture the speaker's accent, dialect, colloquialisms, jargon, specialist language, rhythm, color, tone, emphases, and mood. These attributes of human speech do not give us a full understanding of a person's character, but they do help us "see" the speaker. Be careful not to stereotype or even ridicule by emphasizing too many idiosyncrasies of a person's speech; use just enough of these attributes to give the flavor of the person. Too much emphasis, for example, on someone's poor grammar may make the person seem unintelligent when he or she is merely ignorant. If the person is unquestionably intelligent but unschooled, the writer must get this distinction across, probably not by direct statement but by showing us through a scene this raw, uncultivated intelligence at work. If the quoted person used foul language in practically every sentence of captured conversation, the writer should not report every swear word, but should use some to convey the flavor of the conversation. It would be a distortion to clean up every sentence to make it acceptable to every reader.

In *Do You Sleep in the Nude?,* Rex Reed reported a conversation with Ava Gardner. She didn't speak in four-letter words, but she did speak colorfully—and Reed captured the color:

> Don't look at me. I was up until four A.M. at that goddam premiere of *The Bible.* Premieres! I will personally kill that John Huston if he ever drags me into another mess like that. There

must have been ten thousand people clawing at me. I get claustrophobia in crowds and I couldn't breathe. Christ, they started shoving a TV camera at me and yelling, "Talk, Ava!"

In *The Pine Barrens,* John McPhee reported the following captured conversation with Bill and Fred. Here, the writer captured the essence of conversation with these men, revealing the level of discussion.

> Eventually, I made the request I had intended to make when I walked in the door. "Could I have some water?" I said to Fred. "I have a jerry can and I'd like to fill it at the pump."
>
> "Hell, yes," he said. "That isn't my water. That's God's water. That right, Bill?"
>
> "I guess so," Bill said, without looking up. "It's good water, I can tell you that."
>
> "That's God's Water," Fred said again. "Take all you want."

The main purpose of using captured conversation is to discover and report by indirect means what a person is thinking. The only more direct means would be to tune in on the person's brain and mind— to write an internal monolog.

INTERNAL MONOLOG

Fiction writers have long used internal (interior) monolog as a technique to reveal a character's mental state. Nonfiction writers, by contrast, have had to stay out of cranial territory. After all, nonfiction deals with facts, truth, and objectivity, so how could it use something so subjective, so speculative, as reporting what a person thought? Besides, it's impossible. You can't know what another person thinks without asking.

Tom Wolfe said that you could indeed know what a person thought. All you had to do, he said, was to ask them what they were thinking, and to ask them in depth, not in the superficial way of the hard-news reporter. Wolfe, Gay Talese, and a handful of others involved in the New Journalism of the 1960s, decided that the inner life was accessible to serious, professional writers with high ethical standards. The interior of the mind became a new beat for journalists.

Of all the techniques borrowed from fiction writers by nonfiction writers, this one of entering the mind of another met the most objection. Wolfe's early, persistent, and wonderfully innovative use of the technique almost led to the early demise of the parajournalism movement. It was simply too great a leap for most people, even those sympathetic to this new approach to journalistic writing.

In clever hands like those of Wolfe and Talese, the internal monolog can be the most effective technique for revealing a person's character. We hear his or her innermost thoughts, something we're not normally privy to. Wolfe claims that he doesn't "create" what he puts down as the person's thoughts. He says that the thoughts are expressed to him during a long (sometimes weeks—or months—long) series of conversations, and through letters or diaries. During that extended period of time he also learns how the person expresses him or herself under various conditions of relaxation and stress. This knowledge enables him to make the internal monolog sound "right."

Most of the devices fiction writers use to make internal monologs credible serve nonfiction writers as well. Nonfiction writers, in one sense, have an easier time of it. They don't have to invent the thoughts. All they have to invent are the words, rhythms, diction, emphases, repetitive patterns, unusual punctuation, or lack of punctuation, and other devices traditionally used more by the fiction writer. Well-written internal monolog sounds like unedited, uncensored human thought—or at least what we think it might sound like if we could tap the brain.

Joseph Wambaugh, after considerable interviewing and research, wrote from inside Jimmy Smith's mind as he ran away from *The Onion Field,* where the murder occurred.

En route he thought that maybe Powell will get *himself* killed. Sure, why not? The cop'll make his call and in fifteen minutes there'll be squad cars crawlin' over every inch of that miserable farmland. Powell is nuts. He might try to shoot his way out. Sure.

Or maybe Powell will try to give himself up and the cops might shoot him anyway. Sure. Yeah. The fuckin' cops'll be ready to kill anybody over this. Yeah. And maybe they'll just go ahead and dust him anyway. And then I made it for sure. The other cop won't know nothin' about me. How could he? He knows I'm called Jimmy, that's all. And I kept my hat on and my mouth shut most of the time so he won't even know what race I am. "I got a chance, baby, a hell of a chance!"

An interesting variation on the use of internal monolog is the writing about what goes on (or might go on) within the brain of a non-human being. In the first example, Loren Eiseley, the anthropologist who wrote so creatively about scientific matters, wrote in his book *The Unexpected Universe* about his relationship with his big shepherd dog, Wolfe. Eiseley had laid on the floor a ten-thousand-year-old bison bone that normally sat on his desk. The dog grabbed the bone and mouthed it with sharp fangs. When the master asked Wolfe to put it down, he was met by such low and steady rumbling he couldn't believe it was the same dog. Eiseley decided that we'd understand better what was happening if he wrote for the dog an internal monolog:

> As I advanced, his teeth showed and his mouth wrinkled to strike. The rumbling rose to a direct snarl. His flat head swayed low and wickedly as a reptile's above the floor. I was the most loved object in his universe, but the past was fully alive in him now. Its shadows were whispering in his mind. I knew he was not bluffing. If I made another step he would strike.
>
> Yet his eyes were strained and desperate. "Do not," something pleaded in the back of them, some affectionate thing that had followed at my heel all the days of his mortal life, "do not force me. I am what I am and cannot be otherwise because of the shadows. Do not reach out. You are a man, and my very god. I love you, but do not put out your hand. It is midnight. We are in another time, in the snow."
>
> "The other time," the steady rumbling continued while I paused, "the other time in the snow, the big, the final, the terrible snow, when the shape of this thing I hold spelled life. I will

not give it up. I cannot. The shadows will not permit me. Do not put out your hand."

Another world-renowned scientist, Dr. Lewis Thomas, wrote in *Lives of a Cell* about how animals (including humans) emit odors that communicate. Pheromones, the molecules that create these odors that communicate very specific messages, work under very low concentration—eight or ten molecules in a chain are enough to do the job. He wrote about the thoughts a male moth might have as he got a whiff of bombykol, a pheromone released by the female moth when it would like to be visited by a male. Dr. Thomas is not sure whether the male knows why he's being summoned; all the male moth knows for sure is that he's going!

> The messages are urgent, but they may arrive, for all we know, in a fragrance of ambiguity. "At home, 4 P.M. today," says the female moth, and releases a brief explosion of bombykol, a single molecule of which will tremble the hairs of any male within miles and send him driving upwind in a confusion of ardor. But it is doubtful if he has an awareness of being caught in an aerosol of chemical attractant. On the contrary, he probably finds suddenly that it has become an excellent day, the weather remarkably bracing, the time appropriate for a bit of exercise of the old wings, a brisk turn upwind. En route, traveling the gradient of bombykol, he notes the presence of other males, heading in the same direction, all in a good mood, inclined to race for the sheer sport of it. Then, when he reaches his destination, it may seem to him the most extraordinary of coincidences, the greatest piece of luck: "Bless my soul, what have we here!"

This may not have been the perfect example of internal monolog, but I included it because it's a perfect example of how writing about science can be done in a creative way—the writing of these two men entertaining as it informs. Some scientists would never write an internal monolog for a dog or a moth because, after all, how would anyone know how (or even whether) a moth thinks.

Occasionally, a person's character can be partly developed for readers by letting them hear the character deliver either a formal speech or a shorter but still longish, uninterrupted mini-speech (monolog) in the midst of a conversation. Character comes out through the content of the speech, its level of diction, its method of delivery, and audience reactions.

Other sources besides captured conversation and internal monolog based on close observation can offer dimension to a character. Historic or everyday letters (even love letters from the attic), quoted in part or in total, can add some dimension to character. In an article about an arrest, quoting from official records can shed light on character. Memoirs that offer revealing comments and personal journals or diaries, if available to the writer, can be quoted to give further insights into the character.

ANGLE OF APPROACH/ POINT OF VIEW/VOICE

Character development is affected by the angle of approach you select. If, for example, you plan to write an article about the meltdown of the power plant at Chernobyl in terms of what it means for the future of the world's atomic power industry, you would have no logical reason to develop the character of Chernobyl's chief construction engineer, chief engineers in other plants, or any other individuals. Your concerns would be more global.

If, instead, you decided to approach the story by writing about the poor construction of the plant, you would be allowed by literary convention to bring in the chief engineer's childhood in Siberia; his problems with certain math courses; his attitude toward the Communist Party; and his drinking problems during the hectic days of Chernobyl's construction. All of this background information would give the reader an understanding of this man who will live under a cloud for the rest of his life as "the person responsible."

The potential to develop a character is also affected by the point of view used. Unless you happen to be intimately connected with Chernobyl's chief engineer or with the construction activities and personnel, or did considerable background research, the first person point of view is not the most likely choice. If you did happen to be assistant chief engineer at Chernobyl, of course, you could write an article from the first person point of view and could readily develop for us the character of the chief engineer. You could say things like "I could tell way back in high school that he would become an important person some day—not so much because of his academic abilities but because of his 'political prowess.' Kids always wanted to do what he said would be fun or the right thing to do. I could see that my friend was a born leader."

If you were not as involved with the person and the situation, the likely choice of point of view would be third person. Then you would decide whether to write the story with an objective or subjective voice. If objective, you would use only reports and other available information. If subjective, you would be allowed by literary convention to include your own thoughts on the matter, personal knowledge about the chief engineer's early background, parts of private conversations you had had with the chief, and other information not generally available.

A subjective angle of approach written in the third person would likely be the best way to write this piece, as you could stress not only the construction activity but the character of the man (or people) involved with it. Third person in the subjective angle approach offers the writer the flexibility to write technologically and psychologically.

REALITIES OF GROUP LIFE

A fuller treatment can be found earlier in this book (see page 59), but it's worth highlighting some points here in the context of character development. Since the writer's intention is always to get the reader involved with the character, he or she will include concrete details that will evoke emotions in the reader that trigger memories of other characters who resemble the character being developed. Among the concrete details used by creative nonfiction writers are the details that come from a consideration of the group(s) to which the character belongs. When enough details are used the reader will get an accurate impression of the character. For example, showing us a scene at the noon meeting of the local Kiwanis in which we see that the character is an officer and has been active for years in the good works of the club tells us something about the person's character. I suppose a person could participate in all the charitable activities of a Kiwanis Club and still be a less than desirable citizen, but the chances are slim.

When we learn that the character also works hard for his Congregational Church, acting as Superintendent of Religious Education, we see another dimension of the man. If we read about his dancing only with his wife at the country club's annual dance and about his drinking only Diet Pepsi, we see other dimensions. If, instead, the writer shows him working hard for the Kiwanis and working hard for his church, but in the scene at the country club we see him sloppy drunk and making passes at every unmarried woman while his wife sits out the dances sipping diet cola, we form another impression of the man. We can't make a final judgment from these pieces of evidence, and the writer probably doesn't present his or her own judgment either, but we do have a gradually filling image of the character.

The best technique to reveal these bits of character is to write scene by scene in scenes that show us rather than tell us about a character. Naturally, the writer could summarize (instead of dramatize) and tell us that this character is "the type of guy who attends Kiwanis meetings, teaches Sunday school, and gets smashed at country club dances," but by putting it that way, we have the feeling that the writer has already judged the man and is leading the jury. When we are shown instead of told, we feel more like a jury that's heard the evidence and comes to a decision based on careful thought.

Writers will sometimes give the realities of the character's group life by describing the group's entertainments, clothing, fads, "in" vacation destinations, "in" architectural styles in office and homes, "in" sports, "in" books, and "in" celebrities. If the character is shown fitting perfectly into these group behaviors, we learn one thing; if the character stays away from the activities of the group within which he or she might be expected to be found, we learn something different.

REALITIES OF INDIVIDUAL LIVES

Physical details of a character are best doled out one or two elements at a time—and, if possible, where logic dictates they should appear. It's always a good idea to save the mention of hair color, for example, until a sensible place:

> His long, yellow mane streamed out behind his golf cap in the wind that picked up as they approached the ninth hole....

> The sun glinted from her so-perfect teeth as she took off her glasses and began to speak to the crowd....

> Tripping on the rug, he complained to no one in particular that these damned size fourteens have given me problems since I was fourteen myself....

As you write about real people, consider including elements that describe them through use of gestures. If a person characteristically poses with an elbow resting on the mantle and holds a martini in a certain way, mention it—but only if it seems truly habitual. There's not much sense in wasting precious words on poses that are coincidental and that imply too much by their mention.

Other kinds of gestures can also be used to help create an image for the reader, provided they seem habitual. Some people have minor mannerisms that may delight (or bug) people around them: "He lets his cigar ashes drop wherever gravity dictates." In one case, this might mean that the person is deliberately insensitive; in another case, the same mannerism may be simply the behavior of a theoretical physicist whose mind is not on his ashes—or even on gravity. With the gradual accumulation of other characteristic behaviors the writer includes, the reader begins to form an understanding of what makes that physicist tick.

9 STRUCTURES

Structure is what gives overall coherence to a piece. Many devices and techniques exist for achieving coherence between sentences and paragraphs, but the governing element is the grand, overall structure. Coherence cements together the individual bricks that make up the structure.

The architecture analogy is a good one. Given the purpose of a building, the number of people who will use it, what those people will do in it, and the area allotted it, the architect makes an overall decision on design. Will it scrape the clouds or hug the ground? Once all of the decisions that determine the structure and foundation have been made, the architect brings in other people to make it work. The engineers, carpenters, electricians, and plumbers give it coherence—they cement it together to give it strength and functionality. Then the architect goes another step and invites in the interior decorators who give each floor and the total building an aesthetic unity. The writer constructs a story in much the same way. Within the grand structure of an article or book, the writer works to make each section cohere within itself, cohere with other parts, and to give some measure of aesthetic beauty and unity to the whole. A more delicate metaphor says that good writing requires a thread of coherent logic along which are strung beads of thought. Done well, the necklace coheres (doesn't cascade all over the dance floor) and gives beauty to its wearer and the evening.

Nonfiction writers will often spend a great amount of time considering structure before beginning the composition itself. Some writers just start writing and claim that a structure gradually imposes itself. The trouble with this method is that it may result in a lot of wheel spinning, revision, and rewriting once the structure magically emerges from the mist. Most professional creative nonfiction writers have a structure well in mind before writing at length. The advance consideration of structure is not wasted; in fact, it has value beyond the most obvious: By continually turning over the compost of the mind, the materials become firmly entrenched in memory—and by being in the brain rather than just on paper, the material is promoted in the subconscious. There's no predicting what will grow in this repeatedly plowed and harrowed ground with all its varied nutrients. In such fertile soil sprout the seeds of serendipity.

Faced with the search for structure, sit back and sift, shuffle, and stack. Do any patterns, or things that look like possible patterns, take shape? Is there even a vague shape that promises structural potential? Keep at it for as long as possible. And don't stop sitting and sifting just because one structure occurs to you. Whoever said that the first idea is the best? Consider as many as come to the surface, and think about the possible implications and ramifications of putting each into effect. Don't consider only the problems each presents; think about the positive possibilities. Anyone can think of negatives; think creatively about the possibilities. Any idea will have both negatives and positives. It's a matter of imagining and weighing, discarding, and keeping. It could go on forever, but at some point, usually dictated by deadline or economic pressures, you have to fish or cut bait. Just trust that the waiting and weighing pay off.

I believe that you should know the ending before you begin writing. Knowing this and knowing how to open the piece make the middle rather easy to write. After all, the middle must somehow take off logically from the opening, and it must lead with some inevitability toward the ending you've decided on. Not that you'll necessarily know the actual words of the ending (although you may), but the general thought behind the ending will have been in mind all along, guiding your choice of words and ideas. If the ending is there, it'll act as a magnetic pole drawing everything toward it, at first gently, and then, as the ending nears, irresistibly.

When you know reasonably well how the piece will end, you can relax in the knowledge that everything is nailed down (well, tacked down). You can then concentrate your focus on one section at a time. Returning to the architecture metaphor—the steel is up and the foundation poured, and you can now put all your thought into creating one floor at a time, secure in the belief that things won't fall apart before you can get to them.

Establishing the structure before you start writing may sound terribly mechanical and too linear for the creative mind, but I don't believe that's so. Having the security of structure (even just some structure) enables the writer to relax and play with any number of creative possibilities to perk up each floor (paragraph). To solve any problem creatively you have to let the mind periodically go wild and woolly. This is difficult to do when you're uncertain about what will come next, and what after that, and how it will all end. You are forced to keep asking yourself: If I go with this crazy but interesting idea that right now seems to be evolving, where could I go from there? This continuous, haunting uncertainty dampens our ability to let loose the fetters of conventional thinking. If, however, you are safe within one small segment (floor or paragraph) of the overall structure, and the free-thinking, wildly imaginative moments turn up nothing, all is not lost. You can either try some more of that kind of thinking, or you can simply turn to conventional solutions, the predictable kind some writers turn to right at first for fear of falling fetters. (See—sometimes the playful, alliterative mind dredges up something you'd just as soon it didn't!)

CHRONOLOGIC STRUCTURE

The logic of time (chrono-logic) is perhaps the oldest structure for a story, going all the way back to the storyteller at the fire in front of the cave. "I woke when the sun woke. I left the cave and walked over the mountain and down to the big river. Then I saw a deer come down to drink. I crept up close on quiet feet..." and so on until the embers glow and the story ends, probably with the storyteller's arrival back at the

cave. This follows that, and then that is followed by…and then later.…
The listener (reader) can easily follow the tale because of its logical
"and then" structure of the movement of time. Even before time meas-
urement came along, people knew about the passage of time.

People commonly concern themselves with various segments of
time. Bruce Catton's *A Stillness at Appomattox,* for example, treats one
chunk of time—the final moments of the Civil War. He opens the
book with a scene at Washington's Birthday Ball in an army encamp-
ment near the Rapidan River south of Washington, D.C. We meet
some of the young officers having what for some of them will be the
last joy of their lives on Earth. The author goes on to take us in ensu-
ing chapters down various war roads until the final scene in the town
of Appomattox Court House, Virginia. We watch as the Union com-
manders ride in to accept the sword of surrender from General
Robert E. Lee.

A chronologic structure like that brings contentment to the
mind. It brings closure, which psychologists say the human mind
naturally seeks. (Gestalt psychologists would say that our minds
demand closure—will even create it where it doesn't exist.) Our
comfort comes not only from closure (the resolution of a problem)
but from its linear development. Our understanding increases as we
move from cause to effect, from A to B to C. We understand C
because we've already grappled with and comprehended B, and
before that, A. By the time we reach Z, we can apprehend the entire
progression from A to Z. We see it then not as A to Z, but as *alpha-
bet.* We've understood the constituent parts as we went along, so now
we see the whole for what it is. The trouble is that this attractively
simple, linear sequence is sometimes simplistic, not simply simple.

In the complex world of human affairs, events are not necessarily caused by the immediately preceding event. Sometimes, for
example, actions are caused by a perception or speculation about
what the future might be. When this is done, the future determines
the present as people adjust to prepare for that speculated future. A
chronological construct of time may be inappropriate to use when
trying to explain years later why what happened happened.

A shorter passage of time may call for a straight chronologic structure. The story of a plane crash, a ship collision, or a bank robbery may use the device that shows us at the beginning of the paragraph the precise time—11:43 A.M. As we make our way toward the climax, the time increments may shorten, so that by the end we're seeing the time change every few seconds. At the beginning it may have been by month, day, or hour. In nonfiction, we often know the ending already, yet we're fascinated by the inexorable march of time. Filmmakers love to show us the clock face or the digital counting mechanisms on a time bomb ticking, ticking, ticking. The camera cuts back and forth between the mounting action and the ticking. Suspense mounts. We're affected emotionally by the merciless sweep of time.

Suspense, deliberately planned, has not traditionally been considered appropriate for nonfiction work. Nonfiction writers would sometimes emphasize the passage of time, but they'd be using it simply as a coherence device, as the narrative string. Today's creative nonfiction writers use the passage of time as a device both for the coherence it gives and for the suspense it can develop.

Gloria Steinem used this kind of time device in an article that exposed the lifestyle of one segment of America—"I Was a Playboy Bunny" collected in her book, *Outrageous Acts and Everyday Rebellions*. Steinem (clandestinely) took a job as a Bunny to conduct research for the article, an article that helped make her reputation as a writer in the feminist cause. She worked as a Bunny mole for about a month (long enough, she said, to increase her foot size several times after all the walking and carrying heavy trays). She structured her article chronologically, heading up each minor section with time data: AFTERNOON TUESDAY 5TH; WEDNESDAY 6TH; etc. Some suspense develops as time goes by and we wonder when they'll discover her role as mole.

Steinem structured another article, "Campaigning," also in *Outrageous Acts and Everyday Rebellions,* around a number of essays she'd previously written about the general topic of political campaigning. She used dates as headlines: JULY 1965 (about George McGovern on the trail), and so on, through various other campaigners such as Eugene McCarthy, Robert Kennedy, and Richard Nixon, until the final date, JULY 1972, when the Democratic National Convention convened in Miami. The dates stressed her point about how the women's movement grew into platform planks over that seven-year period of hard work by many men and women. She ended with the significant statement: "But women are never again going to be mindless coffee-makers or mindless policy-makers in politics. There can be no such thing as a perfect leader. We have to learn to lead ourselves."

The same sort of device may be used to cover longer periods of time. The well-known naturalist and philosopher Joseph Wood Krutch named a collection of his essays *The Twelve Seasons: A Perpetual Calendar for the Country,* each chapter named for a month. This works well for coherence and structure in a book where there is no intention of urgency or suspense.

Some of our finest works of nonfiction have followed the seasonal march because it provides a convenient, easily followed structure. It is not only farmers who see life as a series of seasons. The elderly may speak of how many summers old they are. Many people see the spring season as a metaphor for beginnings, renewals. On the Christian calendar, January marks the beginning of a new year; but our bodies and brains tell us that spring, not winter, marks a new year. This gut reaction to our lives and nature's seasons makes a book organized in some fashion around the seasonal flow warmly satisfying.

Henry Beston's *The Outermost House: A Year of Life on the Great Beach of Cape Cod* and Henry David Thoreau's *Walden* each chronicles the life of its author deliberately isolating himself from ordinary city and village life to confront nature head-on in a simple cabin. A structure that follows the flow of the seasons seems a natural for such subjects. *The Outermost House* takes us with the author through a year on Cape Cod, as Beston experiences firsthand the wonders and mysteries of migrating birds, moving dunes, and thundering waves. In his foreword to that book's eleventh printing, he recounts the thoughts called forth by rereading his own words of twenty or so years before:

As I read over these chapters, the book seems to me fairly what I ventured to call it, "a year of life on the Great Beach of Cape Cod." Bird migrations, the rising of the winter stars out of the breakers and the east, night and storm, the solitude of a January day, the glisten of dune grass in midsummer, all this is to be found between the covers even as today it is still to be seen. Now that there is a perspective of time, however, something else is emerging from the pages which equally arrests my attention. It is the meditative perception of the relation of "Nature" (and I include the whole cosmic picture in this term) to the human spirit. Once again, I set down the core of what I continue to believe. Nature is a part of our humanity, and without some awareness and experience of that divine mystery man ceases to be man.

In books like that and *Walden,* the authors not only structure the book tightly (or loosely) around the seasons as a natural order, but they also draw from other events in nature, and that becomes content for the book. Such authors may take off from their contemplation of a specific reed bending (or not bending) in the wind to make a more universal point about the advisability of yielding to the superior force if you wish to survive to win another day. Thoreau would straighten up from watching, with a child's curiosity, an ant's activities, and let his mind spin out universal thoughts.

Diaries, journals, log books, daybooks, and similar writings, though perhaps not written with the public in mind, may eventually be published. Sometimes they'll be published exactly in the chronology written: day by day, year by year, or, in the case of a ship's log, watch by watch. We enjoy seeing how things evolve, especially when we know how everything has worked out, but the keeper of the diary had no idea what life would bring right around the corner. When the diarist speculates about what the future will bring, and we see how close (or far off) the mark he or she was, we enjoy it. The diary gets some of its strength by its innocent march into the unknown future, step by step, day by day.

Chronology may be reworked, reshaped, or reorganized for artistic purposes—within reason. The keeper of the diary, journal, or other form of log may use it someday simply as a source of information to help him or her write an autobiography or memoir. In other cases, a biographer or historian may use the log as a research source, and may jump around through time, quoting now from a diary, now from a journal, now from a local newspaper account. The biographer may use a diary entry from one day to reinforce some speculation of his or her own about how the diarist may have been thinking at some earlier point. An entry at age fifty, for example, might be thought by the biographer to provide insight into the motivation or behavior of the diarist at age twenty-five.

REWORKED CHRONOLOGIC STRUCTURE

For any number of wise reasons—logical, aesthetic, or otherwise—you may decide that a linear, chronologic structure doesn't fit for a particular piece of creative nonfiction. You may turn to the fiction writer for a model of structure that could work better for your purposes. For example, you may drastically reorder chronology by opening up an article or book with a scene that in real time belongs elsewhere in the story, even at the very end.

Tom Wolfe opened *The Right Stuff,* for example, right in the middle of an emotionally moving episode in the life of Jane Conrad as she awaits possible news that her husband's plane has just crashed. The episode is not truly "in the middle of things," but the later chapters do go back to earlier years. Wolfe didn't open by telling us that he was about to tell the story of the astronauts' lives; he didn't tell us about the structure of NASA or the Navy fighter pilot training program; and he didn't tell us that Pete Conrad would survive to become an astronaut. Wolfe took us first into the compelling emotions of a twenty-one-year-old wife of a twenty-year-old fighter pilot as they began married life, a life that would bring to her many moments of terror. The result? We're immediately involved. We're not concerned about all the background. We can't become interested in the astronaut training program until we become involved at a human level with the people participating in it—and Tom Wolfe does this for us. He does it throughout this exemplary book of creative nonfiction, getting us into the mind of someone and then coming out to look around at what's happening.

CONVERGENT NARRATIVES STRUCTURE

The convergent narratives structure is another form of reworked chronology available to the creative writer. This structure is sometimes called "parallel structure," but this geometry metaphor is inaccurate—parallel lines do not converge, according to the geometry axiom. Parallel narratives would best describe stories like those on *NYPD Blue, Law & Order,* and *The Practice,* in which several stories run side by side with cinematic cross-cutting between them. In most episodes, these stories stay truly parallel and never cross each other—never converge. A story can gain in interest when we find out at the last possible minute that two narratives that seemed totally unrelated are, in fact, very dramatically related—and are, unsuspected by us, rapidly converging. In both forms, parallel and convergent, suspense is effectively promoted and entertainment heightened.

THE FLASHBACK

Another fiction device, the flashback, is valuable in the toolbox of the fully prepared creative nonfiction writer. The flashback is another example of how you can rework chronology, re-create time. This device, however, is subject to abuse. It should be used for artistic reasons, not to fill in something you forgot to set up earlier.

Starting out a piece in the middle of things and then going back to pick up the story for a subsequent straight chronological development is not a true flashback. This device is often called a "frame." Starting in the middle is more a "flashforward." A true flashback interrupts a narrative or a scene, but we're soon returned to where we were.

The flashback device, while available to the nonfiction writer, is not too often used. I really had to search to find these examples of its proper use and several methods for using it. In Bruce Catton's *A Stillness at Appomattox,* in the midst of a discussion of how Confederate General Early had sent General Gordon in behind the federal troops to open an attack, we find a flashback to the day before. The flashback is signaled by the opening words of the second paragraph in the excerpt below.

> So the army moved. Very early on the shivery, misty dawn of October 19, with fog hanging in the low places and the darkness lying thick in the graveyard hour between moonset and dawn, the Confederates rose up out of the gorge and came yelling and shooting on the drowsy flank of Sheridan's army.
>
> The day before, certain election commissioners from Connecticut had come into the Yankee lines to take the presidential vote of Connecticut soldiers, and they remained in camp overnight as special headquarters guests. They liked what they saw of army life, and to their hosts at supper they expressed regret that they could not see a fight before they went home. The officers who were entertaining them said they would like to accommodate them, but there wasn't a chance: "It seemed very certain that Early would keep at a respectful distance."

At the end of the subsequent paragraph, author Catton takes us gradually and smoothly out of the flashback with the image of the commissioners leaving more rapidly than they'd arrived.

> Then, suddenly, artillery began to pound, the infantry firing became sustained and intense, and a wild uproar came through the dark mist—and the election commissioners quickly found their clothes and ballot boxes and horses and took off for the North just as fast as they could go.

Loren Eiseley, the anthropologist who wrote a number of creative nonfiction books about science (*The Immense Journey, The Unexpected Universe,* and *The Invisible Pyramid*) also wrote his autobiography creatively (*All the Strange Hours: The Excavation of a Life*). That fascinating book follows a generally chronologic structure, but the author occasionally inserts a flashback to earlier times in his life. In the chapter "The Laughing Puppet," he writes about his problems dealing with college. When other students stumbled into a course they immediately hated, they'd go directly to their adviser and legally drop the course. Loren Eiseley would simply walk away from it, leaving a black mark on his record. Bureaucracy intimidated him. Having set us up with this attitude of his, he writes a flashback to take us back to his high school days. He signals it through the simple phrase, "Once, in high school…" Since readers know that Eiseley is talking about his own college days, they know this is the beginning of a flashback:

> Once, in high school, I had written, more or less blindly, an essay for an English teacher. "I want to be a nature writer," I had set down solemnly. It was a time when I had read a great many of Charles G.D. Roberts' nature stories and those of Ernest Thompson Seton. I had also absorbed the evolutionary ideas of the early century through Jack London's *Before Adam,* and Stanley Waterloo's *Story of Ab.* None of this had come before high school. It had come from books I brought home from the local Carnegie Library to which I used to pedal my coaster wagon. "I want to be a nature writer." How strangely that half-prophetic statement echoes in my brain today. It was like all my wishes. There was no one to get me started on the road. I read books below my age. I read books well beyond my age and puzzled over them. In the end I forgot the half-formed wish expressed in my theme.
>
> I had to seek food, shelter, and clothing. I remember a philosophy professor for whom I had once read and graded papers….

Eiseley reminds us that the high school flashback is over by bringing up the philosophy professor in the first sentence of the third paragraph. A thoughtful writer always makes certain that flashbacks are clearly entered and exited.

Structuring an article or book around chronologies, or their reworked versions, remains popular with creative nonfiction writers because life does proceed chronologically (it can't help it). Other structures may be chronologic, in that they move forward in time, but sometimes the emphasis or intent is not so much upon the march of time as upon how the person functions over time.

STRUCTURE BY FUNCTION

When a writer describes in great detail how something is made or done, he or she is said to write a "how-to" book. When a writer writes a book that shows the reader how to make something perform its intended function, it's called a technical manual. How-to books and technical manuals (and I've written both) are generally not written "creatively"; their purpose is not to entertain but to instruct. Once in a great while, one may be entertaining as well as instructive, but as a genre, they're usually more informative than entertaining.

Two popular variations on structure by function are How Things Function and How Things Come to Be. These are not academically pure categories, but they do give us a way to discuss structure by function.

HOW THINGS FUNCTION

John McPhee has written many articles and books about how individuals function in the world, and frequently about people working at seldom-heralded occupations. His pieces end up as profiles of these individuals, but very often the piece is constructed not so much around the chronology of their lives as around their occupations (*functions*).

In *La Place de la Concorde Suisse,* McPhee didn't follow a structure by function precisely, but many of the chapters concentrated on army units with specialized functions. McPhee also found ways to pull away from talking about this unusual army, an army organized only to forestall invasion by an enemy, to give fascinating descriptions of terrain, geologic history, and individual officers and men. He gives us a popular Swiss expression, which could have been the book's subtitle, "Switzerland does not *have* an army; Switzerland *is* an army," and gives us detailed glimpses of *Sections des Renseignements,* whose function it is to provide army units with important intelligence information: Which farmhouse could shelter how many soldiers? What are the coordinates of that large barn over there where enemy soldiers might stay? How much ammunition and explosives of what type are stored in that camouflaged cave carved out of solid granite? Another chapter gives us an understanding of the important function horses have in such steep terrain and which farmers' horses are certified as suitable should the invasion come today. In another chapter we learn about the possibilities and problems of armored tank warfare in this mountainous land, while another takes us into the artillery units. We find out, too, how the annual maneuvers involve two "armies," the Blue and the Red.

McPhee, in a less well-known early article (the title story in the collection *Giving Good Weight*), gives us a fine profile of New York City's Greenmarket. He opens the piece *in media res* with a scene in that open-air market—people "squeezing the melons," "pulping the nectarines," "raping the sweet corn," and speaking in New York dialects. After we know how such a market functions with its shoppers, he takes us outside the city to other people and places that work to keep the Greenmarket functioning effectively: the huge packing house at Van Houten's farm in Orangeville, Pennsylvania, where cabbage, cucumbers, broccoli, eggplants, and other produce are grown and packed, and then to an area along the New York–New Jersey line where towns stand like small islands in the midst of a black-dirt sea. Pine Island, New York, is the largest and most productive muckland of them all. From this fertile black muck come many of the vegetables bound for the Greenmarket: celeries, beets, iceberg lettuce, carrots—and above all, onions. McPhee says, "What the beluga is to caviar, the muckland is to the onion." From this "ugly black soil" come the Red Globes, White Globes, Yellow Globes, Buccaneers, Bronze Age, Benny's Reds, and Tokyo Long White Bunching onions. This soil functions as onion heaven, a soil so organic it'll burn. By the time the article finishes we know not only what Greenmarket feels, sounds, and smells like, we understand how it functions as a system with lines radiating out from New York City to the still agricultural lands surprisingly close by.

In his collection with the unexpected title *Table of Contents,* McPhee's major piece is a study of a new breed of doctor in rural communities engaging in what's called "family practice." In this long article, "Heirs of General Practice," he lets us watch how these hardworking, often young, doctors function. We learn that these "generalists" have to know so many different specialties that they are now board certified as "specialists" to legitimize the fact that they're not. These "comprehensive specialists" practice family medicine in the belief that if the doctor treats your grandmother, your father, and your niece, he or she will be better able to treat you. These doctors are responsible for the total health care of the individual and the family— and, where feasible, the extended family of two, three, or four generations. Although the piece is not structured entirely on a function basis, McPhee does walk us around with these doctors, listening in and watching them perform many of their multiple functions.

Mark Kramer provides us with a look at a more traditional medical specialist, the surgeon. In this first book by Kramer, *Invasive Procedures,* he takes us into diagnosis sessions with the patient and the surgeon. That's fairly unusual for a writer to do, but then he takes us on a most unusual journey right into the operating arena. We watch the surgeon, doctors, and nurses perform their individual and team-work functions. I recommend reading this book in tandem with McPhee's "Heirs of General Practice."

In a feature article in the *New Yorker,* "A Reporter Aloft: Small Airports" (August 26, 1985), Burton Bernstein flies his readers to a number of what he calls "tenuous airports" in the Northeast. Although he ties the article together organically by flying us to each airstrip, his real purpose is to show us all the various functions involved in the "small airport system." We learn in a most interesting style all kinds of functions performed by the pilot, the air controller, airport manager, and others pivotal or peripheral to the system. We also learn about gliders, ultra-lights, and flying boats, and how these function differently.

HOW THINGS COME TO BE

The second variation on structure by function differs from the first primarily in its purpose. Articles and books of the second type are structured largely around functions but have a primary concern— the early development of a thing, person, or system. Examples include how a new house comes to be; how a new kind of computer comes to be; how a minihydro power generation system develops; how Olympic champions develop; and how one goes about selling to the public a presidential candidate.

Tracy Kidder has written two excellent books that deal with two completely different subjects—houses and computers, but he structured each largely by function. In his book *House,* he chronicles the entire house-creating process from the clients' first dream about a new house, to working with the architect toward a design to approximate the dream, to both groups working with the craftspeople involved to carry out the collaborative vision. Kidder treats other subjects, such as the lumber industry and architectural trends, but he structures the book around three major functioning groups: clients, architects, and builders. This triangle of sometimes opposing, sometimes cooperating forces has the strength inherent in the physical triangle. These major functions, of course, are performed by people, and Kidder does a fine job of making us understand what makes these individuals tick or function. This book could be used as a textbook on how to write nonfiction creatively. At first blush, one would think it unlikely that a writer could treat this topic creatively, but listen to some of the words from *House*:

The air has some winter in it. On this morning in mid-April, 1983, a New England spring snow is predicted. The sky looks prepared. It has a whitening look. Several weeks must pass before dandelions appear, but the urge to build has turned April into May.... Locke [the carpenter] is wearing jeans and work boots and an old brown jacket, a workingman's uniform. His clothes are clean and he is clean-shaven. He has straight brown hair, neatly trimmed and combed, and a long, narrow jaw. There is a delicacy in his features. You can imagine his mother in him. He has a thoughtful air. He studies his transit a moment, laying two fingers to his lips. Then, as he bends again to the eyepiece, he wipes his hair off his forehead and for a moment he looks boyish and defiant. The ceremony can begin as soon as the bulldozer arrives.

Tracy Kidder received a Pulitzer Prize for *The Soul of a New Machine,* his earlier book about how Data General Corporation's new computer, the Eagle (MV-8000), came to be. That book was not structured purely by function, but most of it dealt with function. Chapters on computers, computer people, and computer functions take up such as "The Wonderful Micromachines," "The Case of the Missing Nand Gate," "Midnight Programmer," and "La Machine." Within each chapter Kidder also gives the reader profiles of the key people providing the various functions involved in the design of a new type of computer. The book achieves tension and suspense because the teams are working on a new computer concept while the corporation's administrators believe the teams are simply trying to improve the existing products to compete against rival Digital Corporation's super-minicomputer, VAX. By showing us the individuals and teams functioning, Kidder shows us how a computer came to be.

To demonstrate the all-inclusiveness of structuring by function, consider the best-selling book *The Selling of the President* by Joe McGinniss. The book detailed, as no book had before, just how a presidential candidate is "sold" by the mass media to the American voting public. McGinniss structures the book around various media specialists and their functions in the "selling" or "marketing" of the candidate—in this case, Richard M. Nixon.

The author, using scenes as often as possible, shows specialists at work, or "functioning." He opens in the middle of things with a scene in New York's Hotel Pierre, where television directors, camera people, lighting experts (we mustn't see perspiration glistening on Nixon's upper lip), stage managers (we must have cue cards in the center, so we won't see the candidate's eyes shifting), and others function to produce a one-minute political commercial. (See page 94 for an actual scene from the book.)

Elsewhere in the book we learn how an advertising executive from Madison Avenue functions at higher levels as he tries to sell a man. We also listen in as one of the world's most famous still photographers, Eugene S. Jones, is brought aboard to prepare short commercials. His commercials used the then-new technique of "moving on" the still shots to give the impression of motion pictures but using the advantages of still photography. We're even introduced to an "ethnic specialist" performing his function of critiquing the ten panel shows produced by the campaign group, on which men and women from various ethnic backgrounds speak on behalf of the Republican candidate. McGinniss supplements his vivid descriptions of functions with a lengthy appendix that presents memoranda and reports associated with the campaign, with no comments or opinions by him. The cumulative effect of these eighty-two pages of appended real documents from the Nixon campaign is so devastating that any authorial comments would have been superfluous. McGinniss, wise enough to see that, stayed out of the appendix.

ORGANIC STRUCTURE

Most of the structures so far discussed follow human logic. An organic structure is an even more natural one, one that's somehow inherent in the subject, and one that grows out of it. An organic structure could be called "natural structure," but I don't want to imply that all the other structures are unnatural.

In my book *Getting the Words Right,* I wrote about the various "logics" a writer can use to promote unity and coherence. My example there was of a glaciologist wanting to describe the surface features of a valley glacier. He or she could, of course, use a "chrono-logic" to describe these features on the basis of when they form. But the features could instead be described more organically by following the flow established by the natural downhill direction of the ice's flow. The glaciologist could begin at sea level, where the ice falls into the water as icebergs, and then talk about the glacial forms all the way back up to the glacier's mountain origins. That would be logical, not organic. The organic way would take into account the direction the glacier flows and comes down from the high-altitude snow fields above. It might begin with the wind-blown *sastrugi* forms; proceed downhill with the glacier's flow, describing ice falls and the chaotic crevasses where the glacier fractures as it bends around corners; describe the moraine-forming materials created where tributary glaciers coalesce; and end where the sea cuts a notch in the ice front, giving birth to great icebergs as the giant blocks "calve" into the sea.

To tie this in with structure by function, a glaciologist might in some cases need to describe how a glacier came to be and how it works. In that event he or she might write first about the origin and morphology of the snowflakes that fall high in the mountains; then about how they are gradually converted into ice; then about how the pressure of thousands of feet of ice and snow on top combine with gravity to give the ice its initial shove downhill; and then how that motion causes friction, which causes melting, which provides lubrication that promotes more rapid movement downhill, which causes more melting, more lubrication, more movement, and so on, inexorably to the sea.

John McPhee seems to enjoy finding the possibility of an organic structure in his research materials, but he wants us not to use it too compulsively. If it works, it works; we should not become slaves to it. He works within a form that's logical, yet unobtrusive. Even when we do elect to use an organic structure, we should allow ourselves some flexibility within it when something unexpected pops up.

After Richard West published "Richard West's Texas," he wrote about a completely different but powerful "state"—New York City's restaurant "21"—and published it in *New York* magazine as "The Power of '21.'" He structured this study of a world-class restaurant organically, using the same system as the restaurant's maître d' in seating guests. Depending on your "status," you are seated on a particular floor, in a particular section, and at a numbered table. The table also bears a name: Maxwell's Table of Happy Memories; New Yorker Table; Richard Milhous Nixon President's Table.

Although the hosts like to say, over and over again, "The man makes the table, not the table the man," not everyone believes that wholeheartedly. West moves his "21" story from floor to floor and table to table, spinning fascinating anecdotes about people who have occupied each table at various times during the restaurant's past fifty years. Because this restaurant is hierarchy conscious and seats patrons accordingly, it was natural for West to structure the story by locations that reflect the elitist, hierarchical system. Had he written about a fast-food eatery, hierarchy would have played no role and the structure would have been different. If nothing else, fast-food places treat us all—prince and pauper—alike.

THE TRIP STRUCTURE

One type of organic structure that has always appealed to people is "the trip." The story is any kind of trip, usually told from beginning to end, has the advantage of following the logic of human thought (it proceeds from 1 to 10 or A to Z) combined with the organic logic of following the physical structure of the topic (the trip). This dual logic may explain the continuing popularity of "the trip"—beginning, perhaps, way back with Homer's *Odyssey*. More likely, it began even before the invention of writing—the returning hunter telling the clan around the fire about a trip, its dangers, its failures, and in greater detail, its successes.

Some trip reports concern themselves with the trip itself, a sort of scientific report where the rivers' rapids run; where hostile tribes lurk; where a factory's falls requires a portage; where industrial pollution prohibits drinking from a cup over the side of the canoe; what natural resources line the river; what tourist attractions are near I-95; how many icefalls occur on the Beardmore Glacier before the South Polar Plateau is reached; or where the Blue Nile begins to trickle out of Uganda.

Other stories of trips document not so much the physical side of the trip as what happened along the way. John Steinbeck's *Travels with Charley* tells us some of the physical details of the highways followed, motels visited, etc., but not enough for it to fall into the travelog category. He tells us more about the people he and his poodle, Charley, meet along the way, his thoughts about them, and about the mood of the nation. As he said near the beginning of that book:

> My plan was clear, concise, reasonable, I think. For many years I have traveled in many parts of the world. In America I live in New York, or dip into Chicago or San Francisco. But New York is no more America than Paris is France or London is England. I, an American writer, was working from memory, and the memory is at best a faulty, warpy reservoir. I had not heard the speech of America, smelled the grass and trees and sewage, seen its hills and water, its color and the quality of light. I knew the changes only from books and newspapers. But more than this, I had not felt the country for twenty-five years. In short, I was writing of something I did not know about, and it seems to me that in a so-called writer this is criminal. My memories were distorted by twenty-five intervening years.... So it was that I determined to look again, to try to rediscover this monster land. Otherwise, in writing, I could not tell the small diagnostic truths which are the foundations of the larger truth.

Steinbeck structured the book around the trip, but he didn't care whether we could repeat the same trip ourselves without getting lost on the road. He just wanted the state of the union revealed to us in the same sequence he experienced it. The phrase "creative nonfiction" may not have been around at the time, and I don't know whether he'd approve of it, but that's the kind of writing he was doing in that book.

John Steinbeck seemed to appreciate the organic structure of a "trip." His greatest fiction, *The Grapes of Wrath,* "reported" on farmers driven off their farms near Sallisaw, Oklahoma, forced by the dust to make the arduous trip to Weedpatch, California, the land of plenty. Their trip gave Steinbeck an organic structure along which to string his observations about these people, the economy, and the government during those terrible years. Although he wrote a work of fiction about that trip, Steinbeck had done what a writer of creative nonfiction would have done—he traveled with those "Okies" as they moved westward. He immersed himself in the realities of their lives before writing. *Travels with Charley* gave him a nonfictional way to update himself and us—not a true sequel to *Grapes of Wrath,* but another look, another chance to feel the country. Recognizing this, his editors gave the book its descriptive subtitle, *In Search of America.*

Steinbeck's *Travels with Charley: In Search of America, The Log from the Sea of Cortez,* and *A Russian Journal* all use the trip as an organic structure, but their nonfiction purpose is to tell us something more than details of the trip itself. Sometimes, as in those books listed, the author tells us about things that don't have much to say about the author. Other times, however, a book's primary purpose is to describe an odyssey of personal growth, an odyssey toward a new understanding of Self, of Life. *Zen and the Art of Motorcycle Maintenance,* for example, takes us along with the author, Robert M. Pirsig, and his son, Chris, as they bike and hike around America. The book's subtitle says better what I'm trying to say about the book's real purpose—"An Inquiry into Values." A writer of creative nonfiction articles and books, Edward Hoagland, said in praise of that book that it was "a magic book, full of the elixir of originality, about the majesty of the continent and the frights of the mind." Books structured around a trip but concerned primarily with matters that transcend the geographic are sometimes called "quests." This is a way to structure an odyssey of understanding, an exploration of inner lands.

Blue Highways, by William Least Heat-Moon, chronicles his trip in a van around the perimeter of America, much like Steinbeck and Charley's peregrination. *Blue Highways'* subtitle is an accurate one—*A Journey into America.* Not a journey *around* America, not a journey *through* America, but a journey *into* America. Although he undoubtedly learned things about himself, he certainly learned a great deal about this land and its people. He talks on the first page about the night the idea for the trip occurred to him and why the concept of a circular route appealed to him.

> The result: on March 19, the last night of winter, I again lay awake in the tangled bed, this time doubting the madness of just walking out on things, doubting the whole plan that would begin at daybreak—to set out on a long (equivalent to half the circumference of the earth), circular trip over the back roads of the United States. Following a circle would give it purpose—to come around again—where taking a straight line would not. And I was going to do it by living out of the back end of a truck. But how to begin a beginning?

Blue Highways earned great praise from many quarters. A review by Robert Penn Warren said, in part: "A masterpiece...Least Heat-Moon has a genius for finding people who have not even found themselves, exploring their lives, capturing their language, and recreating little (or big) lost worlds, or moments. In short, he makes America seem new, in a very special way, and its people new...." Annie Dillard said of the book, "His uncanny gift for catching good people at good moments makes *Blue Highways* a joy to read."

To bring the circle full circle, William Least Heat-Moon makes clear on the book's final page what he learned from his quest:

> The circle almost complete, the truck ran the road like the old horse that knows the way. If the circle had come full turn, I hadn't. I can't say, over the miles, that I learned what I had wanted to know because I hadn't known what I wanted to know. But I *did* learn what I didn't know I wanted to know.

ECCENTRIC STRUCTURES

Your writing must be unusually good to succeed with one of the slightly off-center, eccentric structures that follow. Your style, the vividness of your writing, must be of such high quality that your reader will happily (or tolerantly) put up with some vagueness of direction. Your writing must be so enjoyable that the enthralled reader goes along for the ride, figuring you'll end up at a destination at least as interesting as each of the intervening ports-of-call. Not that all writing must be fun, fun, fun; you could be writing about some very serious matters, yet your comments, your imagery, your accurate language, your insights are so interestingly presented that the reader will know you're going to end up at a very interesting, even important, destination—the reader has faith enough to overlook the lack of some more logical, more linear, more expected, more usual structure.

SPIRAL STRUCTURE

Arctic Dreams, by Barry Lopez, provides us with much information about arctic regions, and the author presents it with authority and attractive images. Lopez celebrates the arctic flora, fauna, and peoples, but under it all lie three thematic questions: How does the arctic landscape (and perhaps any landscape) influence human imagination? When we desire to put a landscape to human use, does that desire affect how we evaluate the environment? And what does it mean to "grow rich"—are we here on Earth to lay up treasures, to hunger, instead, after what is truly worthy, or to live at moral peace with our natural world?

Those questions give us significant themes to ponder in a book. Some authors might have structured such a book in a formal way (to match the important themes), but not Barry Lopez. Perhaps it's reasonable to expect that a book with a title involving dreams should use a structure that mimics the way the brain processes thought—by associational chaining from thought to thought, and indeed, that's what Lopez does in this book.

One theory of brain processing says that all our thoughts are stored in some unknown type of files according to what memories are associated with which other memories—from a lifetime. The theory also says that we can think only by associating new information coming into our brains by taking from our brain files memories of any kind of previous experiences that just might be similar enough to help us understand this new experience.

Our language and our thinking seem dependent upon the way our evolutionary ancestors created metaphors from their associated memories. Through metaphors we can move more easily from the thought of the moment to relevant, associated memories. Metaphors are shorthand equations to help us quickly locate in the brain the associated memories needed to understand the moment.

Casual conversation between intelligent, articulate people will proceed from associated thought to connected thought. This process frequently manifests itself in a conversation when one participant says, "Speaking of *that,* did you hear about…?" A good writer like Barry Lopez would not use that as a transition, but he does, in effect, do just that. He moves from one topic to the next by association—one thing makes him think of the next.

In Chapter 1 of *Arctic Dreams,* for example, his associated chaining runs something like this: Standing under the moon of an arctic winter afternoon, Lopez reflects on the fact that the bright moon allows no depth to the sky, but that the stars shine brightly. This thought about stars, associated in his mind (and ours) with the moon, leads him to a description of the stars in the arctic sky; this leads him after a while to another natural association, the North Star (Polaris), which leads him, logically enough, to another associated thought— the North Pole itself; once into that, it's natural enough to go into a scientific review for us of the meaning behind the five different North Poles; and writing about the migration of one of those poles, the North Magnetic Pole, leads him into a discussion of an early scientific expedition that tracked that migration from the year 1600 to modern times. Before long, he's talking about the Sun and its seasonal migrations across the meridians. Through that discussion we learn about the "meaning" of the Arctic Circle, the winter and summer solstices, and even something about the Dutch explorer, Willem Barents, and his icebound (and finally wrecked) ship in 1597.

As he takes us on a hypothetical trip from the North Pole south along the hundredth meridian, he soon associates the variations of Sun positions and its length of stay anywhere with how the various ecosystems have adapted to the seasons—everything from the stunted growth of the subarctic's trees to the retarded development of the region's soils. These are all associated in nature (and in his mind) with rainfall, which gives him a logical opportunity to bring up the fact that the Arctic receives no more precipitation per year than the Mojave Desert—and so the associational chaining goes. Each leap across an associational synapse is logical enough that the reader accepts each of these mini-structures and stays with the writer despite an apparent lack of overall structure—but only, I think, because Lopez writes so well every word, every sentence, every image.

Because associational thinking is so central to all thought, I've decided not to label this variety of eccentric structure "associational" but "spiral." I call it spiral because the writer, like a hunting hawk, spirals around and around the topic, viewing it from different altitudes and distances, different angles, different perspectives. Once certain that the truth or the goal has been spotted and identified, the writer/hawk swoops in and makes the point. During the long, looping, spiraling descent, it may not have been apparent where the hawk might finally strike (or what his prey might be), but the aerial views were attractive all along the way—and we went along for the ride. We had ridden on the hawk's back before, so we knew we'd find the truth down there somewhere and with greater clarity as we swooped down in such dignified swirls. As a hawk has an identifiable shriek while searching, a writer like Lopez has a voice we can hear. This kind of eccentric structure allows the writer's voice to be heard.

Again, my warning—if you have reason to believe that you have not yet achieved an identifiable voice, you'd best stick for the time being with one of the less eccentric, more formal structures discussed earlier in this chapter.

ORCHESTRATED STRUCTURE

We can certainly hear Annie Dillard's voice when she writes in her wonderful, sometimes off-center way. Although she uses associational, highly metaphoric writing that swoops slowly in on the subject, I'll not put it in the spiral category. In her chapter "Seeing," as in many of the other chapters in *Pilgrim at Tinker Creek,* James Moffett said she "orchestrated" the piece. In a very instructive book, *Points of Departure: An Anthology of Nonfiction,* James Moffett, its editor, writes:

> Instead of telling several incidents that show the same thing, Dillard accumulates various firsthand experiences that show different things about the same basic phenomenon. The title indicates the theme, which Dillard develops gradually from differing starting points—old memories, recent observations, passages in books.

Her essay advances in a circular way, like a musical composition in which motifs once sounded are picked up and developed further later, each motif giving new meaning to the others as the whole fills out. She tightly alternates the particular and the general, instance and idea, playing freely up and down the abstraction scale. This draws the reader into the very inductive process of generalizing. No doubt the practice of calling student essays "themes" recognizes that the traditional essay has from its inception with Montaigne—through Hazlitt and Lamb, Emerson and Thoreau—tended toward this musical structure rather than toward either chronology or logical organization.

MOSAIC STRUCTURE

Writers use this eccentric structure, mosaic structure, in several ways. When an article has many quotes from a number of people, often with varied, even conflicting views, it may not be clear at first just where the writer is heading or what his or her overall views will be. Each tile of this mosaic may not make total sense, but after more and more tiles are laid and grouted by the writer's narrative skills, we see the pattern emerge, perhaps a pattern we would never have expected by extrapolating from the first few tiles.

This structure is seen very often in articles about a catastrophic event. The writer interviews the survivors; talks with the victims' relatives; interviews the police, the Coast Guard pilot, etc. When all the tiles are put together by the writer, there's a cumulative effect that influences our emotions and improves our comprehension of the event.

Another situation also suggests the possible use of mosaic structure—multiple scenes. In *The Executioner's Song,* Norman Mailer structures it first into two equal halves; then, within each half, he uses a mosaic structure. His tiles are scenes. In filmic terms, he cuts rapidly among scenes, each scene short, sometimes only several lines long. Where a filmmaker might dissolve, or even fade to black between scenes, Mailer accomplishes the same effect typographically by simply using extra white space after each short scene. This structural technique to create for us the character of convicted murderer Gary Gilmore is dramatically, cumulatively effective.

MEMOIR STRUCTURE

Not to be confused with diaries, which I've placed under chronologic structure, memoirs do not necessarily follow a strict, linear chronology, the way a diary typically does. They generally proceed from youth to old age, but a lot of jumping around through time may happen in a memoir. Tradition allows a memoirist to follow his or her own eccentric route down through the halls of time. Russell Baker's well-received memoir, *Growing Up,* for example, reads almost like a novel except that all the characters are real and made real for us by Russell Baker's narrative ability. He takes us from his youth (and a little bit before) up until his mother, the main character in this story, dies in 1981. Baker's voice is heard throughout the book, as exemplified by the following paragraphs that open Chapter 3.

My mother's efforts to turn poor specimens of manhood into glittering prizes began long before she became my mother. As the older daughter in a family of nine children, she had tried it on her younger brothers without much success. When she married she had tried it on my father with no success at all.

Her attitudes toward men were a strange blend of twentieth-century feminism and Victorian romance. The feminism filled her with anger against men and a rage against the unfair advantages that came with the right to wear trousers. "Just because you wear pants doesn't mean you're God's gift to creation, sonny boy," she shouted at me one day when I said something about the helplessness of women. Of a man vain about his charm with women: "Just because he wears pants he thinks he can get through life with half a brain."

Some memoirs read almost like a diary expanded by later thoughts. Others are more like a historic narrative, one that draws on several sources. *Those Days,* by Richard Critchfield, carries the interestingly descriptive subtitle, *An American Album.* This chronicle of three generations (his own, his parents', and their parents') resembles an old family album in that it includes photographs, diary entries, old newspaper clippings, and letters. It differs from the ordinary family album in that it also includes narrative by the memoirist, interviews by him, and even internal monologs created by the memoirist to bring alive long-dead relatives. This latter album element removes *Those Days* from the category of history or biography and makes it an excellent example of responsibly written creative nonfiction. The chapter "Anne" even ends with a few lines from a familiar song of the day:

> *They'll never want to see rake or plow*
> *And who the deuce can parley-vous a cow?*
> *How ya' gonna keep 'em down on the farm*
> *After they've seen Paree?*

10 🌿 SPECIAL TECHNIQUES

Crafting quality nonfiction takes a combination of things—thorough research, details, description. There are some tricks of the trade, too, that can give the writer an edge and help create a piece that is engaging, dramatic, and vivid. Several of those "tricks" are more commonly associated with nonfiction than with fiction, and I feel it is important to describe them in some detail since they are frequently overlooked by newer nonfiction writers. If you're a more experienced writer, well, it never hurts to refresh your memory or learn some new tips.

LITANY

When you complete your research for an article or book, you'll often find that you can't include all you'd like to because of length limitations. Sometimes the simplest thing is to leave out some information, but when you feel you absolutely cannot leave out certain things, litany is a technique that can be useful.

Litany, because of its vague resemblance to church litany, simply lists single words or short phrases that accumulate in the reader's mind to create and leave the impression of a person, place, or thing. The beauty of this method of compression is that you can accomplish it while simultaneously adding some style. And it may even improve the reader's comprehension and retention.

Saul Pett's litany not only does its descriptive work, it adds style to his newspaper article about former Mayor Edward Koch:

NEW YORK (AP)—He is the freshest thing to blossom in New York since chopped liver, a mixed metaphor of a politician, the antithesis of the packaged leader, irrepressible, candid, impolitic, spontaneous, funny, feisty, independent, uncowed by voter blocs, unsexy, unhandsome, unfashionable, and altogether charismatic, a man oddly at peace with himself in an unpeaceful place, a mayor who presides over the country's largest Babel with unseemly joy.

In *The Harder They Fall,* Budd Schulberg uses several litanies in describing New York City's Stillman's Gym:

You enter this walled city (Stillman's Gym) by means of a dark, grimy stairway that carries you straight up off Eighth Avenue into a large, stuffy, smoke-filled, hopeful, cynical, glistening-bodied world. The smells of this world are sour and pungent, a stale, gamey odor blended of sweat and liniment, worn fight gear, cheap cigars and too many bodies, clothed and unclothed, packed into a room with no noticeable means of ventilation.

In an *Esquire* article, Ken Kesey wrote about the big "Round-Up" rodeo at Pendleton, Oregon, partly with a litany about what was in the parade that opened the rodeo:

The governor in a polished Pierce-Arrow, mayor in a buckboard. Round-up committee in a Conestoga wagon that was drug all the way from Independence by matched oxen seventy years ago. Hay wagon floats, tableaux of hairy trappers skinning beaver, pioneer mothers churning butter, Indian men and WCTU women pounding drums. Oxcarts, chuckwagons, six-line skinners, stagecoaches, and goat carts. Young braves on painted pintos, old squaws on fur-heaped travois.

In his book *Blue Highways,* William Least Heat-Moon told how he went about deciding where to go next on his odyssey around America taking only the byways that show up blue on the map. He would go to the towns whose names intrigued him for one reason or another:

Had it not been raining hard that morning on the Livingston Square, I never would have learned of Nameless, Tennessee. Waiting for the rain to ease, I lay on my bunk [in his van] and read the atlas to pass time rather than to see where I might go. In Kentucky were towns with fine names like Boreing, Bear Wallow, Decoy, Subtle, Mud Lick, Mummie, Neon; Belcher was just down the road from Mouthcard, and Minnie only ten miles from Mousie.

Slightly more complex are the litanies that use short phrases. Jan Morris, in writing about Bergen, Norway, in the *Sophisticated Traveler,* used several variations of this type. Writing about Bergen's market, Morris creates a litany through the repetition of the phrase "there are."

All around, the market bustles like an allegory of Scandanavia. There are stalls of prawns, pickled herrings and smoked trout, there are trestle tables piled high with potted plants and cut flowers, there are lobsters scuttling around tanks, there are men gutting huge salmon in the sunshine, there are women selling reindeer pelts and cucumbers and boxes of mountain berries and hideous ceramic trolls for the tourist trade.

In *North of the C.P. Line,* John McPhee tells the story of cooperation between Maine's airborne and ground-borne game wardens in finding lost hunters. He writes about game warden Sirois searching on the ground for a hunter named Sterling, a man unknown to him. He used variations of "he had no idea" in this litany:

Sirois, who with his wife, Judy, had raised two sons and two coyotes in a warden station so remote it is sixty feet from Quebec—had no idea who Sterling was. He had no idea that a Sterling Drive had been cut into the forest in New Jersey, and that Sterling had built nine imaginative homes there, one with a spiral staircase rising into an octagonal den. He didn't know that after the casinos came Sterling had built houses for Goldsmith of Playboy, Duberson of Harrad's. He didn't know that Sterling drove a diesel Olds with air, or that he possessed an Indy 600 three-cylinder snowmobile which he had driven at speeds up to ninety miles an hour. Sirois, whose own history had become as endangered as Sterling's, didn't know any of that, nor did any of it matter. A man was lost, and another meant to save him.

John McPhee wrote about what an airborne game warden (coincidentally and confusingly also named John McPhee) carried in his Super Cub plane. This litany is a variation in that after each element of the litany he inserts a quote from interviews with the warden or some other narrative material the writer is reminded of. Pilot McPhee has just slowed the plane until it's making no headway over the ground below. Writer McPhee had just innocently asked how fast the headwind was blowing to keep the plane hovering:

> "We're indicating forty-five miles per hour," he said. "There's your answer. That's how fast the wind is blowing." There were snowshoes on the wing struts—two pairs. He said, "You never know when the airplane is going to refuse to go." He had skis and poles and an M-1 rifle. ("The sound of a revolver doesn't carry.") A five-foot steel ice chisel was mounted on the fuselage. There was some kero dust ("kerosene and sawdust, it burns for quite a while") and strike-anywhere matches in a waterproof steel case. There was some trail mix, but no regular stores of food. ("If I carry a lot of food in the airplane, I just eat it. I carry trail mix the way some people carry chewing tobacco.") There were goose-down warmup pants and extra down parkas that were supposedly good to seventy below zero....

In *Slouching Towards Bethlehem,* Joan Didion wrote in one of the opening paragraphs about California itself, before she went into the story of Lucille Marie Maxwell Miller's murder. Joan Didion used three litanies, allowing variations within a litany to keep it from getting boringly repetitious:

> This is the California where it is possible to live and die without ever meeting a Catholic or a Jew. This is the California in which a belief in the literal interpretation of Genesis has slipped

imperceptibly into a belief in the literal interpretation of Double Indemnity.... Here is where the hot wind blows and the old ways do not seem relevant, where the divorce rate is double the national average and where one person in every thirty-eight lives in a trailer. Here is the last stop for all those who come from somewhere else, for all those who drifted away from the cold and the past and the old ways. Here is where they are trying to find a new life style, trying to find it in the only places they know to look: the movies and the newspapers.

Ernest Hemingway, whose style favored compression, wrote this litany of "definitions" about what living is. The words are put in the mouth of the dying El Sordo in *For Whom the Bell Tolls*:

> Dying was nothing and he had no picture of it nor fear of it in his mind. But living was a field of grain blowing in the wind on the side of a hill. Living was a hawk in the sky. Living was an earthen jar of water in the dust of the threshing with the grain flailed out and the chaff blowing. Living was a horse between your legs and a carbine under one leg and a hill and a valley and a stream with trees along it and the far side of the valley and the hills beyond.

Litany's appeal comes partly from its inherent rhythm. Listen to the rhythmic effect achieved by David McClintick, writing in *Esquire* about Bill Paley of CBS:

> He was determined to overtake NBC and marshaled all the powers of his formidable personality to the task. Paley the persuader, Paley the charmer, Paley the dogged negotiator, Paley the master salesman went into action.

PAIRS

Another slight variation on the litany technique is the use of paired words or phrases. Jan Morris made very effective use of this technique near the opening to her essay "Not So Far: A European Journey" collected in *Journeys:*

Mrs. Thatcher's Britain is an uneasy kingdom, a kingdom of anomalies. It is poor but it is rich. It is weak but it is resilient. It is very clever in some ways, thick as mutton in others. It wins more Nobel Prizes per capita [sic] than any other nation, yet it can hardly keep its head above bankruptcy. It is socially at loggerheads with itself, but it is united in a sentimental passion for the charade of monarchy.

Even the sensations of a motorway drive like ours are muddled and puzzling, as we pass out of the poor wild mountains of Wales, where there are far more sheep than humans, so swiftly into the most thickly populated and intensely developed landscape in Europe.

John McPhee, again in his *North of the C.P. Line,* used a litany, but this time he repeated a two-word sentence for its rhythm. Flying Warden John McPhee is taking an airborne census of how many fishermen are fishing with and without a shack on the ice:

> Party of five on Second Musquacook Lake. No shack. Party of five on Clear Lake. No shack. No shack. No shack. Party of two on Big Eagle Lake. No shack.

Lest we think that this technique of litany began recently with writers of creative nonfiction, here is a paragraph from Francois Rabelais's *The Cake-Peddlers' War.* The excerpt comes from a section titled "Why It Is Monks Are Shunned by Everybody, and Why It Is That Some Have Longer Noses Than Others."

> Similarly, a monk—I mean the lazy ones— does not labor, like the peasant; he does not guard the country like the soldier; he does not cure the sick like the doctor; he does not preach to nor teach the world like a good evangelic doctor and pedagogue; he does not bring in commodities and public necessities like the merchant. And that is the reason why they are all jeered at and abhorred.

The French satirist and humorist wrote that litany back in the 1500s.

CLUMPING

Frequently, especially at the beginning of an article, you may want to give some kind of background (historical, geographical, etc.) before launching into the topic. Or, research has turned up much more information than the article could stand, yet the writer believes that at least the gist of that background is essential for the reader. If it's simply a series of facts, the writer may use one of the forms of litany as a way to compress the information. If the information can't be compressed into single words or short phrases, the writer may make use of what Peter Jacobi has called "clumping."

I've subdivided such clumping into three types. The most common use for clumping is historical. As succinctly as possible, the writer wants to give sufficient historical background that the reader will more readily understand the article. The writer can leap across centuries with this technique—and the reader will accept it because it's obviously done intentionally. A note of caution: If you use this technique you must know your subject well or you'll unknowingly distort history, and your readers may know it.

HISTOROCLUMPING

In a not terribly serious way, Ken Kesey wrote in *Esquire* (June 1985) about the history of Oregon that led up to their Round-Up rodeo in "The Blue-Ribbon American Beauty Rose of Rodeo."

> In the 1700s, explorers. Then pioneers. Then settlers tired of the Oregon Trail, this is fur damn piece enough, by gadfrey! Then ranchers and stock, riders and roundups. Finally the wheat farmers draw lines, and more lines, gathering space, creating a county.
>   ...In 1865 the county seat was Umatilla Landing, where the Umatilla River meets the Columbia.
>   Point of departure for pack trains bound for placer mines in Idaho. In 1868 the railroads push inland; kills the river trade. Umatilla Landing dwindles in size and importance, becoming barely a ghost port. Farsighted go-getters sign petition

demanding county seat be moved to Pendleton. Shoot, the only saloon in the territory is located there, stands to reason the county business oughter follow suit. Even build a courthouse to accommodate it....

Jan Morris, after an opening paragraph in which she describes contemporary Native American traders under the portico of the Palace of Governors Museum in Santa Fe, New Mexico, gives her readers a quick review of what these Native Americans have gone through over the past several hundred years.

> They have been around here for ever. Long before the gringos came in their wagons, long before the Spaniards with their cavalry, centuries even before the wandering Navajos or the raging Apache reached these parts, the Tewa and the Keres Indians lived in their adobe pueblos along the valley of the Rio Grande. The arrival of the white man has left them more or less cold to this day. Once in 1680, they rose in rebellion against the Spaniards, but they were soon put down, and ever since they have lived in a condition of reasonably amiable but unforthcoming resignation, coming into town each day to plonk themselves down there beneath the venerable arcade....

Jan Morris also used historoclumping when she wrote about her first visit to mainland China in a piece titled "Very Strange Feeling," collected in *Journeys*. She wrote of a Chinese dance band playing a Glenn Miller song in Shanghai. They sounded to her as though they had played it once too often:

> They have been playing it, after all, since they and the song were young. Their musical memories, like their personal experiences, reached back through Cultural Revolution, and Kuomingtang, and Japanese Co-Prosperity Zone, back through all the permutations of Chinese affairs to the days of cosmopolitan Shanghai—those terrible but glamorous times when European merchants lived like princes here, Chinese gangsters fought and thrived, the poor died in their hundreds on the sidewalks, and the Great World House of Pleasure offered [here Morris segued

seamlessly into a litany of services offered] not only singsong girls and gambling tables, but magicians, fireworks, strip shows, story-tellers, mah-jong [sic] schools, marriage brokers, freak shows, massage parlors, porn photographers, a dozen dance platforms and a bureau for the writing of love-letters.

In 1985, Gary Wills wrote in *Esquire* about the 1960s, giving in one paragraph a rapid cultural history of that decade:

The fads and tragedies came and went, barely distinguishable. We had camp weddings—Tiny Tim's on the Johnny Carson show. Camp assassination—the S.C.U.M. woman attempt on Andy Warhol. Camp patriotism—Abbie Hoffman in flag drag. Camp religion—Billy Graham going disguised in fright wig to a rock show. And it grew harder to find a difference between the camp and the straight versions of—what? Reality? Between Billy Graham with a wig and without one; between Abbie's flag and Anita Bryant's anthem; between Valerie Solanas and Lee Oswald; Johnny Carson's bridegroom and Johnny Carson.

GEOCLUMPING

A brief, compressed "clump" of information given before getting too deep into the topic can include geographical or geological background. Ken Kesey, in the very next paragraph after giving us that rapid bit of historoclumping about the establishment of Umatilla County, Oregon, decided we need a geographic feel for it:

Umatilla County. Two million acres. Drained by McKay Creek, Birch Creek. Out of the Blue Mountains. Towns. Hermiston, Stanfield, Echo, Adams, Helix, Athena, Milton-Freewater. And, as county seat, the biggest little city north of Reno—Pendleton, Oregon.

When Jan Morris wrote about her journey across Texas from Oklahoma in *Trans-Texan,* she gave readers a rapid ride across before giving us the details of her trip. In geoclumping, we leap across space the way we leap across time in historoclumping.

It is rather more than 600 miles down 281, from Red River in the north to Rio Grande in the south, across pleasant flatland counties with names like Jack or Archer, through the wooded hill country of the center, across the wider rolling ranchlands south of San Antonio into the tropic territories of the Rio Grande valley, where the palm trees stand in lordly enfilade, where the fruit and vegetables grow like lush weeds, and there seems to hang upon the very air some potent radiation of the south.

In *Slouching towards Bethlehem,* Joan Didion set the stage for a piece titled "Some Dreamers of the Golden Dream," about a woman murdered on Banyan Street, by giving us directions to Banyan Street. The concrete details about the area are a form of geoclumping. She manages to compress a lot of information (which was probably in her field notebooks) by using this device.

> Imagine Banyan Street first, because Banyan is where it happened. The way to Banyan is to drive west from San Bernardino out Foothill Boulevard, Route 66: past the Santa Fe switching yards, the Forty Winks Motel. Past the motel that is nineteen stucco tepees: "SLEEP IN A WIGWAM—GET MORE FOR YOUR WAMPUM." Past Fontana Drag City and the Fontana Church of the Nazarene and the Pit Stop A Go-Go; past Kaiser Steel, through Cucamonga, out to the Kapu Kai Restaurant-Bar and Coffee Shop, at the corner of Route 66 and Carnelian Avenue. Up Carnelian Avenue from the Kapu Kai, which means "Forbidden Seas," the subdivision flags whip in the harsh wind. "HALF-ACRE RANCHES! SNACK BARS! TRAVERTINE ENTRIES! $95 DOWN." It is the trail of an intention gone haywire, the flotsam of the New California....

CHRONOCLUMPING

A writer can sometimes effectively compress time, not in a historic sense but in the sense of a day or hours. One examples comes from John McPhee's "A Textbook Place for Bears," collected in his book *Table of Contents.* He writes here of Pat McConnell, whose profession it is to trap bears for the State of New Jersey.

On the seat between us now was her loose-leaf Bear Book, a running diary of captures and sightings. On August 24, 1981, in Sussex, she had captured a four-hundred-pound bear and hung a radio on him. After he took off, the radio beeped for ten minutes and he was never heard from again. On September 16, 1981, and May 2, 1982, she had captured a four-hundred-pound bear and had given him the nickname Flasher. She had nicknamed other bears Pain, Buckwheat, and Mo. May 14, 1982, Passaic County, she caught a three-hundred-and-fifty-seven pounder, who was, in a manner of speaking, too close to Fifth Avenue, and she moved him over to Warren. May 27, 1982, bear reported on Shades of Death Road, in Allamuchy. December 12, 1981, twenty-three-pounder under Bearfoot Tower, in the Newark Watershed, Passaic County.

TELECLUMPING

Teleclumping is a term that describes writing that resembles the terse succinctness of a telegram's compressed language. Teleclumping is similar to chronoclumping except that the writing that follows the chronological references is in short and sometimes incomplete sentences, is typically present tense, and is sometimes laconic. Two examples come from John McPhee's *Table of Contents,* the first from "A Textbook Place for Bears." Here, the police get calls about bears and enter the complaints:

> The bears go onto the blotter.
> Sussex County, 1981. Bear shows up at a barbecue, goes straight upwind to the charcoal-broiling hotdogs, takes them from the grill.
> Morris County, 1981. Fox terrier trees bear. Bear refuses to descend, largely because a hundred people have collected under the tree. Address: Denville.
> Morris County, 1982. Bear plays with back-yard swing, takes clothing from clothesline, mounts ceramic deer.
> Passaic County, 1982. Bear in private garden attempts to pass through opening in dry wall. Bear too wide, knocks down dry wall.

In McPhee's *North of the C.P. Line,* he writes about airborne game wardens flying over Maine during hunting season, ready to help find lost (temporarily confused) hunters. The flier monitors the C.B. radio:

> "Two Two Five Two. Two Two Six Seven. I'm over the St. John near the Big Black Rapid, eastbound. Is there anything we can do for you while we're here?"
>
> The voices of wardens come up from the woods. A hunter near Seven Islands has lost his bearings, has no idea where he set up his camp. Jack (the pilot) has a look and finds the camp. A party at Nine Mile is missing one hunter. Jack hunts the hunter and finds him walking in a brook.

The techniques of litany and clumping can help you write more creatively or compress information. Consider them first as ways to make your writing more interesting, and second, as ways to compress your ideas to fit length limitations.

TO BE OR NOT TO BE?

Intransigent verbs (yes, I made that up) frequently infest sentences and wreak more havoc than many writers realize. They come in disguise as *am, is, was, were, been, had been, to be, be.* My teachers and college professors told me time and again to avoid any passive verbs, but no one ever stressed the prohibition dramatically or thoroughly enough to make a lasting impression. In subsequent years I've come to understand their reasoning.

I call these verbs "intransigent" because they behave so inflexibly that one has trouble rooting them out. They keep popping up as though they believe they belong in every other sentence. They don't.

The reader's eye/brain system reacts to images and preferably images that move. Our eye/brain system, in its still animalistic way, reacts to anything that shows us an image, especially if the subject *does* something. The intransigent verbs don't *do* anything. Their subjects just sit there, passive. Get them doing something and they come alive on the page.

Your reader's brain dozes in the shade with passive verbs (forms of "to be"), but leaps into action when propelled by almost any other verb. "Killer be's" do have their role in passive places, but rarely.

"To be" doesn't conjure up any image in the brain. It says only that the subject exists—and we already knew that. Tell us something new. Better yet, "show" us something new. "To be or not to be, that is the question"—the bard gives us a moment's pause, and then we remember we have the answer—NOT to be.

Let's look at some real-life examples of improving the imagistic content of sentences by rooting out intransigent "killer be's," no matter how bullheadedly they resist.

> The marines **are** dropped on the landing zone by helicopters. (10 words)
>
> *Revised to:*
>
> The marines **slide** rapidly down ropes dangling from the helicopters hovering above the landing zone. (15 words)

True, I had to add five words to rid us of that "are," but look what we gained. As the writer, it forced me to picture those marines in my mind and, when I did, I saw those ropes dangling. I added "rapidly" for its accuracy—and then I saw how well it alliterated with "ropes," and then I saw the alliterative strength of "hovering helicopters." Serendipity strikes again.

I achieved all those bits of better writing simply by creating something more active than "are." The original version "expressed" for the reader what happened, but the revisions "impressed" a lasting image on the brain. We want our sentences vivid (vivid deriving from the Latin *vivere*—to live). Give life to sentences by substituting accurate, vivid verbs for the intransigent forms of *to be:*

He **was** enticed by her black hair.

Revised to:

Her black hair **knocked** him for a loop.

She **was** embraced by the clown.

Revised to:

The clown **grabbed** her and **hugged** her.

Note that I got rid of the "killer be's" by providing a subject that is active. In the first example, "her black hair" became the subject that acted upon "him." The revision in the second example also shifted focus by changing subjects: She was no longer passively embraced; the clown actively grabbed and hugged her. In a sentence that takes an intransigent verb, the subject is often disguised as the object. All you have to do is make the object the subject; the rest will come easily.

When that solution is not available, try eliminating or minimizing an infestation of "killer be's" by simply combining phrases and sentences.

His hair *was* blond and his forehead *was* glistening. His blue eyes were bright but unreadable. (16 words)

Revised to:

His hair was blond, his forehead glistening, his blue eyes bright but unreadable. (13 words)

I eliminated a "was" and a "were" and combined two sentences, but did we lose any imagery? I couldn't easily get rid of the first "was" because I wanted to retain the rhythm of the three phrases, but, hey, two out of three ain't bad.

We found the writing program *to be* very complete and well documented. (12 words)

Revised to:

We found the writing program very complete and well documented. (10 words)

As he walked up to the bar, he quickly scanned the handful of customers who *were* scattered around the tavern. Reggie *was* zeroing in on a blonde who was sitting at the bar, and positioned himself next to her. Reggie *was* a sucker for blondes, and he wanted this one. (50 words)

Revised to:

As Reggie walked up to the bar, he quickly scanned the handful of customers scattered around the tavern. He zeroed in on a blonde sitting at the bar, and positioned himself next to her. A sucker for blondes, he wanted this one. (42 words)

We can eliminate a weak-kneed "be" by making the subject do something more than merely exist.

There *was* a battle.

That tells us that a battle existed. Pretty weak. Let's sit back and think about it. What do battles do besides exist? Battles *break out.* Battles *start up.* Battles *explode.* Any one of these would go a long way toward developing a feeling for the battle—and would certainly be better than the use of "was."

Revised to:

Suddenly, there was the sound of heavy naval guns.
Or:
The roar of heavy naval guns broke the stillness of the night.
Or:
Heavy naval guns cracked the stillness of night.
Or:
Heavy naval guns roared and flashed in the pink of dawn.

I've forced myself to think with more accuracy about the imagery I wanted to create in your brain.

"Suddenly, there was the sound of heavy naval guns" merely expressed what I had in mind, gave the basic facts. It fell short of impressing on your brain the sights and sounds of that battle's beginning moments. Don't merely express something; impress it on the neurons of your readers' brains.

I suspect that we infect our writing with intransigents because the is's, was's, and were's come so trippingly to the tongue. After all, these verbs expressing simple existence probably arrived early in our language-skills development, and we've had millennia of practice using them. Anything so long practiced becomes second nature, an autonomic response.

Since *to be* forms come so automatically, I recommend we let them take their place on the page in all their primordial abundance—provided we have the self-discipline to go back through this first draft and hunt for them. Circle those "killer be's" on a read-through and make the changes necessary to eliminate most of them. Aye, there's another rub. How many? I've decided to allow myself and my students one intransigent verb per one hundred words of text (1/100). A one thousand-word piece, for example, should have no more than ten. That's Cheney's Rule of Thumb; don't blame anyone but me.

And don't get carried away, aiming for zero tolerance of intransigence. To the extent you try to meet the suggested ratio, you'll be a better writer. Oops—I meant, you'll write better.

SNAPSHOTS

When introducing a character for the first time, or when introducing a minor character into the narrative, you may wish to present what I call a snapshot—only a glimpse—of him or her. Later, you may want to describe the person in greater depth, but everything in its own time.

A snapshot of a person is not an oil painting, not even a good photograph; it's not a biography, not even a profile or a sketch. It's a mere snapshot designed to give the essence of a person. It's detailed, however, and neither a caricature nor a cartoon. Snapshots take considerable thought.

SNAPSHOTS OF PEOPLE

Here are two excellent examples from Tobias Wolff's *This Boy's Life: A Memoir,* and one from Frank McCourt's *Angela's Ashes.* Each runs only fifty to seventy words, yet look at the powerful images they achieve.

> She made the world seem friendly. And somehow, with her, it was. She would talk with anyone, anywhere, in grocery stores, or ticket lines or restaurants, drawing them out and listening to their stories with intense concentration and partisan outbursts of sympathy. My mother did not expect to find people dull or mean; she assumed they would be likeable and interesting, and they felt this assurance, and mostly lived up to it.
>
> **Tobias Wolff**
> *This Boy's Life: A Memoir*

> Delia and Philomena were large women, great-breasted and fierce. When they sailed along the sidewalks of Brooklyn lesser creatures stepped aside, respect was shown. The sisters knew what was right and they knew what was wrong and any doubts could be resolved by the One, Holy, Roman, Catholic, and Apostolic Church. They knew that Angela, unmarried, had no right to be in an interesting condition and they would take steps.
>
> **Frank McCourt**
> *Angela's Ashes*

SNAPSHOTS OF PLACES

Snaps of places share the attributes discussed under snaps of people: You're giving us a glimpse or two of the environmental context. As with snapshots of characters, this is not a profile, but just the essence of the place. Photographic terms lend themselves well to this concept. There is the microshot, the macroshot, and the megashot, each offering widening degrees of coverage.

Frank McCourt uses the microshot in this excerpt from *Angela's Ashes*.

> The room had a fireplace where we could boil water for our tea or an egg in case we ever came into money. We had a table and three chairs and a bed, which Mam said was the biggest she'd ever seen. We were glad of the bed that night, worn out after nights on the floor in Dublin and in Grandma's. It didn't matter that there were six of us in the bed, we were together, away from grandmothers and guards, Malachy could say *ye ye ye* and we could laugh as much as we liked.

The perspective is wider in Jill Ker Conway's snapshot from *The Road from Coorain*. Take a look at this macroshot.

> We never saw such things in the west [of Australia] because the sun and the dust faded them too quickly. Now there was the intoxicating blue of the ocean, the rich designs of the rugs and curtains, and the unfailing wonder of the garden, where everything was always green. The sudden comfort was overwhelming when contrasted with years of fighting the drought. Every garden and house on the street was an object of wonder to be examined and reexamined.

And here, from the same book, a megashot.

> The cars would sweep home over the dusty roads, their lights visible like pillars of fire across the plains. If one arrived home first, one could stand on one's veranda and watch the other departures, visible for twenty miles or so. On regular nights there were only the stars, the cry of a fox, and the sound of the wind. Then, if a car traveled very late at night it meant an emergency. Distant watchers would crane their heads to see where it went and wonder what had gone wrong.

THINK SCENE

The same dramatic need that exists in fiction exists in nonfiction. We like to see scenes in front of us. After all, life does seem to occur as a series of scenes.

Before starting to write, ask yourself what could be transmitted to the reader best by a scene. Some of these potential scenes will be embedded in narrative summary, but it's important to first identify the scenes that make up a story.

What constitutes a scene? A scene in creative nonfiction includes who, what, where, when, what people said, and even what people said they thought at the time (using interior monologs). A scene occurs in a specific place (where); usually the narrator and one or more others are there (who); at a particular time (when); something happens (what); people converse (dialog or captured conversation); and sometimes someone thinks about something (interior monolog). When these elements change significantly, it may be a new scene.

Scenes can begin in several ways.

DESCRIPTIVE NARRATIVE

A snapshot of a person or the people who will soon be in the scene—or a snapshot of the place where the scene will immediately occur—can be useful here. Although usually done sparingly, you might introduce your thoughts on the situation or the people. You are the narrator. You can tell your reader what you were thinking, feeling, and/or how you reacted. This is known as interior monolog (for more, see page 138).

DIALOG

Dialog may begin between those present. Several kinds of dialog may be used:

- *Summary Dialog*—a brief report that suggests a longer conversation. Not a quote.

- *Indirect Dialog*—gives more details than summary dialog and gives the feeling of the conversation without quoting it.

- *Direct Dialog*—conversation between quotation marks. It's as if we're overhearing the actual conversation, hearing the actual words and phrasing. Its purpose is not as much to convey information as it is to "show" us the dynamics of the relationship(s). This dialog may tell us things, for example, about power: shared power, power taken, power abdicated, power reversed, or even power unrecognized.

- *Unsaid Dialog*—hidden dialog (subtext) read between the lines. After all, sometimes the reader can learn more about a person by what he or she leaves unsaid. Some subtext can be revealed through gestures, and the gestures may connote the opposite of what the words are saying at the same time. Actions sometimes speak louder than words.

The special techniques described in this chapter (litany, clumping, avoidance of intransigent verbs, snapshots, and dramatic scene construction) will help you transform ordinary writing into more interesting, more dramatic writing, writing more enjoyable to read.

11 🌿 RESEARCH METHODS

Although I've set aside this section to discuss research in the creative nonfiction writing process, it's not too different from research done for any good nonfiction writing. Readers today expect creative nonfiction writers, journalists especially, to provide not only a complete and objective treatment; they also expect some subjective treatment, which usually means treating the emotional content of the story. They want the complete picture, a picture that includes fully developed scenes, captured conversations, and even internal monologs (although they don't all agree on this technique). Through these, and other techniques discussed in earlier chapters, the creative nonfiction writer deliberately excites the reader emotionally as well as intellectually—our minds use emotions to add meaning and clarity to straight, factual information. This, of course, sets the creative nonfiction writer aside from the journalist who believes, or is instructed, that emotions should not play a role in understanding the news of the outer world. To gain an appreciation for the central importance of the research work required by this kind of writing, I recommend that you read any or all of *The Right Stuff* (Tom Wolfe), *Common Ground: A Turbulent Decade in the Lives of Three Families* (J. Anthony Lukas), *House* (Tracy Kidder), or *Those Days* (Richard Critchfield).

Creative nonfiction writers still use the basic research method—interviewing—but they also use many more methods. They talk with the people immediately involved in the story to flush out, and later to flesh out, the who, what, where, when, why, and how elements of the traditional news story. The traditional reporter on a daily newspaper barely has time to ferret out all those elements with the accuracy and completeness he or she desires. Since the creative nonfiction writer isn't usually constrained by a similarly tight deadline, there is much more time to get the story as accurate and complete as possible.

SATURATE AND IMMERSE

This highly involved research effort, sometimes called, appropriately, "saturation reporting" or "immersion research," requires that the writer be willing (and financially able) to stick with a story for weeks, months, or even years. The writer also has to be willing to move in on the lives of complete strangers and to dig deep into those lives, warts and all. Gay Talese, speaking on a panel at Yale ("New Journalism—Two Decades in Perspective") told the audience of students and writers, "You've got to do deep and thorough research—you've got to have an affair with your subject."

Mark Kramer said that he spent several years living among or around the men and women he wrote about in *Three Farms,* a book that takes the reader through the lives of people operating farms of different types, sizes, and locales.

The fiction writer can hole up in a garret or a cabin and work largely out of his or her memory and imagination, but the creative nonfiction writer can't work out of those sources alone. He or she must conduct research out in the real world, the raucous world, the dirty world. This requirement to work away from the studio or the study turns some writers away from this form of writing. Others love that side of the profession—it's what draws them in. I write this not to discourage you from the profession but to suggest that you keep the requirements clearly in mind: the need to work away from home, family, and friends for long stretches of time; the need sometimes to sleep in strange beds under alien roofs; and the need sometimes to live for long periods with no income other than the publisher's advances on royalties (not always available to the beginner in this field).

Not only must you undertake great amounts of research when writing creative nonfiction, you must be absolutely sure that every piece of information you produce is verifiable. On that Yale University panel, Talese said, "In creative nonfiction, the rules of accuracy must not be violated. All that we write should be verifiable." Everyone on that remarkably talented panel (Didion, Dunne, Lapham, Plimpton, Talese) moderated by Shelley Fisher Fishkin, stressed this requirement of accuracy. (They may have been reacting, too, to allegations made against the New Journalists that they ignored accuracy in the pursuit of drama. In those early days, the sixties and early seventies, some self-proclaimed New Journalists, or parajournalists, were enamored more with the joys of self-expression than with journalistic accuracy. Some were not journalists so much as advocates for favorite persons or causes—and because all of this was fairly new, they figured they must be New Journalists.)

Some of his early critics were surprised and pleased with the thoroughness and accuracy of the research conducted by Tom Wolfe in preparing to write *The Right Stuff*. That book presents one of the best models for writers who want to write creatively about well-researched subjects. His readers learn a great deal about NASA's space program and about the astronauts' lives in a book whose style makes it fun to read, even while acquiring all this information.

Traditional journalists have only to report the variations or versions of "truth" given them by a variety of sources and simply enclose the versions of truth in quotation marks. They're not required to figure it all out and come to some synthesis of what the truth is—in fact, they're constrained by journalistic tradition (and editors) not to introduce their feelings or interpretations at all.

Creative nonfiction writers, however, may well bring themselves into a story, either overtly or subtly, believing it only fair to let the reader gauge the writer's credibility and thus the accuracy of the facts presented. For creative nonfiction writers, concealing themselves, in a sincere attempt at objectivity, gives the reader no reference point. The innocent reader has no choice but to believe the facts, or reject them totally. According to Norman Mailer and others, facts are not "nuanced"—and we need to read of the unspoken forms of communication, the gestures; we need the nuance.

Many creative nonfiction writers feel, too, that if they include character sketches about the people central or peripheral to the story, the reader will be able to gauge the credibility of the facts presented by those people. If a person is merely named, the reader can't be sure what credibility to assign. If the person is also identified by a title, especially by an impressive-sounding title (say, director), but with no other personal background, the reader may ascribe too little or too much credibility based solely on name and title. This places considerable responsibility on the writer's shoulders to provide accurate and objective character sketches.

The only way you can be sure your work will be accurate is to do your research well. What does that mean? First of all, it means not to stint. Dig in. Read. Observe. Interview. The terms "saturation research" and "immersion research" describe it best. You must saturate your mind with information by immersing yourself in the subject as deep as you can go. The result? Your writing yields something beyond what might be expected, whether that means unexpected information or information expressed in an unexpected (creative) way.

It takes time to gather information—as I've said before-weeks, months, sometimes years. To write in a style that is appropriately creative requires time. The complexity of the subject affects the time needed. Conducting the necessary interviews involves time. There may be many people to interview, or the interviews may be few but geographically diverse. The person being written about may have such a complex life that you find it necessary to study him or her far longer than you might have anticipated. The chances are that anyone worth spending a lot of research and interview time on for a major article or book will be a very busy, complicated person living a complex life—so expect the project to take a long time; it comes with the territory.

THE PURPOSE OF INTERVIEWING

Interviewing is usually a great part of the research effort for this kind of writing. Almost any feature article for a newspaper, a story for a news magazine, or a story for a corporate employee magazine or newsletter requires that you talk with people involved. The interview is the cornerstone for most nonfiction articles and books because interviews add so much. They add fresh ideas, ideas you might never have come up with on your own. They provide different angles, views, perspectives, insights on the person or the topic under study. They give you names of other people you might interview, people you might never have thought of or heard of while sitting back at home in your study. The interviewee may mention other authorities you should read for further information. You may hear of journals, book titles, and even specialist conferences you might attend. And, very important, interviews will provide you words, jargon, specialist language, and more detailed knowledge that will lend authority or credibility to your article or book. Lastly, interviews enable you to "people" your article or book, an extremely important element in most creative nonfiction. An article that never gives us people tends to turn us off after a while. We identify with people. Naturally, people give life to a piece of writing.

PREPARING FOR THE INTERVIEW

Anything that will provide you all the above information should be well worth preparing hard for. For instruction in the art of interviewing, refer to books such as *The Craft of Interviewing* (John Joseph Brady); *Creative Interviewing* (Ken Metzler); and *Interviews That Work: A Practical Guide for Journalists* (Shirley Biagi). But here are a few tips:

1. Be certain about seemingly trivial items: the interviewee's exact address, floor number, room number. Check at least once on the agreed-upon date and hour for the meeting and confirm these details at least several days in advance.

(There's nothing worse than flying to Chicago and finding that you were to have interviewed your person the day before.)

2. Arrive early so you can go into the interview relaxed. Come well-groomed yourself, and have with you well-groomed equipment: a tape recorder with fresh (and extra) batteries, clean tape heads, working pens and pencils, plenty of appropriate tapes, and a notebook.

3. Take prepared questions to explore. These questions grow out of your own curiosity, your own intuitive understanding, your library or other research, your interviews with significant others, and from holes you've discovered in your information wherever obtained. This list is a MUST list-those questions you must not leave the interview without answers for. During the interview, of course, more questions will occur to you to ask.

I subscribe to the notion that you should prepare yourself thoroughly for the interview, but John McPhee, an interviewer of great skill, says that he acts on a different premise. He says he'd rather begin his interview as a *tabula rasa,* his mind a clear slate. Someone of his obvious intelligence and knowledge is never a completely clean slate, but he says that he likes to walk into the first interview with only his intelligence and curiosity to guide him. He fears that if he has studied up too much on the topic or the person, he may appear to know more than he does, perhaps unintentionally encouraging the interviewee to hold back some essential information on the presumption that McPhee already knows of it. McPhee may have a point; there's a very human tendency to show off just how much the interviewer knows— in an attempt to impress the interviewee and perhaps establish good rapport. It is better, McPhee says, to risk sounding a little on the dull side so the interviewee will take on a teacher role and provide all kinds of information that might otherwise be held back. The interviewer should, however, demonstrate that the interviewee's points are getting through and that he or she (the interviewer) is a quick and appreciative learner, just enough that the teacher-interviewee will continue in the role clandestinely assigned by the interviewer.

CONDUCTING THE INTERVIEW

The interview is an unnatural act. There's a pretense, an artificiality to it. Because of that, both the interviewee and the interviewer are generally uptight about the interview process. An analogy would be the situation when you tell someone that you want to take some candid photographs of them. Almost everyone feels obliged to act before the camera's eye. They're suddenly not themselves; they're actors on stage. Some people freeze up before the camera's implacable eye. Since most of us go through life watching other people in the spotlight, we're embarrassed and self-conscious when the spotlight suddenly puts us center stage. The interviewer must do whatever is necessary to defuse the situation as soon as possible and get things into a conversational mode.

USING THE TAPE RECORDER

Only that rare person with almost photographic (or audiographic) memory should attempt to rely on memory or note taking. Recording on paper what's said while it's being said is the time-honored method, and many interviewers, especially those working before the arrival of dependable tape recorders, swear that this is the best method. But I believe in the tape recorder. Tape recording has so many advantages that it's hardly worth discussing. It's been argued that a tape recorder, no matter how small and unobtrusive, makes it more difficult to develop that feeling of a conversation, which I've said is so important. But consider the alternative: What's so conversational about one of the two people scribbling away like mad, flipping back through the notebook to find something said earlier, scratching something out, asking for a quote verification, and periodically flipping back to the list of prepared questions?

Compare this with two people conversing comfortably about the subject while a tape recorder silently records everything. Certainly, the interviewer may occasionally also write something on a pad, but most of the time he or she retains good eye contact with the interviewee—one of the most important attributes of a conversation. How can you retain good eye contact while scribbling in a notebook? Plus, there's no better way to get accurate and complete quotes that can be edited down later, if necessary.

The interview is one of the most complex mental exercises you are apt to be called upon to conduct, considering how many distinct activities the brain must undertake simultaneously. I liken it to that of an air traffic controller at Chicago's O'Hare Field during the Christmas holidays, with a heavy snowfall during prime landing time. It's not unlike the simultaneous thinking processes going on in the brain of a television technical director producing a live news show with multiple "feeds" coming in live from around the world, slides coming in from a projector, film coming in from a film chain, and three cameras operating, not to mention a live radio feed from Beirut supplemented by a videotape that's just arrived by plane. In the midst of voices coming over the headphones and people handing him or her notes, the director has to instruct and coordinate (in real time) the activities of a half-dozen people—and the living-room viewer must not be allowed to sense the chaotic control room scene. Everything must seem under cool, professional control. If that seems an exaggeration, consider what goes on in the interview situation. I remind you of this not to frighten you unduly but to point up why you should be prepared—and why a tape recorder just might be your best friend.

SIMULTANEOUS ACTIVITIES

1. You're asking questions from the prepared MUST list.

2. You're writing down the answers to the prepared list.

3. You're asking new, unplanned questions that evolve.

4. You're writing down the answers to the new questions.

5. You're thinking about all that's being said and all that's going on. (What's the idea behind that response? What other possible meanings lurk between the lines? Is something being held back? What? How can I get at any of this through a new line of questioning? Should I phrase it evocatively or provocatively?)

6. You're recapping the interview, internally and sometimes externally. (Am I getting it? Like the air traffic controller—have I got the whole picture of the situation upstairs? Am I alert to everything that's going on, or am I too hung up on the prepared Q & A's? What else should I ask now or later in view of what's being said at the moment? Should I stick to my prepared "must" questions, or follow up right now on this fascinating new stuff that's developing before my eyes, stuff I never dreamed would come up when I was making up my list? Which will finally be of more interest to my readers—answers to the prepared questions or answers to this new, intriguing but tangential material?)

7. You're monitoring the interview externally and internally—you're periodically monitoring the tape recorder dials and reels; you're monitoring your subject's answers for any contradictions occurring between what the subject said a few minutes ago and what he or she is now saying, and what the subject said in some other place and what he or she is now saying. And you're asking yourself, How can I explore that contradiction with new questions or with provocative statements? Do I sense duplicity in that apparent contradiction, or simply a change of mind—remembering that everyone does not have to be consistent forever. And you're listening for any contradictions between the words used now versus those used earlier; is the tone the same? Is the body language consistent or contradictory as the subject gives this apparent contradiction or inconsistency?

8. You're observing the dynamics and the details: Are there any repetitive gestures (that might vivify a narrative); any repetitive words or phrases; any characteristic body language by the interviewee. Is your own body language betraying your feelings (to yourself and, perhaps involuntarily, to the interviewee)? Are there environmental details that might lend authority or sensory interest to the narrative, or give insight into the person's character or lifestyle? What is the "texture" of the setting—people around, weather outside, ambient conditions in the room; any extraneous events surrounding the interview but not a part of it (e.g., the sound of workers hammering outside may affect the thinking and the emotional response of the inter viewer and interviewee—and that sound may have different "meanings" to each participant). What is the subject's behavior toward outside interruption (e.g., the phone or the intercom) during the interview?

9. What are the interactions, physical and psychological, between you and the person interviewed; between the interviewee and his or her staff, friends, associates, spouse, pets, etc. that may happen within the time of interviewing?

10. Have you taken in all you can about the exterior environment: his or her office, outer office, lobby, the building's exterior architecture, the neighborhood?

THE TWO BASIC INTERVIEW TYPES

THE SHOPPING LIST INTERVIEW

The shopping list interview uses the familiar question/answer (Q & A) format. It's a quick-in/quick-out technique that depends solely on the list of planned and written-down questions (sometimes given in advance to the interviewee).

Because it goes so fast and so efficiently, this style of interview tends not to be so effective. Its great disadvantage is that there's no time to develop a good rapport between participants. Without rapport, little trust is developed in either direction. Without trust, there's little credibility. The interview is marked by superficiality and artificiality, appearing to offer the interviewee conversation, but providing a formal list of questions with little leeway for the free flow of ideas. The result of its formality is that the interviewee will be guarded in his or her responses and responds with answers as short as the questions. If you're in a hurry, of course, that's to your advantage, but if you want a useful exchange, it has to be a conversation, not an interrogation. A conversation, or the feel of it, can be achieved only by the in-depth interview format.

THE IN-DEPTH INTERVIEW

To establish the rapport required for a good interview, begin by having (or cultivating) a genuine interest in the person or subject of your interview. If your interest is nonexistent or minimal, it will show in your voice, in your eyes, in your body language, in the framing of your original questions—and certainly in your responses as the interview progresses. If you can bring sincerity and empathy into the interview, you'll be 80 percent there. Sincerity, empathy, and genuine personal interest are the ingredients that promote trust and rapport with the interviewee. And be wise in how you conduct yourself. If you are doing multiple interviews about the same person or topic, word will get around quickly that you are interviewing. If you do poorly, for whatever reason, with the first several interviews, you'll enter subsequent interviews at a distinct disadvantage. If you have been too pushy, judgmental, or insensitive, or if you've spoken ill of the first interviewee to the second one, imagine your reception and lack of rapport with interviewee number three. People will open up fully only with someone careful, trustworthy, and sensitive.

SOME DOS AND DON'TS

THE DOS

1. Before you can get into the meat of an interview, you've got to slip into something comfortable—a conversational mode. At first, it may feel stiff, but if you handle the first few minutes well, this unreal conversation will evolve into a real one. Naturally, a lot depends on the person interviewed and his or her willingness or ability to slide into a genuine conversation with a stranger. I'm talking here only about what you can do from your end to establish this conversational feeling as soon as possible.

   Many interviewers take a list of warm-up questions, questions they've found through experience will put a person at ease and from which they can fall easily into conversation. I think of them as "fall-back insurance," something to have along in case you can't find a more natural way into a conversational mode.

   If possible, use a more organic method. Find something relevant to the situation, the setting, the day's news (even the weather) to get the two of you talking in a relaxed way. If, for example, you see on the person's shelves a series of golf trophies, it would be better to ask about those (an organic entry) than to ask a typical warm-up question: "What sports do you like?" or "What do you do to relax when not working?" If you see photographs or paintings of children, comment about them, rather than using your list of warm-up questions to ask, "Do you have any children?" Even if the photographed children turn out to be nieces and nephews, you are off on a very human level, talking about children who are obviously significant to the interviewee for some reason. And what is that reason?

   Listen, really listen, to the responses about the children. If you're lucky, you may learn something about the interviewee from which you can logically (and organically) launch the actual interview. The discussion, for example, might bring out that the children are, indeed, the interviewee's children and they were, at the time of the photograph, living at Yahats, Oregon. That's where she was born, too, and where she still returns every summer to work on her books. (Ah ha!) "What book are you working on now?" "What is it about Yahats that helps you write?" "Which of your other books did you write there?" "Do you think many authors have certain places that seem to turn on their creative juices?" "I've read many definitions of creativity, but what is it?" There's no telling where that last discussion will go, but it may lead to other writers' and friends' names that will provide you further questions—or lead you to them for follow-up interviews.

2. Go with the flow of the conversation, bringing it back into line with new, cleverly invented questions (or prepared ones you've been waiting to ask from your list and can now slip into the conversation organically).

3. Act and react as you would in a true conversation. Don't jump on certain answers with an accusatorial tone, unless you are an investigative reporter deliberately trying to provoke the person. If an answer stimulates you, pursue it…but perhaps a little later on. If you are perceived as a pouncer, the person will put his or her guard back up, the guard you've been trying so hard to lower.

4. Keep your opinions to yourself, no matter how difficult it may be for you. True, this makes it an unreal conversation for you, but, remember, your readers are more interested in the interviewee's opinions than in yours. Feel the person out to plumb the dimensions of his or her opinions, but don't offer yours too often or too obviously. Just ask evocative questions, the kind that pull out further meaning, not the kind that might make the person wish they'd never offered the opinion in the first place. Your job is to find out for

your readers what this person thinks about anything. If you're too confrontational in your questioning, the source will soon dry up, and you'll be forced back into a shopping list mode.

5. Ask open-ended questions, the type that cannot be answered easily by a simple yes, no, or maybe.

6. Ask why. A simple "Why?" may be the most productive question you'll ever ask. Even when you think you know the answer, ask it. Don't be afraid to look less than a genius; ask it. The answer may surprise you.

7. Probe the abstract or vague answer. Sometimes, an abstract or vague answer will be completely innocent of deception; at other times, such an answer may be the obvious head of obfuscation rising up to confound you. The only way to find out, for sure, is to ask for details. You'll want details for your readers' ease of comprehension anyway, but the asking for details may flush out obfuscatory intentions. If that happens, PROBE, PROBE, PROBE.

8. Ask simple questions. They are often the most fertile, growing the best answers. Oriana Falacci, one of the best-known interviewers, has often been cited for the simple question she asked an astronaut, the type of question most of us would hesitate to ask someone presumably so brave: "Were you scared?" The straightforward reply was informative, interesting, and surprising. "Hell yes," he answered, and that led to a relaxed conversation between them from that point on. She may have known very well what he would say; she wanted to hear him say it—and what he had to say about it. Unasked, the subject would not have been addressed.

9. Elicit anecdotes. During your preliminary interviews with significant others, you have undoubtedly collected a few

anecdotes about your main person or about the topic of your research, but once you're in that interview with your subject, it is time to get some of the most useful ones. Ken Metzler, author of *Creating Interviewing*, advises us not to ask for them directly, "Have you got an interesting anecdote that I can use to delight my readers?" Such an open-ended question with an inherent expectation ("interesting," "delight") will often draw a blank, or some long, involved story that you can't use. Instead, just keep your ears open for "little stories" the person tells—those are the anecdotes.

Keep alert, too, for the potential for a "little story" in what the person is saying at the moment. If the interviewee has mentioned something general about some kind of behavior, ask whether that's ever happened to him or her. Let your subject spin out the little story—and be quiet for a few seconds after he or she stops speaking; the first story may well trigger another one. If you allow the person to keep pulling up a whole string of memories, you may get all you need. If, however, he or she doesn't come up with a second one (after you've let a few seconds of silence go by) tell one on yourself. That will not only develop further rapport between you, it may also elicit further ones from the subject as he or she sort of "tops" yours.

Unless the interviewee is also a writer, he or she may not understand what an anecdote is and how you may use it, so just ask for examples. Asking for stories may elicit more than you wanted—more words, anyway. The word "example" connotes brevity, and that's probably what you seek. If you then want more words about the example, just ask "Why?" or "How come?" or "How's that?" or "Why do you feel that way?" These are all open-ended questions meant to elicit or evoke responses.

If you want to encourage the interviewee to come up with more and better anecdotes, act interested, enthusiastic, enthralled, or fascinated by the "little story" evoked. People like to be appreciated for what they say, so show your appreciation (even if you have to stretch a little). Your subject will be tempted to find better and better stories that will elicit from you further appreciation of his or her talent at storytelling. You may use only one or two of the little stories, or pieces of them, but your reader will benefit from your clever eliciting.

10. Be as gracious at the end of an interview as you were in the beginning: You may want to come back for a second interview; you may want to ask further questions by telephone later; or you may want to interview this same person (or his or her colleagues) for a different article or book at a much later date. To use the common aphorism, "Don't burn your bridges behind you."

A part of being gracious and professional is to inform the interviewee at the end of the interview just how things go from there—what happens to the tape—and some inside information about the writing, editing, and publishing process, if the person seems unfamiliar with the process. You probably will not want to send the person drafts for approval, but you may say that you'd like to be able to call back to verify any facts, dates, etc. When the article is published, send a copy to your interviewee(s) immediately. After all, they've given you their time and expertise—the only thing in it for them now is the article's publication.

11. Probe for the human side. When you write about a person, especially an "important" person, you must find ways to remind your readers that this person is a human being not too terribly different from them. They know that he or she is, in fact, very different, but if they can identify with some common element behind the mask, they'll feel they under stand the person better.

THE DON'TS

1. Don't stick rigidly to your prepared list of questions, but have it ready. Try, instead, to play off the conversation in progress. Appear to be inventing the questions on the spot (don't use the formal language found on your list). Try to include in your wording something just said in the inter view. Even when that question was far down on your list, work it in now when it has arisen naturally in conversation.

2. Don't lead the jury. Be careful how you word your questions so as not to lead the interviewee (even unconsciously) in a direction you wish to pursue. An apparent tangent may lead to an even more interesting destination, given a chance.

3. Don't fill in conversational gaps. In everyday conversations, we all have a fear of "dead air." We jump into a silence and fill it with anything. The interview is not a normal conver-sation (try as you might to achieve that feeling), so you should act accordingly. Deliberately leave long pauses unfilled. The possible benefit to your purposes is that, fearing that the interview will look like it's not going well, the interviewee will jump into the gap and start shoveling desperately to fill it—and may fill it with material he or she didn't intend to bring up at all. You may hear things tum-bling out that you would never in the world have asked, either through sensitivity or through ignorance. After the person says something genuinely interesting, say "wow" or something else to show that you "got" it and liked it, but don't follow it up with other words or a further question. Just leave that conversational gap for the interviewee to fill.

4. Don't be afraid of "dumb" questions. It has been said that "The only dumb question is the question not asked." We all hesitate to ask something that may expose our innocence or our ignorance. Ignore that self-protecting temptation; ask

the question. You're not in the interview to demonstrate how much you know about something; you're there to find interesting and informative materials for your readers. Asking questions will uncover what you're looking for—and sometimes the seemingly dumb question will unearth things you never dreamed of.

5. Don't hesitate to revisit earlier questions and answers. Don't be afraid to return to an earlier answer that you didn't fully understand, one that seemed fertile, but then the interview went off on some new tack. With the benefit of hindsight and further information as the interview has proceeded, your question may seem even more significant now than it did originally. Ask the question in a new way, so the interviewee won't feel abused by being asked the identical question again. Research inconsistencies. If the inconsistency is great, you may want to probe more right now, or revisit again in a few minutes to see what answer then comes out. And revisit any question that obviously struck a sour note at the time it was asked. You didn't follow it up then because you didn't want to offend, or you wanted time to consider the implications before probing a bit more. The trick is to revisit with different wording each time you recycle—and you may wish to recycle a particular question several times.

Revisiting or recycling serves several useful purposes. You may get better answers the second time around, after a better rapport has developed; you may get altogether different answers; and you may get something totally new, something not even mentioned in the previous answer(s).

INTERVIEWING FOR SUBJECTIVE REALITY

All the discussion about interviewing and other research methods thus far has had to do with what is sometimes called "objective reality." The writer conducts his or her research to develop material that will be useful in re-creating for the reader just the way things occurred and looked at the time. For creative nonfiction writers, objective reality is not the only reality. There is also the subjective reality—the emotional life of a person, what goes on in his or her mind. Critics of subjective reality think that as soon as the writer leaves objective reality and begins to dip into a person's emotions and thoughts, he or she is leaving the world of journalism and entering the world of fiction. Creative nonfiction writers maintain that one can present the reader a more complete, more accurate picture of reality by presenting the objective *and* the subjective realities of a situation. Everyone lives in a world made up of both realities, so why not report on them?

How can you possibly know what another person thinks? the critics ask. They forget, of course, that when *they* interview people, they accept what an interviewee says—presumably because he or she doesn't merely think it or feel it, but actually says it. Why not accept what a person says in an interview about what he or she thinks or feels—and report it? If you do report this subjective reality, you must make it clear to the reader that this is what the interviewed person said about his or her feelings and thoughts.

Some creative nonfiction writers, like Tom Wolfe, invent internal monolog for the interviewed person. Wolfe says he can do it because he has researched and interviewed at length, frequently for weeks and months, so that he can accurately capture what that person would be likely to think during some event. Some would say that a person of Wolfe's imagination and willingness to dig deep probably can create a monolog that approximates what a person might think, feel, or say— but in how many other writers would we have that much faith?

John McPhee, interviewed by Norman Sims for his book *The Literary Journalists,* said that we cannot get into another person's head and think for him or her. In McPhee's series of excellent books, he tells us in one way or another how the characters feel about something, but he says he never invents what they feel—that always comes from the interview. Like Wolfe, McPhee practically lives with the people he writes about, so that what he writes about their thoughts and feelings is undoubtedly accurate in the details and in the tone.

Tom Wolfe wrote this about subjective reality in Chapter 2 of his book *The New Journalism*:

> The idea was to give the full objective description plus something that readers had always had to go to novels and short stories for: namely, the subjective or emotional life of the characters. That was why it was ironic when both the journalistic and literary old guards began to attack this new journalism as "impressionistic." The most important things one attempted in terms of technique depended upon a depth of information that had never been demanded in newspaper work. Only through the most searching forms of reporting was it possible, in nonfiction, to use whole scenes, extended dialogue, point-of-view, and interior monologue. Eventually I, and others, would be accused of "entering people's minds"...But exactly! I figured that was one more doorbell a reporter had to push.

Wolfe's use of the word "impressionistic" does not mean to imply an analogy to Impressionism, the style of painting where much of the detail is left out. Creative nonfiction is actually more of a realistic painting than is regular news reporting. Regular, objective, news reporting is more impressionistic; it leaves out the entire realm of the subjective and gives an impression painted by a pile of facts hastily dabbed on the canvas and information from sometimes rather rapid-fire interviews smeared across to give a semblance of truth.

Gay Talese, in Ronald Weber's *The Reporter As Artist,* said this on writing about what another person is thinking:

> I attempt to absorb the whole scene, the dialogue and mood, the tension, drama, conflict, and then try to write it all from the point of view of the person I am writing about, even revealing whenever possible what those individuals are *thinking* during those moments that I am describing.

Talese has said, too, that he believes he can more accurately reflect a person's thoughts about something than could that person him or herself, particularly if that person is not a writer. Talese added that this presumes he's been studying the person for a long time, perhaps months. He's interviewed his subject on many occasions on various topics, and he's asked what the person thought about the particular topic. He feels that a clever writer (like himself) can bring out meanings through words much better than the average person he interviews can—especially if the person is merely quoted in casual conversation. No one speaking extemporaneously uses words as well as a professional writer with lots of time to compose. Talese even concludes that he is fairer and more accurate in his reporting when he uses indirect quotes than when he uses the expected direct quotes.

In a direct quote, the writer captures the interviewee's words as verbatim as possible within quotation marks. By contrast, in an indirect quote, the writer uses his or her own words to render what the interviewee said, and often sets the paraphrase off with the word "that." "John said *that* the war seemed to go on interminably" is an example of an indirect quote, while a direct quote might read, "'The war seemed to go on and on and on,' John said." Although direct quotes give the impression of objectivity and accuracy, if a professional writer revises the interviewee's words into a clearer statement, it may, in the end, represent a more accurate expression of the person's thoughts. Talese reminds us always to do as he does: Attribute any indirect quote to its source. This practice requires the ultimate in careful thinking and working, or one can either unintentionally distort the person's message or intentionally make the person seem to support some point the writer desires to make. The ethical journalist must always keep this in mind.

Two examples from Gay Talese's *Honor Thy Father* demonstrate how he puts indirect quotes into practice by telling us what a person was thinking at the time:

> The men slept in shifts through June and July, constantly on the alert for any intrusion, but nothing happened. The monotony,

Bill thought, the monotony is maddening, and he was tempted at times to leave again for California, but each time he resisted, fearful that a disaster would strike moments after his departure.

The children talked quietly, and Rosalie sat quietly next to Bill, feeling frustration and guilt. She wished that she had found out ahead of time the main reason why both parents had been invited; if she had, she might have protected Bill from that which made him most vulnerable: his ego.

In the second quote, Talese used two approximate equivalents of thinking: "feeling" and "wished." Whether using "thinking," "feeling," or "wished," he was not thinking *for* Bill or Rosalie—he had gotten these thoughts, feelings, and wishes from them in a long series of interviews.

OTHER RESEARCH RESOURCES

Library research used to eat up a writer's life. You had to get to the library through sleet or snow, figure out the library's systems, get cooperation from an overworked staff, in some cases, photocopy relevant materials because the books or articles could not leave the building, or lug home the books and other sources that *might* prove useful and then lug them all back again.

Then, to the rescue, on a white steed rode THE INTERNET, now readily accessible on the writer's own desk (or lap). Now, the contents of libraries all over the world can be accessed at the touch of a finger. Moira Anderson Allen's extremely useful book, *writing.com* is a must for anyone researching on the Internet. With this fabulous resource at your side, you'll find materials on the web—government documents, current research studies, databases—that are otherwise extremely difficult to track down, even through Interlibrary Loan programs.

THE CHALLENGES OF RESEARCH

The research phase of writing creative nonfiction involves a different set of difficulties than those of the hard news, deadline writer. If you do not have the time, funds (for airplanes, cabs, trains, hotels, research assistance), or persistence enough to pursue research in great depth, you'd best seek out a different line of work. Reporters speak of how much legwork they have to do to cover a beat or follow a story. Their legwork resembles that needed for the hundred-yard dash; with creative nonfiction we're speaking of the legwork required for the marathon.

Some writers may change their minds about going into creative nonfiction when they see that it requires getting out from behind the word processor, getting up from the comfortable chair, and getting out into the sometimes uncomfortable world outside. They may also change their minds when they discover that they have to follow their people around for weeks or months, almost like a bird dog, immersing themselves in the subject, saturating themselves in data and details.

If you go into this line of writing, you'll want to work with all your senses operating at peak efficiency all the time. You'll try to sense the world with your antennae erect and alert—you've got to try to take it all in. Without this sensory inventory to draw on, once you're back in the office your writing will not have the creative edge required for this kind of writing. You have to willingly (and happily) dig into that which smells bad as well as that which smells wonderful, and listen to that which repels as well as that with which you agree. All of this sensory acquisition will provide the concrete and sensory details you'll need to create the objective reality of the situation for your reader. You'll need, too, to dig deep into the emotional side of those interviewed, uncovering their innermost thoughts and feelings, if you're to give your readers that subjective reality which, when combined artfully with the objective reality, will paint for them as honest and accurate a picture of the world as it's possible for you, a fallible human, to paint. Emotional content enables us to create dramatic, vivid, accurate scenes. A scene that lacks emotional content will likely be less than successful as a scene. An article full of scenes without emotional content may not fail, but it would probably not qualify as creative nonfiction.

One difficulty associated with staying close to a subject is that you may get too emotionally involved, a problem the deadline writer doesn't generally face. After weeks or months of research and interviewing, you may love or hate the person. In either case, your writing may tear your heart out. You know that what you finally write will affect this person's future. Can you stay neutral about the subject to be fair? *Should* you? Should you take a position and then build your case while remaining as objective as you can? Should you withhold anything from your article or book? Should you withhold anything from legal authorities? As a sensitive writer, such questions, quandaries, and dilemmas may hurt you deeply. You may feel guilty about your necessary voyeurism. You'll have to ask penetrating questions that probe where the person is extra sensitive. That may be just what needs probing, but your sense of propriety may prevent your probing deep enough. If you think that your personality cannot handle such questions without shattering itself, you'd better look around for other writing jobs.

Much creative nonfiction revolves around events and people, and unless you're writing history, you'll want to be present—on the scene—when the events happen. Since you can't control when an event will occur, and since you can't force your interviewees to adapt to your schedule, you almost always have to work within someone else's framework—certainly within the sometimes unpredictable framework of events. They happen when they happen—not when you wish they would happen.

If you're profiling a person, his or her "events" or "scenes" may have no predictable schedule at all—they just happen when life wants them to happen. Luck may put you there when the great scene unfolds, the scene that'll make your article or chapter leap to life—or you may have gone to Oregon to research some facet, and miss it. You can't be everywhere at once, though you know you should be. This is a built-in difficulty—it comes with the territory.

You can see that this kind of research depends a lot on luck and serendipity—things you can't control—so stay clear if you find you need predictability in your life. Be aware that every so often, a project evaporates. You've put in weeks or months of effort, perhaps all on speculation (without a contract), and then something happens—the circumstances, unpredictable when you started, fall apart, leaving you with your research languishing in notebooks or computer memory.

A book project evaporated on me once. When then-President Reagan fired my daughter and her soon-to-be husband from their jobs as air traffic controllers, I thought (even in the midst of all that family heartache) that I had the basis for a book about "our air traffic controllers and where they flew," which I'd publish to commemorate the fifth anniversary of the strike and the firing of those 11,400 controllers. Like most of them, my daughter couldn't find a job in her chosen profession. After a year of bartending and chimney sweeping, her husband was hired, along with forty other men, by the Australian equivalent of our FAA. When all these people and their families went Down Under to work, I proposed to write a book centered on this intrepid group and touching lightly on the other thousands. Since that firing so dramatically distorted the lives of so many young families, I thought it a natural—and I had an "in" that most writers would not have. I went to Australia for preliminary interviews and research, came back, and, through my agent, proposed the book to a number of publishing houses. I couldn't understand their general response. They said, "By the time the fifth anniversary comes around, no one will even remember the strike, let alone care what happened to all those controllers." I did some more research, before giving up. When the fifth anniversary came around, I found that, indeed, no one remembered the strike, or if they remembered it, couldn't care less about it. History had moved on—earthquakes had occurred, floods and fires had come and gone, and the United States had attacked Libya. History has a way of doing that—moving on to other projects. You have to select those topics or people that will endure—or research and write more rapidly and get the book out there as soon as possible.

The last issue I'll mention concerns the research itself, and that is *over*-researching. If you love the research phase of writing, and many do, you may not know when to stop. If the topic has any substance at all, you could probably do secondary research forever. You might even conduct primary research yourself (multiple national mail surveys of public opinion, for example) and just keep going. At some unpredictable time, however, you'll cross the point of limited returns. Your article or book can handle only so much information, and you'll have to eliminate much of what you've worked so hard to get. The very human tendency is to include as much research-derived information as possible—after all, look at all the time, money, and effort you've put into the research phase—it just seems so wasteful not to include this, and this, and that, and of course, that. Don't do it.

Professional writers may collect a wealth of information, but they do this knowing that from it they'll whittle it down to a small pile from which they'll select the best material. Winnowing the wheat from the chaff gets more difficult as the chaff gets excessive. The other problem of over-researching comes from the time, effort, and money involved in the researching itself. Where does it fail to pay off? A piece of work not supported by enough research will show it; a work suffocating under an avalanche of research-derived information will show it, and may be so burdened as to be unreadable—or, at least, unread. A writer unread might just as well have stayed in bed.

Ethical considerations run through all these discussions of research methods typically used in writing creative nonfiction. The writer must design any research with accuracy in mind, report results with accuracy, and conduct and report on any interviews within ethical standards and guidelines. The next chapter explores some of the ethical issues inherent in research and writing.

12 🌿 ETHICAL CONSIDERATIONS

Consideration of ethics intrudes on any serious discussion of facts, accuracy, thoroughness, credibility, creativity, or professionalism in any nonfiction writing, but especially in journalistic writing. We can't get into the legal implications of unethical behavior; ethicists and lawyers sometimes clarify these issues for writers. And, as many books have been written on the subject of ethics in journalism, we won't go into great depth on the subject, fascinating as it is. I want only to provide some tips about how a writer can remain ethical. I'll also mention several cases where otherwise excellent writers apparently lost track of the absolute requirement to be honest with the reader.

Traditional journalists have fewer difficulties with ethics because they adhere as closely as possible to the facts. The creative nonfiction writer, however, may run into problems because the craft uses techniques borrowed from the fiction writer, making it almost inherently suspect. Skeptics abound in this world, and especially in the world of journalism. This skepticism puts an additional burden on the writer of creative nonfiction, or, as Norman Mailer has called it, the writer of "applied creative writing."

When we write personal nonfiction—nonfiction (journalistic and otherwise) in which we deliberately insert ourselves into the story—ethics problems diminish in one sense. Since reader skepticism usually derives from the question of credibility, readers of personal nonfiction can assess for themselves the reliability of the writer. Traditional journalists, of course, try hard not to write personally, fearing it will destroy their objectivity. Their readers have to accept at face value the statements made by this faceless, anonymous writer.

When we write "impersonal nonfiction"—nonfiction in which we avoid revealing our presence to the reader—we have the inherent problem of credibility. Skepticism may sometimes be justified, because the seemingly anonymous creative nonfiction writer, especially when using fiction techniques heavily, may embroider the facts to make the piece more dramatic and appealing. As soon as that is done, the writer may cross ethical boundaries, vague as they are. It's very easy to wander innocently across those fuzzy borders. Creative nonfiction writers therefore need to keep their wits about them and behave scrupulously, bending over backward to be professional and responsible.

ETHICAL IMPLICATIONS OF TECHNIQUES

I'll proceed here from a discussion of writing techniques that may seem almost outside any concern about ethics, to techniques considered ethical by some, borderline ethical by others, and definitely unethical by yet others. It's quicksand terrain, this matter of ethics in writing.

ETHICAL IMPLICATIONS OF DICTION

William Safire, in his *New York Times* column in 1985, "On Language," first brought to my serious consideration the ethics implications of diction. In the column "Caviar, General?" he referred to a "dilemma" that I translated for myself as "an ethical dilemma." He worried around, in that delightful way he does, the problem every writer faces all the time—if you have in mind the perfect word, *le mot juste,* should you use it in the interest of accuracy, even though you realize it will sail loftily over the heads of most of your readers?

Safire posed the dilemma like this: "Do you settle for a more generally understood term, thereby pandering to our audience's ignorance—or do you use the unfamiliar word, thereby failing to communicate, and appearing to be a showoff?" Then he summed it up eloquently: "Is your job to communicate or to educate?"

Safire questioned whether to ever use a word that will fly over the audience's heads, and I enjoyed his answer: "Fly over everybody's head only when your purpose is to teach or to tease." He went on to suggest that we should never do it when our purpose at that moment is to persuade.

Since much of creative nonfiction writing tries to educate (inform) our audience while persuading them, we should take his suggestion and go ahead and use the occasional high-flying, accurate word, provided we do so in a context that makes the meaning clear. We can even do it by slipping in a phrase or word nearby that's closely synonymous, with the dual effect of making the meaning clear and educating the audience about the meaning of the word. This technique, handled without empathy for a reader's sensitivity, can unintentionally take on a tone of condescension. Better, I think, to gamble that the context will gradually clarify matters, than to condescend, or even appear to condescend, to the reader. A well-educated audience actually enjoys learning a new word or having a new use for a familiar word (and they'll go through the trouble of looking it up), but they can smell condescension a paragraph away—and they won't come back for more.

Closely related to such "elitist" writing comes jargonistic or specialists' writing. Michiko Kakutani brought this business to mind in her book review column in the *New York Times* (January 30, 1983), when she reviewed John McPhee's *In Suspect Terrain*. She made one extremely interesting point not frequently made. She said that the ethical dilemma here was whether the author of a technically oriented book, in this case, a book largely about geology, should use specialists' terminology or somehow simplify it for the reader. The review reports McPhee's defense of a particularly arcane exchange between two geologists: "It doesn't matter that you don't understand them. Even they are not sure if they are making sense. Their purpose is to try to." In effect, the reviewer said that you don't have to understand all the details of the talk as long as you understand the talk's significance. It would become an ethical problem only when the writer hides his or her own ignorance behind the jargon or specialists' language, or in any other way tries to obscure, distort, confuse, or fabricate facts behind the convenient screen of specialists' words.

In the case of elitist language, as in the case of specialists' language, the governing criterion is whether you have been honest with the reader. If you can say to yourself that your use of either kind of language was designed only to clarify facts, establish mood, or create a tone to the reader's overall benefit, go ahead and use the language that does the job best.

ETHICAL IMPLICATIONS
OF IRONY AND HUMOR

Irony and humor also have ethical implications. The possibility that irony and humor could have an ethical dimension came to me in the 1970s while reading an article by Richard Bernstein in the *New York Times*. He described the interesting competition for French readers between France's major, and largely establishment-oriented, newspaper *Le Monde,* and the "alternative" paper once headed up by Jean-Paul Sarte, *Liberation. Liberation* had pulled many readers away from the traditional, very staid, very serious-to-the-point-of-somber *Le Monde* by writing "creatively" about serious topics. Its tone was not funny, it was ironic. Bernstein quoted French writer Alain Finkelkraut as saying, "You can hear the chuckle of the journalist audible behind the headlines."

If *Liberation* had only poked fun at the news and at the government bureaucracy, it would have stayed a small humor sheet, but under it all its writers are serious journalists. Unlike most French papers, which featured pages filled with commentary and analysis, not reportage, *Liberation* took to sending reporters to the scene to relate what was happening. There would be no ethical implications if all they did was go for the laughs alone, while calling themselves a humor or parody sheet, but they put themselves forth as a *news*paper, so there is the potential for problems. They behaved ethically, however, by taking the news and the facts seriously, even though they presented them in an arresting, if sometimes playful, way. As long as they approached matters like this, there should be no major ethical problems. The French, who are said to have a word for everything, may not have a word for the kind of writing produced by *Liberation,* but I'd probably call it creative nonfiction.

Irony and humor have a respectable place in journalism. Since irony, however, very often gets its strength by stating the exact opposite of what's intended, the opportunity for misinterpretation exists. A literal-minded person would not have been too well warned by the title of Jonathan Swift's essay back in 1729 ("A Modest Proposal for Preventing the Children of Poor People from Being a Burden to Their Parents or the Country"). Would he or she have been aware of Swift's irony when he wrote the following in that essay?

> I shall now therefore humbly propose my own thoughts, which I hope will not be liable to the least objection. I have been assured by a very knowing American of my acquaintance in London, that a young healthy child well nursed is at a year old a most delicious, nourishing and wholesome food, whether stewed, roasted, baked, or boiled; and I make no doubt that it will equally serve in a fricassee or a ragout.

If you write with irony, provide sufficient hints that it is not to be taken as the truth. Ask yourself with all honesty: Will my presumed audience "get" it?

ETHICAL IMPLICATIONS OF INTERNAL MONOLOGS

The use of internal (interior) monolog by creative nonfiction writers has been, and continues to be, the most hotly debated issue in the battle over how far we should go in applying fiction's techniques to nonfiction. Journalists worry most about the use of internal monolog because it appears to overlap too much into fiction, thereby lowering its credibility in the mind of a skeptical reader. It is the most creative technique used in creative nonfiction in that the writer *invents*.

Tom Wolfe and Gay Talese, who have been using this technique longer than most, say that they use it cautiously and responsibly. They maintain that it is not pure invention, as it is in fiction. They always write it only after completely immersing themselves in the mind of the person they're writing about. They get into the person's mind through interviewing in great depth; observing how the person interacts with others over a long period; working out of letters the person has written and received; using diaries, journals, and anything else that enables them to believe that they can speculate responsibly about that person's thoughts on a subject. They are sure that what they do in writing an internal monolog is ethical because they have dug so deep.

Readers may worry about how much of an internal monolog to believe because of the way it sometimes appears on the page. Like fiction's internal monolog or stream of consciousness, the monolog is often in italics; sentences are often incomplete or interrupted by random, disconnected thoughts; and, especially in Wolfe's case, the punctuation may be eccentric, bizarre, unique, and visually exciting.

Some creative nonfiction writers choose not to write internal monologs, believing them to be too far over the line into the territory of fiction. John McPhee, for example, never uses it, saying that a writer cannot get into another person's head. To him, to imply through internal monolog that the writer has entered and is reporting intracranial happenings borders on the unethical.

In the hands of the inept or unscrupulous, internal monolog is an easy device behind which to hide unethical writing. The beginning writer is best advised to stay away from internal monologs to avoid unintentionally lapsing into unethical writing.

ETHICAL IMPLICATIONS
OF COMPOSITES AND FABRICATIONS
IN PURSUIT OF THE LARGER TRUTH

A fiction writer very often creates a character by combining facial features from someone the writer knows, a limp from another, and a deep-cracked voice, totally out of his or her own imagination. Creating composite characters is not only acceptable and ethical behavior for the fiction writer, it's expected.

However, when the journalist or creative nonfiction writer creates a composite character and puts that character forth as real, the writer violates the rules of ethical conduct for nonfiction writers. When a writer creates a composite scene made up of bits and pieces of actual scenes or settings, he or she also violates the ethics of the profession. Again, the fiction writer does this all the time to create a more interesting, more dramatic scene or setting and it's expected. Creative nonfiction writers sometimes do it with the same motivation—but in their case, it's unethical.

On June 18, 1984, *Wall Street Journal* reporter Joanne Lipman wrote in a front-page article that Alastair Reid, writer for the factually scrupulous *New Yorker* magazine, had for years been creating composite characters and places, and had been publishing them in that magazine as nonfiction. After the *Wall Street Journal* article broke, the *New York Times, Time* magazine, and all the other major newspapers, magazines, and radio and television broadcasts jumped on Reid and his *New Yorker* editor, the highly respected William Shawn, who spoke up for Reid. Now, they seemed to jump a bit more gleefully than one would expect, probably because the *New Yorker,* more than any other publication, had regularly boasted consistently about its scrupulous and hardworking fact-checking department and the magazine's general devotion to accuracy and truth.

Alastair Reid said to reporters that he had spent his career since the 1950s creating composite characters and scenes, all in a sincere effort to get at "the larger truth." *Time* magazine, on its "Essay" page of July 2, 1984, reported that Reid had said, "A reporter might take liberties with the factual circumstances to make the larger truth clear." Essayist Roger Rosenblatt went on to write that Reid was wrong in assuming that "larger truth is the province of journalism." He added that "where the larger truth is sought, the answer is where it's always been: in history, poetry, art, nature, education, conversation; in the tunnels of one's own mind."

Reporter Lipman complained that in the December 2, 1961, issue of the *New Yorker*, Reid had written in his piece "Letter from Barcelona" about a "small, flyblown bar by the harbor, a favorite haunt of mine for some years because of its buoyant clientele." Well, *New Yorker* readers loved that flyblown bar, and he says he received letters from people swearing that they'd tracked it down. Unfortunately, Reid now admits that the bar by the harbor doesn't exist—although he insists that it did at one time, but not when he was writing about it, and the conversations he said went on in it actually went on in some other place—in some cases, just in his own head.

The attitude that gets Reid into trouble was conveyed in the statement that "whether the bar existed or not was irrelevant to what I was after." He said that he is always after "the poetic whole," that he's like a poet in his concern for conveying the image rather than the mere facts. Coming to his defense, fellow writer for the *New Yorker* Paul Brodeur said that he himself figures that quotes are accurate so long as they "don't do violence to the intent of what was said." Reporter Lipman wrote that "Brodeur himself subscribes to a form of creative journalism."

William A. Henry III wrote on *Time*'s "Press" page on July 2, 1984: "To critics, it did not matter than Reid's deviations were largely inconsequential. Any departure from fact is the first step on a slippery slope toward unbelievability. Facts are what people can agree on. Truth can be determined by each reader."

Reid, Shawn, and Brodeur may have genuinely been in pursuit of a greater reality, a larger truth, when they created and published their composite characters and scenes, but when a writer gets comfortable with using that fiction technique on inconsequential matters, couldn't he or she slip easily over into using it on more consequential matters and thus truly violate professional ethics? The consensus of professional writers seems to be that we should not use composites or fabrications of any kind, even for the most inconsequential matters, thereby staying well within the ethics of the profession.

Janet Cooke, a reporter for the *Washington Post,* wrote a story, "Jimmy's World," which won a Pulitzer Prize. A problem of journalistic ethics, and a clear case of it, developed after she received the award. Jimmy, it was discovered, was not a mere composite; Jimmy was a total fabrication of Janet Cooke's imagination. In its embarrassment, the *Post* returned the Pulitzer Prize, and Janet Cooke resigned. Her letter of resignation, published in the *Post,* said that "'Jimmy's World' was in essence a fabrication. I never encountered an eight-year-old heroin addict. The September 28, 1980, article was a serious misrepresentation which I deeply regret. I apologize to my newspaper, my profession, the Pulitzer board, and all seekers of the truth. Today, in facing up to the truth, I have submitted my resignation."

Because the story was so well written and contained such believable dialog and concrete details, her editors went along with it even without corroborative evidence in lieu of the principals' identities. They said they had, at first, no reason to suspect her of fabrication. It was a fascinating, if terrifying, story, and they felt it had to be told.

The *Washington Post* provides its reporters, writers, and editors a guide to ethics in writing for that paper. "Standards and Ethics" is very detailed, having evolved out of the simple set of principles first laid down by Eugene Meyer when he bought the paper in 1933. These statements for ethical writing could apply well to any nonfiction writing—and perhaps particularly to any efforts toward creative nonfiction:

> The first mission of a newspaper is to tell the truth as nearly as the truth can be ascertained.
> The newspaper shall tell *all* the truth, so far as it can learn it, concerning the important affairs of America and the world.
> As a disseminator of the news, the paper shall observe the decencies that are obligatory upon a private gentleman.

What it prints shall be fit reading for the young as well as the old.

The newspaper's duty is to its readers and to the public at large, and not to the private interests of its owner.

In the pursuit of truth, the newspaper shall be prepared to make sacrifice of its material fortune if such course be necessary for the public good.

The newspaper shall not be the ally of any special interest, but shall be fair and free and wholesome in its outlook on public affairs and public men.

These Principles are reendorsed herewith.

ETHICAL IMPLICATIONS OF THE PLAIN STYLE

One of the most disquieting pieces I've ever read was one by Hugh Kenner, the highly respected author of books about contemporary literature. His article in the *New York Times Book Review* (September 15, 1985), "The Politics of Plain Style," made me clip it out, highlight line after line, and read it time after time. I'm sure I can't do justice to this wonderfully disturbing article, but I'll try to provide its essence.

I found the piece disturbing because I thought at first Kenner might be saying that all the advice I've given in this book might lead my readers into unethical writing—hardly my intent. I do find some comfort in the fact that such world-renowned writers as John McPhee, George Orwell, Joan Didion, and E. B. White have all counseled us to "write plain." Even Jacques Barzun titled his excellent and practical book on rhetoric *Simple & Direct*—another way of saying, "Write in the plain style."

Kenner said that the plain, unadorned style began about two hundred years ago in reaction to the previous "high styles" that were esteemed in proportion to their ornateness. The plain style came with the "arrival" of straight, nonpolemical, nonpolitical journalism in newspapers. He says that "the hidden premise" in this new, plain style was that "a man who doesn't make his language ornate cannot be deceiving us." This is the speech of merchants and artisans who handle things and would thus handle words with equal uprightness and honesty, not like the wits and scholars who handle only ideas—and thus are not to be trusted too highly.

Then comes the terrifying premise of his article: "Handbooks and copy editors now teach journalists how to write plainly, that is, in such a manner that they will be trusted. You get yourself trusted by artifice."

His point, apparently, is that there's something artificial about writing clearly. Therein lies my concern. Is it a problem in ethics if you deliberately disguise the fact that you're trying to persuade a reader to your way of thinking by writing with plain words, plain images?

He reinforces this notion by writing: "The plain style feigns a candid observer. Such is its great advantage for persuading. From behind its mask of calm candor, the writer with political intentions can appeal, in seeming disinterest, to people whose pride is in their no-nonsense connoisseurship of fact. And such is the trickiness of language that he may find he must deceive them to enlighten them."

It took a few readings of the article to leave behind my first interpretation, that we should not use the plain style because it's potentially deceptive—that it only feigns honesty. Finally, I realized that his real message was for the innocent reader, not the honest writer. I had missed the point on the first several times through, but he had made it clear four paragraphs from the end:

> It is clarifying to reflect that the language of fiction cannot be told from that of fact. Their grammar, syntax, and semantics are identical. So Orwell passed readily to and fro between his two modes, reportage and fiction, which both employ the plain style. The difference is that the fictionality of fiction offers itself for detection. If fiction speaks political truths, it does so by allegory.

That is tricky, because it transfers responsibility for what is being said from the writer to the reader....

I guess this all boils down to two points for us to remember. When we're writers, use the plain style, but understand its potential power to deceive and write honestly; and, when we're readers, be aware and wary of any style, by any writer. Anthony Brandt's column for *Esquire,* "Truth and Consequences: For a Writer Telling the Public What It Has to Know Is Only Half the Battle" (October 19, 1984), ends with an admonition that could serve us all:

> I've learned to pull in my horns. I've learned discretion, I've learned to doubt myself more. I advise my reader to do the same. Beware. Doubt me, doubt my brethren. That way lies the healthy skepticism that will keep us all, readers and writers alike, relatively honest.

You have an unspoken, unwritten, implicit contract with your reader, a contract to tell the truth—whether you're writing fiction or nonfiction. In fiction, you must stay true to the story, which is different from nonfiction, where you must stay true to the facts as you know them.

FICTIONAL BITS WITHIN NONFICTION

It doesn't come up too often, but there are times when a nonfiction writer wants to write a short fictional piece, perhaps a paragraph or so, right in the midst of a straight, nonfiction narrative. He or she may want to lapse into fiction to protect someone's privacy (or forestall a libel suit); to make the same point better, more colorfully, more entertainingly, more emotionally, and thus more memorably; or to get at the "whole truth," the "larger truth," the "greater reality" by introducing some subjectivity—fiction. Recall, however, that Alastair Reid of the *New Yorker* thought he was doing just that.

We can use pure fiction in the midst of nonfiction provided we flag it. We must alert the reader that we've crossed, or are about to cross, over that fuzzy border into fiction territory. We must, for we have a contract with the reader, and without our beloved reader, we writers would whistle in the wind.

Writers have found several flag signals to alert the reader, some more subtle than others. The more subtle, the more artistic, the more artistic, the more dangerous. A balance must be struck between not wanting to be too obvious, too intrusive about it, and wanting to be sure that the code of ethics is not violated by being so subtle that the reader fails to see where the nonfiction leaves off and the fiction begins.

One subtle yet clear way is to italicize the fiction parts. A writer may "get away with" the fiction-i.e., be within the bounds of ethics—if he or she merely uses italics to flag the fictional parts, but it would be more professional and ethical to also make some reference outside the italicized portion to the "previous speculation," or "that fictional look at the future," or some such supplemental signal.

Sometimes the fiction will be in the form of a short internal monolog. The reader who stops to think about it will, of course, realize that the writer could not have known exactly what the person was thinking, but it's more ethical to use additional flagging or warning devices, such as "she may have been thinking," "he could well have thought to himself," "perhaps she said to herself that day," or "perhaps he said something to himself like...."

We can use words like "probably," "possibly," or "apparently" periodically to reinforce that we are using speculative writing—fiction. Even though you think you've set it out clearly enough earlier on, your implicit contract to deal honestly requires that you remind the reader that you've slipped out of nonfiction territory into the land of fiction.

I've talked so far only about those regular nonfiction articles in which fiction, true fiction, is inserted, for whatever motivation, into the nonfiction narrative. Creative nonfiction articles and books may do that too. The same contract stands—you must be honest with the reader.

It is easy to violate unintentionally our implicit contract in creative nonfiction writing, which in some critics' minds is always right on the edge, if not over the edge, of fiction. Obviously, it's impractical to flag every place where we're being "creative" and not "factual" (because we're always true to the facts while presenting them in a creative way). But we've got to honor our contract and tell the reader what we're up to.

The lead editorial in the *New York Times* (October 5, 1986) gave us a fine example of a major newspaper using a creative nonfiction technique. Try to identify the technique, and consider whether the readers were adequately informed that the *Times*—("All the News That's Fit to Print")—was playing with fiction.

The President, Imagined
No, says a spokesman, the President won't have a news conference before he leaves to meet Mikhail Gorbachev in Reykjavik. It's a special shame, and not just because Mr. Reagan has averaged only seven a year. Rarely has the public so needed to hear from the President.

Then what's the next best thing? A simulation. It's easy to imagine reassuring Presidential answers to three urgent questions.

Q. Mr. President, you've left much confusion about your policy on lying to the public. Did your Administration lie in order to promote news articles that would rattle Libya's Colonel Quaddafi?

A. Well, it has never been our policy to mislead or lie to the media, ever. If a misguided official might have done so in this matter, I regret it and want now to reaffirm our commitment to truth. We know how freely Communist... (and the answer went on).

Q. Sir, you took an unusually stubborn position on sanctions against South Africa, even after Congress passed them. Now both houses have overridden your veto, will you carry out the law ungrudgingly?

A. Well, I'm not happy about Congress taking over executive branch responsibility for conducting foreign policy. But the law stands higher than... (and the answer went on).

Q. Mr. President, some of your supporters think you made a bad deal for a Soviet spy and fear you'll come back from Reykjavik empty-handed.

A. Well, it's way too early to second-guess a deal because so far, there is no deal. What there is between... (and on).
Thank you, Mr. President.

I have to admit that when I first skimmed (too rapidly, perhaps) that editorial on the morning it arrived, I thought it was truly a typical Q & A exchange with a *Times* reporter, or perhaps at a presidential press conference. After a while, it dawned on me that the whole exchange was a cleverly written bit of creative nonfiction intended to make me think it was just that—temporarily. The danger of inserting that bit of fiction into a paper noted for its careful handling of news is that it will be taken for "news that's fit to print."

I went back to see whether the editor had lived up to what I believe about running up flags for the reader, warning of any such change away from the expected course. Yes, they certainly had tried to warn me in the head: *The President, Imagined.* "Imagined"—that was the first flag (although it fluttered by me at first reading). The first paragraph sets me up beautifully; it's straightforward narrative reporting.

The second paragraph hints broadly enough with "A simulation," but I skimmed right by it—we're always reading about simulations. The editor, still worrying about whether the warning is clear (but without ruining the fun by being too obvious), says that "it's easy to imagine…." Looking back through it, I realized what had been done to me—and I loved it. I thought, however, that the editor hit me too cleverly when the editorial ended with an italicized, "Thank you, Mr. President." That looked so familiar, so real, so nonfiction, that I took in the line, the hook, and the sinker. Had the editor not flown all those warning flags, I would have had an excellent example of how even the great *New York Times* had slipped up—but it hadn't and I didn't. It did provide an excellent example of responsible, ethical, creative nonfiction—and an example of how a reader, given half a chance, will not read something the way you intended. Ethics require open-eyed caution.

In a book-length work, some writers will put a short (and sometimes a long) statement up front, even as a foreword, that explains how the research was conducted, and just how much fiction is involved. This enables readers to carry that understanding with them as they work their way through the words. Gay Talese added a five-page section (titled "Author's Note") at the end of *Honor Thy Father* explaining his relationship with the Bonanno family and how he went about researching and interviewing for that book about the

Mafia. Such a statement *must* be made somewhere, and must, in itself, be honest and clear. Statements of this kind can include details about the writer's research methods: if he interviewed by tape, by notes, by memory; how long he was in the field with the subject or the characters; whether he had full access to diaries, journals, day-books, ships' logs, etc. They may also talk about the writing, especially about the fiction techniques used, addressing such issues as how valid were any conversations used; on what did they base any internal monologs; whether the central characters had read the manuscript and if they approved of it in whole or in part; whether the central characters had the right of text approval.

In short, our professional ethics demand that we be honest with the readers, honest with the characters involved, honest with ourselves, and that we, in general, lay our cards on the table for all to see. Without that honesty, there may be creativity, lively writing, and many other good things—but not honorable and esteemed creative nonfiction.

APPENDIX ❧ APPLICATIONS
OF CREATIVE NONFICTION

Throughout the book, I've used examples from some of the top creative nonfiction writers to illustrate the use of fiction techniques in nonfiction writing. This final chapter takes a look at specific applications—history and biography, personal histories (memoir), travel, nature, science and technology, and journalism, or "hard" news. If you're a teacher, you might ask students to identify the fiction techniques being used in each excerpt. I hope, too, that when you read these short excerpts you'll be inspired to read the complete book or article. I've used only the best, so you're in for a treat.

HISTORY AND BIOGRAPHY

History and biography are more closely related than an "and" between them would imply. I'm not the first person to think about their close relationship. Emerson's biographer Jean Strouse wrote that Emerson had said, "There is properly no history, only biography." In "The Real Reasons," collected in *Extraordinary Lives,* Strouse says, "Good biographers combine the arts of the novelist, the detective work of the historian, and the insights of the psychologist."

The great American biologist, Leon Edel, says in his book *Writing Lives*:

The writing of lives is a department of history and is closely related to the discoveries of history. It can claim the same skills. No lives are led outside history or society; they take place in human time. No biography is complete unless it reveals the individual within history, within an ethos and a social complex. In saying this we remember Donne: No man is an island unto himself.

In a later chapter ("Dilemmas"), Edel quotes the founder of the new biography, Lytton Strachey, describing biography as "the most delicate and humane of all the branches of the art of writing." "Delicate," Edel added, "because the biographer seeks to restore a sense of life to the inert materials that survive an individual's passage on this earth—seeks to recapture some part of what was once tissue and brains, and above all, feeling, and to shape a likeness of the vanished figure."

Edel then gives what amounts to a credo for writers of creative nonfiction within the "new biography":

> The writer of biography must be neat and orderly and logical in describing this elusive flamelike human spirit which delights in defying order and neatness and logic. The biographer may be as imaginative as he pleases—the more imaginative the better—in the way in which he brings together his materials, *but he must not imagine the materials.* He must read himself into the past; but he must also read the past into the present. He must judge the facts, but he must not sit in judgment. He must respect the dead—but he must tell the truth.

In his chapter, "The New Biography," Edel presents four of his principles of biographic writing, and then sums up the chapter with a list of devices the new biographer legitimately steals from the fiction writer, all of which will sound familiar to students of creative nonfiction.

> And the task and duty of biographical narrative is to sort out themes and patterns, not dates and mundane calendar events which sort themselves. This can be accomplished by use of those

very devices that have given narrative strength to fiction—flashbacks, retrospective chapters, summary chapters, jumps of the future, forays into the past–that is the way we live and move; art can be derived from this knowledge.

Let's read a few examples of how some historians and biographers apply that credo and those fiction techniques to make their work more interesting, yet just as informative as other historians and biographers we may have read.

> Under Prince Henry's stimulus, Lagos, a few miles along the coast from Sagres, became a center for caravel-building. Oak for keels came from Alentejo, bordering on the Algarve. Pine for the hulls grew along Portugal's Atlantic seaboard, where it was protected by law. The cluster pines also produced resin to waterproof the rigging and to calk the seams of the hull. Around Lagos there soon developed the flourishing crafts of sail-making and rope-making. While Prince Henry at Sagres did not actually build a modern research institute, he did bring together all the essential ingredients. He collected the books and charts, the sea captains, pilots, and mariners, the map-makers, instrument-makers, and compass-makers, the shipbuilders and carpenters, and other craftsmen, to plan voyages, to assess the findings, and to prepare expeditions ever farther out into the unknown. The work Prince Henry started would never end.
>
> **Daniel J. Boorstin**
> *The Discoverers*

> Whether Pitt [England's secretary of state in 1756] possessed the strategic eye, whether the expeditions he launched were part of a considered combination, may be questioned. Now, as at all times, his policy was a projection on to a vast screen of his own aggressive, dominating personality. In the teeth of disfavour and obstruction he had made his way to the foremost place in Parliament, and now at last fortune, courage, and the confidence of his countrymen had given him a stage on which his gifts could be displayed and his foibles indulged. To call into life and action the depressed and languid spirit of England; to weld

all her resources of wealth and manhood into a single instrument of war which should be felt from the Danube to the Mississippi; to humble the house of Bourbon, to make the Union Jack supreme in every ocean, to conquer, to command, and never to count the cost, whether in blood or gold—this was the spirit of Pitt....

Winston S. Churchill
A History of the English-Speaking Peoples,
Volume III: The Age of Revolution

If any decade could be called the decade of the consumer, it was the fifties: the money rolled in, the living was easy, appetites expanded, and television nightly tickled greed. Twice in that decade the Bureau of Labor Statistics revised the consumer price index to make it reflect the changes in what the average American bought with his pay—an ever smaller percentage, it turned out, for food. Likewise for clothing. But more and more on housing, more and more for leisure, more and more for doctors and medicine. All essentials were easily met by the rising economy, but luxuries and indulgences, what the economists call "discretionary purchasing power," were themselves becoming an essential to the growing national economy, the growing national market. We at *Colliers* wanted our share of this growing market, but we were being shouldered away from the trough.

Theodore H. White
"The Fifties: Incubating the Storm,"
In Search of History

So it could happen badly with him [Ulysses S. Grant] when he was alone and cut off and the evils of life came down about him. Marooned in California, far from his family, tormented by money problems, bored by the pointless routine of a stagnant army post under a dull and unimaginative colonel, he could turn to drink to escape. He could do the same thing back in Missouri as a civilian, working hard for a meager living, all the luck breaking badly, drifting into failure at forty, Sam Grant the ne'er-do-well. Deep in Tennessee, likewise, sidetracked by a jealous and petty-minded superior, the awful strain of Shiloh lying ineradicable on his mind, his career apparently ready to end just as it was being reborn, the story could be the same. There was a flame in him, and there were times when he could not keep the winds from the outer dark from blowing in on him and making it flicker. But it never did go out.

Bruce Catton
"Glory Is Out of Date,"
A Stillness at Appomattox

In the White House Robert Lincoln and John Hay sit gossiping pleasantly, Nicolay away at the Fort Sumter flag-raising. The doors burst open and several voices at once tell them the news. They run downstairs, take a carriage, cannot quite believe what they have heard. Slowly their carriage plows a path through the gathering thousands of people around Tenth Street. Dr. Stone gravely and tenderly tells Robert the worst: there is no hope. He chokes. The tears run down his face. After a time he recovers and does his best during hours of the night at comforting his mother.

At about the same hour and minute of the clock that the President is shot in Ford's Theatre, a giant of a young man rides on a big one-eyed bay horse to the door of the Seward house on Lafayette Square, gets off his horse, rings the doorbell, says he is a messenger from the attending physician and has a package of medicine that must be personally delivered to the sickroom of the Secretary of State. The servant at the door tries to stop the young man, who enters and goes up the stairs, suddenly to turn in a furious rush on Fred Seward, beating him on the head with the pistol, tearing the scalp, fracturing the skull and battering the pistol to pieces.

Carl Sandburg
Abraham Lincoln: The War Years

The commander of the division to which I belonged, as soon as we were on board the ship, appointed me boatswain, and ordered me to go to the captain and demand of him the keys to the hatches and a dozen candles. I made the demand accordingly, and the captain promptly replied, and delivered the articles; but requested me at the same time to do no damage to the ship or rigging. We then were ordered by our commander to open the hatches, and take out all the chests of tea and thrown them overboard, and we immediately proceeded to execute his orders; first cutting and splitting the chest with our tomahawks, so as thoroughly to expose them to the effects of the water. In about three hours from the time we went on board, we had thus broken and thrown overboard every tea chest to be found in the ship; while those in the other ships were disposing of the tea in the same way, at the same time. We were surrounded by British armed ships, but no attempt was made to resist us. We then quietly retired to our several places of residence, without having any conversation with each other, or taking any measures to discover who were our associates.

Alfred F. Young
The Shoemaker and the Tea Party: Memory and the American Revolution

The next morning, the *Caird* gave a sudden, sickening roll leeward; the painter carrying the sea anchor had been severed by a block of ice that formed on it, out of reach. Beating the ice off the canvas, the men scrambled to unfurl the frozen sails, and once they succeeded in raising them, headed the *Caird* into the wind. It was on this day, May 2, that McNish abruptly gave up any attempt to keep a diary.

"We held the boat up to the gale during that day, enduring as best we could discomforts that amounted to pain," wrote Shackleton, in an uncharacteristically direct reference to their physical suffering. The men were soaked to the bone and frostbitten. They were badly chafed by wet clothes that had not been removed for seven months, and afflicted with saltwater boils. Their wet feet and legs were a sickly white color and swollen. Their hands were black—with grime, blubber, burns from the Primus and frostbite. The least movement was excruciating.

"We sat as still as possible," wrote Worsley. "[I]f we moved a quarter of an inch one way or the other we felt cold, wet garments on our flanks and sides. Sitting very still for a while, life was worth living." Hot meals afforded the only relief. Shackleton ensured that the men had hot food every four hours during the day and scalding powdered milk every four hours of the long night watches.

Caroline Alexander
The Endurance: Shackleton's Legendary Antarctic Expedition

Students at The Salt Institute for Documentary Studies, associated with the University of Maine and located in Portland, produce an annual book, *Omnibus,* in which they publish writings and photographs of life in Maine. This article, "Pounding Ash," documents Native American basketmaking as practiced in the past.

Moose spits on his hands and twirls the ax between them, studying the brown ash log in front of him. He lifts the ax over one shoulder, his right hand at the base of the ax, his left hand near its head. His hands join as he brings the blunt end down hard over the brown ash log he has already stripped of bark. The sound echoes through the Pleasant Point Passamaquoddy reservation, bouncing off his neighbor's house, reverberating even after the initial impact. He immediately lifts the ax again above his head, brings it down, and that sound echoes once more through the reservation. It is rhythmical, powerful.

When they finish pounding, Moose uses his ax to notch two places at the end of the log. It is an ax that has been in Moose's family for at least four generations of basketmakers. It has pounded so many logs that the blunt end of its iron head has curved inward. In between the notches he pulls off a strip the length of the log and the depth off a growth ring. If he or Chris have missed even an inch while pounding, the strips Moose pulls off will not separate smoothly from the tree. Later, Moose's father, Fred Moose, Sr., will scrape the rough parts of the strip with his knife. These strips are the beginnings of a basket.

Sally Steindorf
collected in *Omnibus 2000*

PERSONAL HISTORIES (SKETCHES, PROFILES, MEMOIRS)

No perfect definitions exist to cleanly separate profiles from sketches. Different editors and writers call a sketch a profile or a profile a sketch, so I'm not trying here to make a final statement about which is which. I separate profiles and sketches on the basis of depth of treatment and purpose. A profile tries to give us a short (say 1,000- to 10,000-word) biographical summary of a person. The sketch tries only to get at the essence of a person, not his or her life story. Personal histories (autobiographies) are written by the person involved, whereas profiles and sketches are written by someone other than the subject. A personal history, by my loose definition, is of book length (say 50,000 words or more) and may be written with almost any structure the person wants.

SKETCHES

Melvin Maddocks's twice-weekly column for the *Christian Science Monitor* was frequently a sketch about a leading figure. The two excerpts that follow show how much a good writer can get across in fewer than one thousand words, and how a writer gets at the essence of the man. The first comes from "The Flower of Ice Hockey Takes His Last Turn," written upon the retirement of the Montreal Canadiens' Guy LaFleur; and the second is from "Remembering the Late, Great Count Basie—the Swinging Never Stopped," a column commemorating the pianist-composer upon his death.

> Though deceptively strong, he appeared less burly than the players around him, like a figure skater who had blundered in among the heavy hitters. But there was a special intentness to LaFleur. Even when he coasted on the ice for a routine face-off, he brought drama, urgency. The eye followed him, as the eye follows an actor on stage who has the gift of presence. The tempo of excitement lifted just because he was there. When the puck was dropped, LaFleur moved for it with a bright-eyed hunger. He is one of those players so drawn to the puck that the puck seems drawn to them.
>
> **Melvin Maddocks**
> "The Flower of Ice Hockey Takes His Last Turn,"
> *Christian Science Monitor* (December 5, 1984)

> Basie had a subtlety to match his power. His humor was irrepressible. A Basie solo in the middle of a piece often took on the

character of a family joke played back and forth with bassist Walter Page or guitarist Freddy Green or drummer Jo Jones, to name three old hands. Modest to the point of deference in these dialogues, Basie nonetheless had a way of getting in the final witty topper. Everything he played possessed a kind of joy so central to his being as to be beyond his power to suppress. Even his blues came out happy.

Melvin Maddocks
"Remembering the Late, Great Count Basie—
the Swinging Never Stopped,"
Christian Science Monitor (May 4, 1984)

PROFILES

The first excerpt comes from a section of the *New Yorker* called "Profiles." Calvin Trillin and other writers for that magazine write some of the best, most thoroughly researched, and longest profiles of any publication. Calvin Trillin wrote one about Edna Buchanan, a crime reporter for the *Miami Herald* in the 1980s.

In the newsroom of the Miami *Herald,* there is some disagreement about which of Edna Buchanan's first paragraphs stands as the classic Edna lead. I line up with the fried-chicken faction. The fried-chicken story was about a rowdy ex-con named Gary Robinson, who late one Sunday night lurched drunkenly into a Church's outlet, shoved his way to the front of the line, and ordered a three-piece box of fried chicken. Persuaded to wait his turn, he reached the counter again five or ten minutes later, only to be told that Church's had run out of fried chicken. The young woman at the counter suggested that he might like chicken nuggets instead. Robinson responded to the suggestion by slugging her in the head. That set of a chain of events that ended with Robinson's being shot dead by a security guard. Edna Buchanan covered the murder for the *Herald*—there are policemen in Miami who say that it wouldn't be a murder without her. Her story began with what the fried-chicken faction still regards as the classic Edna lead: "Gary Robinson died hungry."

Calvin Trillin
"Covering the cops," *New Yorker* (February 17, 1986)

New York magazine also runs many profiles and sketches written in a creative way. Tony Schwartz, who covers the media waterfront so diligently and so well, wrote a profile (or is it a sketch?) about Dan Rather:

> The son of a ditchdigger, he wants above all to hold on to what he's got. But he also wants to do it on his own terms. He is determined, for example, to be seen with CBS as a company man and head cheerleader. But he also sees himself as heir to Ed Murrow, the conscience of a corporation he increasingly doubts has the best interests of the news division at heart. He is zealous about protecting his *Evening News* turf and his authority as managing editor. But he is also, by nature, deeply reluctant to confront his adversaries and extremely eager to get along. He sees himself as a fierce guardian of traditional journalistic values. But he is also committed to winning a ratings battle in which non-journalistic values such as promotion and pizzazz are more and more a factor.
>
> **Tony Schwartz**
> "Dan on the Run,"
> *New York* magazine (February 3, 1986)

A weed—in the vernacular of groundsmen in England—is known as a volunteer, and there are no volunteers in the Centre Court at Wimbledon. Robert Twynam, who grows the grass there, is willing to accept a bet from anyone who is foolhardy enough to doubt this. Twynam's lawn—nine hundred and thirty square yards, one fifth of an acre—is the best of its kind, and Twynam has such affection for it that he spends a great deal of time just looking at it. He takes long, compact walks on the Centre Court. At times, he gets down on his hands and knees and crawls on it, to observe the frequently changing relationships among the various plants there. Twynam keeps a diary for the Centre Court ("February 4: very sunny spells, Centre Court fine," "February 5: cooler, little sun, Centre Court O.K."), and, in the words of one member of Wimbledon's Committee of Management, "Mr. Twynam regards each blade of grass as an individual, with its own needs, its own destiny, and its own right to grow on this blessed piece of lawn." Twynam has been at Wimbledon forty-four years. Nearly all of the greatest stars of tennis have played under his scrutiny, and—while he knows a great deal about the game—his appraisals of all of them seem to have been formed from the point of view of the grass. "When Emmo puts his foot down…," Twynam will say, in reference to Roy Emerson, of Australia, "when Emmo puts his foot down, he is stepping on forty or fifty plants."

John McPhee
"Twynam of Wimbledon,"
A Roomful of Hovings

MEMOIRS

Filmmaker and author Ben Logan recalls growing up on a different field of grass in his personal history, *The Empty Meadow.* Brought up on a Wisconsin farm, Ben writes below of one of his first teenage encounters with a member of the opposite sex.

> She bit her lip and wouldn't look at me or let me turn her face toward me. "Everything goes too fast."
> "You mean us? Last time?"
> She nodded. "I didn't mean to let you kiss me."
> I laughed and squeezed her shoulder. "Why did you then?"
> She jerked away from my hand. I thought she was going to slap me. "Oh you're something aren't you? You think boys are so different! You think girls are just starched marshmallows or something! You think you can do anything you want with us just so you don't get us wrinkled up or pull off any buttons!"
> From a long way off I could hear myself thinking, God-almighty, what the hell is going on?
> She looked at me, waiting. The moon had come up and was on her face. She was prettier than ever. She took a deep breath. The front of the suit raised up and down. I watched that happening, thinking about the anatomy of it and almost forgot what we were talking about.

Ben Logan
The Empty Meadow

Clyde Rice's memoir, *A Heaven in the Eye,* won the 1984 Western States Book Award for creative nonfiction. Begun when Rice was seventy-five, the book is a memoir of his life from age sixteen until he was thirty-four. He says that the publisher didn't want to hear about his first sixteen years, and he, himself, felt that no one would want to read about what happened after his thirty-fourth year. This short excerpt has to suffice to describe the entire wild and wonderful story, but it does provide some of its gusto.

> I was invited to a few of the fine homes of the old first families of Portland [Oregon]. Scattered throughout the downtown areas, these houses were very grand, but the impression I had about the people I met there was of lap dogs atop embroidered cushions, nor did their young impress me any more favorably. Life, my mother's death had recently reminded me, was rich and priceless and soon gone, but here in their fabulous boxes these people were the quiet antithesis of gusto. The sap of life was lost here. After visiting four or five of these fine houses, I said out loud, not to the mirror but with some self-consciousness, "What you seek you won't find in money or prestige." I added this motto to the things I already knew about myself—for example, that I never watched to catch myself simpering in the acclaim of however many mutts, and that I was going to do the sexual thing with Miss Nordstrom.
>
> **Clyde Rice**
> *A Heaven in the Eye*

TRAVEL AND A SENSE OF PLACE

Although the writers quoted below all write about their travel experiences, they are not, in the usual sense, travel writers. Travel writers intend to help us plan our trips to places they discuss, letting us know important information about transportation, sleeping accommodations, restaurants to seek out (or avoid), passport/visa requirements, and the costs of everything. Their purpose is pragmatic.

The writers collected here have a purpose more poetic than pragmatic. They try their best to give us a vicarious sense of place—they give us its feel. The best travel writers also try to give us a feel for the place, but they don't consider their purpose literary. Perhaps those quoted here do not think themselves literary, but their nonfiction writing is creative and entertaining as it informs. The traditional travel writer transports us; the creative travel writer speaks of transport.

> At starlight we dropped down the stream, which was a deadwater for three miles, or as far as the Moosehorn; Joe telling us that we must be very silent, and he himself making no noise with his paddle, while urging the canoe along with effective impulses. It was a still night, and suitable for this purpose—for if there is wind, the moose will smell you—and Joe was confident that he should get some. The harvest moon had just risen, and its level rays began to light up the forest on our right, while we glided downward in the shade on the same side, against the little breeze that was stirring. The lofty, spiring tops of the spruce and fir were very black against the sky, and more distinct than by day, close bordering this broad avenue on each side; and the beauty of the scene, as the moon rose above the forest, it would not be easy to describe.
>
> **Henry David Thoreau**
> "The Moose Hunt,"
> *The Maine Woods*

> And so we walked, hour upon hour, over rollercoaster hills, along knife-edge ridges and over grassy balds, through depthless ranks of oak, ash, chinkapin, and pine. The skies grew sullen and the air chillier, but it wasn't until the third day that the snow came. It began in the morning as thinly scattered flecks, hardly noticeable. But then the wind rose, then rose again, until it was blowing with an end-of-the-world fury that seemed to have even the trees in a panic, and with it came snow, great flying masses of it. By midday we found ourselves plodding into a stinging, cold, hard-blowing storm. Soon after, we came to a narrow ledge of path along a wall of rock called Big Butt Mountain.
>
> **Bill Bryson**
> *A Walk in the Woods*

Even in the dark sky, the big rock seemed to cast a shadow over our course. I thought this reach a terrible place to die, and that turned me again to the depth finder: under us lay the Catskill Aqueduct, large enough to carry a locomotive and deep enough, were the Empire State Building placed on the tunnel floor, to leave only the top hundred feet of the skyscraper rising above the river surface. Inside the aqueduct each day, transverse to the flow of the Hudson, five hundred million gallons of cold mountain water rush down to New York City. Could tourists see that immense thing under the river, they might visit to gawk there as they do at Hoover Dam.

William Least Heat-Moon
River-Horse: A Voyage across America

It was not a popular train, this Simla Mail. Its odd twisted route was undoubtedly the result of the demands of the imperial postal service, for the British regarded letter writing and mail delivery as one of the distinguishing features of any great civilization. And Indians feel pretty much the same.

"Use the shutters," the ticket collector said, "and don't leave any small articles lying around."

The whistle of the Simla Mail drowned the sounds of music from the bazaar. I was soon asleep. But at midnight I was woken by rain beating against the shutters. The monsoon which had hit the Punjab only the day before had brought another storm, and the train struggled through it. The thick raindrops came down so hard they splattered through the slats and louvers in the shutters, and a fine spray soaked the compartment floor.

The guard knocked on the door at 5:20 to announce that we had arrived at Kalka.

It was green and cool at Kalka, and after a shave in the Gentlemen's Waiting Room I was ready for the five-hour journey through the hills to Simla. I could have taken the small, pottering "Simla Queen" or the Express, but the white twenty-seat railcar was already waiting at the platform. I boarded, and snoozed, and woke to see mists lying across the hills and the heavy green foliate in the glades beside the line.

Paul Theroux
"Making Tracks to Chittagoing,"
Sunrise with Seamonsters: Travels and Discoveries

For all these reasons, to come to Kathmandu expecting it to resemble a spotless mountain city like Zurich or Geneva would be foolish. Apart from anything else, the largely Hindu community lets a plethora of sacred cows wander unobstructed in the middle of the steadily growing vehicular traffic. By changing blocks, one can transport oneself back and forth over various centuries in a way that is almost unimaginable in a Western city. In the course of a few streets, I encountered a Tibetan wearing a T-shirt that said "The University of Hawaii"; a Nepalese who tried to sell me hashish or his sister; and a poster in the window of a travel agency describing a night-club act called "Rags to Riches." The poster read "Rags to Riches roaming around the world now in Kathmandu...featuring Jonathan from France on guitar and Philip from Iceland on flute. Cheering you up with folk music, jokes, and skits in a friendly atmosphere." I also overheard a woman in the elegant Chinese restaurant in the Annapurna Hotel say delightedly, "Oh, they have American chop suey."

Jeremy Bernstein
"The Himalaya Revisited,"
New Yorker (February 3, 1986)

The guesthouse really did exist, but two men stirring a tureen in its open-air kitchen explained indifferently that the owner was away and all the rooms were locked. We sought assistance at the mayor's house (an old trick), and the incumbent, well-fed man of Pickwickian geniality listened to our story, took a key from a hook next to his front door and led us to an unoccupied adobe cottage on the other side of the street. "Have you got candles?" he asked, scratching his crotch. We had, and we fetched them from the jeep and followed him inside, seeing off several dozen mice. Matthew lit the candles, and we sat on two camp beds positioned in the middle of the front room.

The mayor eyed a mouse in the corner. "I hope you'll be comfortable here," he said, his expression indicating that he thought this was unlikely. "When you leave, pay me whatever you like. If you want food, ask for Violeta at the top of the street. Er, I'll be off now."

Sara Wheeler
Travels in a Thin Country: A Journey through Chile

It is as though the British Isles are tilted permanently to one corner—the southeast corner, bottom right, where London stands seething upon the Thames. Everything slithers and tumbles down there, all the talent, all the money, and when I got on the M4 motorway that morning I felt that I was being swept away helter-skelter, willy-nilly across the breadth of England. Around me all the energies of the place seemed to be heading in a single direction—the trucks from Cornwall and South Wales, the tourist buses, the ramshackle No Nuclear estate cars, the stream of expense-account Fords, their salesmen drivers tapping their steering-wheels to the rhythm of Radio One. London! London! Shouted the direction signs. London! Screamed the blue and white train, streaking eastwards beside the road, and when I turned off to the south and made for Dover, still I felt the presence of the capital tugging away at me, as it tugs commuters from their mock-Tudor villas day after day from the far reaches of Surrey and pastoral Hampshire.

Jan Morris
"Not So Far: A European Journey,"
Journeys

Writers frequently use a "run-up" of several lines to set the environmental context for the scene or narration and to provide a sense of place. Tobias Wolff uses this technique effectively in *This Boy's Life: A Memoir,* as does Ian Frazier in *On the Rez.*

We drove farther into the mountains. It was late afternoon. Pale cold light. The river flashed green through the trees beside the road, then turned gray as pewter when the sun dropped. The mountains darkened. Night came on.

Dwight stopped at a tavern in a village called Marblemont, the last settlement before Chinook. He bought a hamburger....

Tobias Wolff
This Boy's Life: A Memoir

I was on the road by 6:45 in the morning. Mist rose from the Clark Fork River and hung up in the bushes beside it like packing material; a man stood on the front of a log loader and wiped the mist off his windshield with full gestures of his arm. I took

Interstate 90 almost all the way—up the Clark Fork Valley to Butte, over the Continental Divide, over more ranges of mountains, then along the valley of the Yellowstone River to Billings. Beyond Billings the road headed south into Wyoming, past the site of the battle of the Little Bighorn, then across the creased and empty near-desert in the northeastern part of the state.

Ian Frazier
On the Rez

NATURE AND HUMAN NATURE

Many creative nonfiction writers find topics of great interest within nature and the out-of-doors. Some writers tell us about the wonders of nature, ecological systems, and life in the wild without drawing any moral message, except, perhaps, that we should preserve nature. Other writers use nature as a jumping-off place to wax philosophical about the nature of humankind. Like most things, neither category is purely one or the other. People writing about the wonders of nature will often briefly digress to make some point about how people could learn something from Mother Nature, but their main message is not philosophical. The more philosophical writers, on the other hand, may also give us much interesting information about nature along with their main messages about the nature of humankind.

> You might think, after many years of teaching a class called "Nature Writers," that I would know what nature meant, but I do not. Perhaps this is of little importance. The word comes from the Latin, *to be born,* which is fundamental enough, and puts it under the heading of abiding mystery. Then we have the essential character of something, like a rock, or a child; plus physical power, according to the dictionary, causing the phenomena of the material world; or for one grand definition, the sum of the surrounding universe. When I hear it said in caustic tones that "Everyone knows man is a part of nature," I have only the vaguest idea what that means either. The last time I heard such a remark, it came from a teacher of philosophy who did not seem to be particularly interested in what is often referred to as "the lower forms of life." There is reason

to suspect the assumptions of the human brain when it becomes too elevated from the earth that nurtured it.

John Hay
"The Nature Writer's Dilemma,"
collected in *On Nature*

These three excerpts give us three writers' thoughts on meeting up with an exciting part of nature.

The first time I ever saw a bear in the wild, I was on my way back from fishing in a beaver meadow on state land next to the Flathead National Forest, about ten miles from the town of Bigfork, Montana. I was coming around a bend on an overgrown logging road when I saw up ahead a large black animal see me and duck into some thimbleberry bushes. I knew it was a bear. I didn't move and he didn't move for maybe three minutes. There was no likely tree nearby for me to climb. Then the bear hopped out of the bushes, took a look at me over his shoulder, and galloped like crazy down the trail. As he ran, his hind feet seemed to reach higher than his head. He splashed water up and made the rocks clack as he crossed a little creek, and then he went into the brush on the other side with a racket that sounded like a car crashing through there. For some reason, I picked up a rock. I felt the weight of the rock in my head, I smelled the breath from a wild rosebush, I saw the sun on the tops of the mountains, I felt the clothes on my back. I felt like a man—skinny, bipedal, weak, slow, and basically kind of a silly idea. I felt as if I had eyes all over my head. I proceeded, a procession of feelings, down the trail where the bear had run. I saw dark blots on the trail where he had splashed water from the creek. I kept saying, "A bear! I saw a bear!"

Ian Frazier
"Bear News,"
New Yorker (September 9, 1985)

By June the Elk are in alpine meadows. There are deer where there is browse; and these black-tailed deer love the river bottoms. The bear are numerous. I remember one bright August day when August Slather had the oars, holding the middle of the Bogachief on a long slow drift in flat water as I whipped the river with a fly. As we rounded a bend we saw a large black bear on the next point, a couple hundred yards distant. Augie gave me a knowing look and pointed the boat directly to the animal. The wind was right and, as fortune would have it, the rear end of the bear was pointed our way. He had flipped a big fish from the water and was leisurely engaged in eating it. When the boat was within three feet of the bear, I reached over and gave it a slap on the back, shouting, "What are you doing here?" It was seconds before the message reached the bear's brain. Meanwhile his sympathetic nervous system went into operation. His rear legs stiffened, his back seemed to freeze. Then the danger signal reached consciousness and the animal was off through the dense brush, not once looking behind.

Justice William O. Douglas
My Wilderness: The Pacific West

Black bears rarely eat creatures larger than squirrels. They prefer little ones. They eat wasps' nests with the wasps in them. They eat living yellow jackets. When eating honeycombs, they also eat the bees. In 1976, a tagged Pennsylvania bear was caught stealing from a beehive in New Jersey. It was dart-gunned and extradited—home to Pennsylvania. A bear will sit on its butt beside an anthill, bomb the anthill with a whisking paw, then set the paw on the ground and patiently watch while ants swarm over the paw. The bear licks the paw. A bear will eat a snake or a frog. But all these sources of protein do almost nothing to pack that mattress of fat. Fruit and nuts make the fat. Bears eat so many apples sometimes that they throw up the pulp and retain the cider, which ferments in the stomach no less effectively than it would in a pot still. The bears become drunk. By the Deerfield River, in Massachusetts, a dozen years ago, two inebriated bears full of hard cider lurched all over a nearby road, wove about, staggered, lolled, fell, and got up on the hood of a police car. Massachusetts closed its bear season for the duration of the hangover.

John McPhee
"A Textbook Place for Bears,"
Table of Contents

The following excerpts are from writings about an experience of nature that is less exciting than bear sightings. Its emphasis is on the beauty of the wild and its appeal to our senses. These examples come from a category of books about nature and about human nature—books written by people who have deliberately removed themselves from society to reflect on that society, on nature, and on themselves. Henry David Thoreau may not have been the first writer to take himself outside the workaday world to live for a time confronting nature, reflecting on it, and then reflecting on the nature of humankind, but he's one of the more familiar ones.

> For sounds in winter nights, and often in winter days, I heard the forlorn but melodious note of a hooting owl indefinitely far; such a sound as the frozen earth would yield if struck with a suitable plectrum, the very lingua vernacular of Walden Wood, and quite familiar to me at last, though I never saw the bird while it was making it; Hoo hoo hoo, hooer hoo, sounded sonorously, and the first three syllables accented somewhat like how der do; or sometimes hoo hoo only. One night in the beginning of winter, before the pond froze over, about nine o'clock, I was startled by the loud honking of a goose, and, stepping to the door, heard the sound of their wings like a tempest in the woods as they flew low over my house. They passed over the pond toward Fair Haven, seemingly undeterred from settling by my light, their commodore honking all the while with a regular beat.
>
> **Henry David Thoreau**
> *Walden*

All of us have special places of great beauty. One of my favorites at sunset in the winter is looking across a barren hillside with a rim of birches silhouetted against its color. It has always fascinated me and I have often wished I could paint that delicate tracery against the reddening sky. Another is a high ridge that commands a view of many miles to the east. To see a moonrise there, to watch a certain notch begin to brighten and finally see the golden rim slip above the dark horizon never fails to fill me with awe and wonderment.

In a lifetime of seeing beauty in the wilderness, I always feel a lift of spirit and an afterglow of serenity and content. I also know one must take time and wait for the glimpse of beauty that always comes, and one must see each as though it were his last chance.

Sigurd F. Olson
Reflections from the North Country

The Weddell teems with large animals in the austral summer, even in early winter, when the *Palmer* entered pack ice on its northern perimeter, when we found large numbers of crabeater and Weddell seals, fur seals, and predacious leopard seals; chinstrap, Adélie, and emperor penguins; sei whales, mink whales, and orcas. After the barren vistas of heavily-utilized seas to the north, the Weddell seemed like a refugium. Knowing that whales one had only the vaguest notion of—the Southern bottlenose whale, Arnoux's beaked whale—roamed here along with the largest animal that ever lived, the blue whale, made some of us keenly observant. We studied every patch of open water.

Barry Lopez
"Offshore: A Journey to the Weddell Sea,"
collected in *American Nature Writing 1995*

About five miles north of my house in Ames, Iowa, is a state-designated "prairie remnant," a 25-acre piece of land that escaped the plow. In mid-September of a very wet year, the dominant color here is rich green. The five- or six-foot-tall stems of Indian grass are fully headed-out—tan seed heads wave and rustle in the stiff westerly breeze. Other vegetation, mostly partridge pea, with its small yellow flowers and vetch-like leaves, clusters and creeps around the base of the taller grasses, entirely covering the soil beneath. Behind the stand of grass is a grove of trees, a few evergreens and some oaks. A crow sits on the uppermost branch of a dead tree, steadying itself against the breeze.

Jane Smiley
"So Shall We Reap,"
collected in *American Nature Writing 1995*

The *Patagonia Express* dropped anchor directly opposite the ice cliffs. I cannot say it was beautiful; it was beyond all that. I stood on the deck in the painfully cold air watching icebergs calve into the still water. The fall blocks boomed in the silence, like blasts of dynamite on some distant planet. It was impossible not to think of Coleridge's vision of ice in *The Ancient Mariner* ("The ice did split with a thunder fit"); even Norman's eye glittered obligingly.

Some of us strapped on lifejackets and climbed into a Zodiac. The tallest ice cliffs, at least 180 feet high, revealed themselves to be cleft with deeper blue caverns of cold air stretching back into the inner world of the earth. Gulls with black spindly legs landed on ice floes, and under the water I could see spectral outlines of secret things. We motored through the pack-ice along all one-and-a-half miles of the shining glacier. It radiated coldness. A crewman shouted and pointed behind us, and we turned our heads to see a tower of ice the size of a multi-storey carpark plunging into the lagoon, the foundations bouncing upwards with ostentatious languor as the top disappeared.

Sara Wheeler
Travels in a Thin Country: A Journey through Chile

PERSONAL REFLECTIONS

Personal reflections are usually written in essay form, but I've not called the following "essays" because we tend to associate that form with those dull things we were required to write back in school. Also, personal reflections are written in more forms than the essay, so I chose to use the more accommodating phrase.

E. B. White, the modern master of the personal essay, said in the foreword to *Essays of E. B. White*: "There are as many kinds of essays as there are human attitudes or poses, as many essay flavors as there are Howard Johnson ice creams."

Novelist Maureen Howard, editor of *Contemporary American Essays,* wrote in her introduction to that collection: "An essay, though it takes as many shapes as weather or daylight, always has the immediacy of a real voice...."

The examples that follow have distinct voices that we hear in the reflections.

I have noticed on my trips up to the city that people have recut their clothes to follow the fashion. On my last trip, however, it seemed to me that people had remodeled their ideas, too—taken in their convictions a little at the waist, shortened the sleeves of their resolve, and fitted themselves out in a new intellectual ensemble copied from a smart design out of the very latest page of history. It seemed to me that they had strung along with Paris a little too long.

I confess to a disturbed stomach. I feel sick when I find anyone adjusting his mind to the new tyranny which is succeeding abroad. Because of its fundamental stricture, fascism does not seem to me to admit of any compromise or any rationalization, and I resent the patronizing air of persons who find in my plain belief of freedom a sign of immaturity. If it is boyish to believe that a human being should live free, then I'll gladly arrest my development and let the rest of the world grow up.

E. B. White
"Freedom,"
One Man's Meat

At eighteen I longed to die for it. When World War II ended in 1945 before I could reach the combat zone, I moped for months about being deprived of the chance to go down in flames under the guns of a Mitsubishi Zero. There was never much doubt that I would go down in flames if given the opportunity, for my competence as a pilot was such that I could barely remember to lower the plane's landing gear before trying to set it down on a runway. I had even visualized my death. It was splendid. Dead, I would be standing perhaps 4,000 feet up in the sky. (Everybody knew that heroes floated in those day.) Erect and dashing, surrounded by beautiful cumulus clouds, I would look just as good as ever, except for being slightly transparent. And I would smile, devil-may-care, at the camera—oh there would be cameras there—and the American flag would unfurl behind me across 500 miles of glorious American sky, and back behind the cumulus clouds the Marine Band would be playing "The Stars and Stripes Forever," but not too fast.

Russell Baker
"The Flag,"
So This Is Depravity

I have pursued my own chronology not so much to record it as to explore it. Remembering a particular house often brings back a predominant mood, a certain weather of the spirit. Sometimes, opening the door of a till-then-forgotten room brought on that involuntary shiver, that awed suspension. These sudden rememberings are gifts to writers, like the taste of the madeleine—for much of writing is simply finding ways of re-creating astonishments in words. But as I began to reel in my itinerant past I found that I was much less interested in recording it than in experiencing the sense it gave me of making tangible a ghostly dimension; for an instance of rememberings can, without warning, turn into a present moment, a total possession, a haunting.

Alastair Reid
"Hauntings,"
New Yorker (December 23, 1985)

A very, very long time ago (about three or four years), I took a certain secure and righteous pleasure in saying the things that women are supposed to say. I remember with pain—

"My work won't interfere with marriage. After all, I can always keep my typewriter at home."

Or:

"I don't want to write about women's stuff. I want to write about foreign policy."

Or:

"Black families were forced into matriarchy, so I see why black women have to step back and let their men go ahead."

Or:

"I know we're helping Chicano groups that are tough on women, but that's their culture."

Or:

"Who would want to join a women's group? I've never been a joiner, have you?"

Or (when bragging):

"He says I write like a man."

I suppose it's obvious from the kinds of statements I chose that I was secretly nonconforming. I wasn't married. I was earning a living at a profession I cared about. I had basically—

if quietly—opted out of the "feminine" role. But that made it all the more necessary to repeat the conventional wisdom, even to look as conventional as I could manage, if I was to avoid some of the punishments reserved by society for women who don't do as society says. I therefore learned to Uncle Tom with subtlety, logic and humor. Sometimes I believed myself.

If it weren't for the women's movement, I might still be dissembling away. But the ideas of this great sea-change in women's views of ourselves are contagious and irresistible. They hit women like a revelation, as if we had left a dark room and walked into the sun.

Gloria Steinem
"Sisterhood,"
Outrageous Acts and Everyday Rebellions

There is a housing project standing now where the house in which we grew up once stood, and one of those stunted city trees is snarling where our doorway used to be. This is on the rehabilitated side of the avenue. The other side of the avenue— for progress takes time—has not been rehabilitated yet and it looks exactly as it looked in the days when we sat with our noses pressed against the windowpane, longing to be allowed to go "across the street." The grocery store which gave us credit is still there, and there can be no doubt that it is still giving credit. The people in the project certainly need it—far more, indeed, than they ever needed the project. The last time I passed by, the Jewish proprietor was still standing among his shelves looking sadder and heavier but scarcely any older. Farther down the block stands the shoe-repair store in which our shoes were repaired until reparation became impossible and in which, then, we bought all our "new" ones. The negro proprietor is still in the window, head down, working at the leather.

These two, I imagine, could tell a long tale if they would (perhaps they would be glad to if they could), having watched so many, for so long, struggling in the fishhooks, the barbed wire, of this avenue.

James Baldwin
"Fifth Avenue, Uptown,"
Nobody Knows My Name

During the months that have passed since that September morning some have asked me what understanding of Nature one shapes from so strange a year? I would answer that one's first appreciation is a sense that the creation is still going on, that the creative forces are as great and as active to-day as they have ever been, and that to-morrow's morning will be as heroic as any of the world. *Creation is here and now.* So near is man to the creative pageant, so much a part is he of the endless and incredible experiment, that any glimpse he may have will be but the revelation of a moment, a solitary note heard in a symphony thundering through debatable existences of time. Poetry is as necessary to comprehension as science. It is as impossible to live without reverence as it is without joy.

Henry Beston
*The Outermost House: A Year of Life
on the Great Beach of Cape Cod*

JOURNALISM

Journalism presents a broad, almost limitless opportunity for writers of creative nonfiction. Before the early 1970s, traditional newspaper reporters and editors would never have believed for a moment that writing in their publication would be increasingly creative. The word "creative" connoted that reporters would make up the news, create facts out of whole cloth, or, at best, would write subjectively about the news, instead of objectively, as they had been taught in school and by their editors. They didn't want to accept the increasing evidence that they would have to write more creatively—interestingly and dramatically, that is—to compete with magazines and the broadcast media. Magazines, especially the growing number of special-interest magazines, have been giving the public more exciting, more attractive, more dramatic presentations of the news and its background for years. Difficult as it may be to accept, there has been a rapid "magazining" of newspapers in America and more recently, a "magazining" of television news broadcasts.

Today, most newspapers have accepted the fact that if newspaper journalism is to survive as a medium against the powerful and more attractive media, it has to adapt—a sort of species adaptation for evolution and survival. If the newspaper species takes on too many of its competitors' attributes, of course, it is in danger of losing the primary attributes that have enabled it to survive so far—adherence to objective, accurate reporting of the facts. Newspapers must continuously monitor their adaptive efforts, but there are writers who are leading the way, writers who manage to keep the facts straight while surrounding them with colorfully written narrative that borrows from certain fiction techniques, as described in this book. These excerpts of journalistic writers show that such adaptive mechanisms can work, and work splendidly, whether written on a deadline or not. I've not been able to include one variety of journalism, sportswriting, but that field offers many opportunities for the creative nonfiction writer.

NEW YORK—A healthy 17-year-old heart pumped the gift of life through 34-year-old Bruce Murray Friday, following a four-hour transplant operation that doctors said went without a hitch.

Early Thursday morning, three surgeons at Presbyterian Hospital lifted Murray's flabby, enlarged heart from his chest cavity and replaced it with a normal heart that had been flown in from St. Louis inside an ice-filled beer cooler. The operation lasted from 3:45 a.m. to 7:30 a.m.

As Murray's diseased heart sat in a stainless-steel bowl at the foot of the operating table, doctors gradually weaned Murray away from the heart-lung machine that had kept him alive throughout much of the operation. The new heart, beating slowly at first, gradually took over the task of pumping blood through Murray's body. And by 5:25 a.m., Dr. Eric Rose emerged from the 19th-floor operating room and proclaimed the procedure a success.

Jonathan Bor
"It Fluttered and Became Bruce Murray's Heart,"
Syracuse Post-Standard (May 12, 1984),
collected in *Best Newspaper Writing 1985*

ST. PETERSBURG, Florida—Suspense is building at the track. Fans mill around the staging area to get a glimpse of what a woman describes as the "fantastic chest" of her favorite contestant. When the runner's name is finally announced, he gets a long ovation. One man hops around, shouting: "Give me a K! Give me an E! Give me another E! Give me an...."

The cheers are for a greyhound named Keefer. Few dogs ever attract so much attention, but when it comes to Keefer, people here get downright dogmatic. They say he is the smartest or the best-looking or the most affable young racing dog they have ever seen. They even applaud when his victories are replayed on the track's closed-circuit television system.

Keefer's trainer, James Schulthess, is his most outspoken fan. He calls Keefer "the best dog in the world, and maybe the best dog that ever lived."

Such biased views aside, this much is certain: At the tender age of two, the big beige hound from Kansas is one hot dog....

Francine Schwadel
"Red-Hot Racing Dog Wins People's Hearts
Even When He Fails,"
Wall Street Journal (April 16, 1986)

Craig Stedman, a South Kingtown patrolman, headed down Worden's Pond Road to the Tucker house. The rain was really something. He found Charlie lying nine feet from the porch.

There was a loaded .38-caliber pistol near his left elbow and a nine-pound iron bar against his right arm. He had bad head injuries and a sporadic pulse. Stedman knocked on the door and wrote down the first thing that Lucy Tucker said to him.

"I didn't want to kill him, but he had a gun and said he would kill me and the children. He had a gun and wouldn't stop so I hit him. Oh, God, he wouldn't stop."

Stedman radioed for help and then went back outside to check Tucker again. This time there was no pulse. It was 12:15.

Mark Patinkin
"I Didn't Want to Kill Him, But He Had a Gun,"
Providence, R.I. Evening Bulletin (March 20, 1981),
collected in *How I Wrote the Story*

It used to be easy to put together the qualities that made for a good, honest tavern. That's because there were only two basic kinds: simple neighborhood places with the owner serving the drinks and popping for an occasional round, and dim Formica joints that called themselves cocktail lounges, where a hired hand mixed the drinks and shorted the register.

Now there are bars for every taste, or lack of same. We have the California-inspired fern bars, where you can get a sliver of goat cheese in your martini; a sports-theme bar, with youngish customers living for the day a TV crew will record them holding up a finger, shrieking that they're number one; and activities bars, where the owners take the place of suburban moms and dads by organizing outings, softball games, dwarf-tossing competitions, and an occasional wedding.

Mike Royko
"A Clean, Well-Lighted Place,"
Esquire (June 1986)

For the last 50 years, the increasing speed of computers has been as much a constant as the outstretched arm of the tax collector. While that good fortune is bound to come to an end eventually, teams of scientists and engineers continue to produce faster and faster machines. They accomplish that by a mixture of clever new designs and an old-fashioned devotion to cleanliness.

None of the dire predictions about the end of innovation have come true yet, said Robert Dreyer, a former Intel chip designer who is now studying at Harvard. "The end is always 10 years away," he said. "As you get closer to the end, the engineers find new ways to push it back."

Computer chips are enormously complicated machines, but their operation can be explained by a few simple principles. All the decision-making about where the pop-up windows will be on the screen, which monster will explode or how the modem will squawk depends upon the movement of packets of electrons between transistors, the switches that direct the flow of current on a chip. A full packet means one thing to a transistor, and an empty packet or, more precisely, the absence of a packet, means the opposite. Each chip has millions of tiny packets moving among millions of transistors at the same time, and somehow they manage to do the right thing.

Peter Wayner
"The Incredible Shrinking Chip...Circuits,"
New York Times (January 13, 2000)

HELSINKI, 1952—Sauna (pronounced *sowna*) is a Finnish bath, and a great deal more. It is a sacred rite, a form of human sacrifice in which the victim is boiled like a missionary in the cannibal islands, then baked to a turn, then beaten with sticks until he flees into the icy sea, then lathered and honed and kneaded and pummeled by the high priestess of this purgatorial pit.

Nothing relaxes a Finn like this ritual of fire worship, water worship, and soap worship. It is an ancient folk custom dating from forgotten times, and it explains why Finland produces so many great marathon runners. Anybody who can survive a sauna can run twenty-six miles barefoot over broken beer bottles.

Red Smith
"Good, Clean Fun,"
The Red Smith Reader

SCIENCE AND TECHNOLOGY

Since science and technology are frequently lumped together, despite their great differences, I've kept them lumped here as a category. Science and technology might have been included under "journalism" in another classification system, but I wanted to separate them out here. Until fairly recently, science and technology writers rarely allowed themselves to be creative. As a society, we need more fine writers of creative nonfiction to keep us (enjoyably) abreast of what's happening in those rapidly growing fields. The subjects of science and technology require excellent writing, especially if they are to be made understandable for the layperson. Writing clearly about these subjects for professional colleagues is difficult enough, but to write clearly for laypeople requires even greater skill. Add the requirement to also write in a style that is engaging, and you have a serious challenge in front of you.

If you are searching for a writing niche, and you enjoy science or technology, these fields are wide open to good writers. And the public desperately needs good writers to inform us clearly about all the sciences and technologies that surround us, affect us, change our lives, determine our futures—perhaps even determine the survival of our species.

An informed electorate lies at the very foundation of democracy—and yet we all feel less and less informed about the progress of science and technology. Some of us feel we're sufficiently informed by television news and documentaries, but those media give us a false sense of security about how well informed we are; we just think we're informed. We need writers to inform us in greater depth, but we also want to enjoy our informative reading—and that requires creative nonfiction writers like those that follow.

SCIENCE

We have allowed these chemicals to be used with little or no advance investigation of their effect on soil, water, wildlife, and man himself. Future generations are unlikely to condone our lack of prudent concern for the integrity of the natural world that supports all life.

There is still very limited awareness of the nature of the threat. This is an era of specialists, each of whom sees his own problem and is unaware of or intolerant of the larger frame into which it fits. It is also an era dominated by industry, in which the right to make a dollar at whatever cost is seldom challenged. When the public protests, confronted with some obvious evidence of damaging results of pesticide applications, it is fed little tranquilizing pills of half truth. We urgently need an end to these false assurances, to the sugar coating of unpalatable facts. It is the public that is being asked to assume the risks that the insect controllers calculate. The public must decide whether it wishes to continue on the present road, and it can do so only when in full possession of the fact. In the words of Jean Rostand, "The obligation to endure gives us the right to know."

Rachel Carson
"The Obligation to Endure,"
Silent Spring

They were generalists. Those primitive early cockroaches possessed a simple and very practical anatomical design that remains almost unchanged in the cockroaches of today. Throughout their evolutionary history they have avoided all wild morphological experiments like those of their relatives, the mantids and walking sticks, and so many other bizarrely evolved insects. For cockroaches the byword has been: Keep it simple. Consequently, today, as always, they can live almost anywhere and eat almost anything.

Unlike most insects, they have mouthparts that enable them to take hard foods, soft foods, and liquids. They will feed on virtually any organic substance. One study, written a century ago and still considered authoritative, lists their food preferences as "Bark, leaves, the pitch of living cycads (fern palms), paper, woolen clothes, sugar, cheese, bread, blacking, oil, lemons, ink, flesh, fish, leather, the dead bodies of other Cockroaches, their own cast skins and empty egg-capsules," adding that "Cucumber, too, they will eat, though it disagrees with them horribly." So much for the cucumber.

David Quammen
"A Republic of Cockroaches,"
Natural Acts: A Sidelong View of Science and Nature

It is not that there is more to do, there is everything to do. Biological science, with medicine bobbing somewhere in its wake, is under way, but only just under way. What lies ahead, or what can lie ahead if the efforts in basic research are continued, is much more than the conquest of human disease or the amplification of agricultural technology or the cultivation of nutrients in the sea. As we learn more about the fundamental processes of living things in general we will learn more about ourselves, including perhaps the ways in which our brains, unmatched by any other neural structures on the planet, achieve the earth's awareness of itself. It may be too much to say that we will become wise through such endeavors, but we can at least come into possession of a level of information upon which a new kind of wisdom might be based. At the moment we are an ignorant species, flummoxed by the puzzles of who we are, where we came from, and what we are for. It is a gamble to bet on science for moving ahead, but it is, in my view, the only game in town.

Lewis Thomas, M.D.
"Making Science Work,"
Late Night Thoughts on Listening to Mahler's Ninth Symphony

TECHNOLOGY

One holds the knife as one holds the bow of a cello or a tulip— by the stem. Not palmed or gripped or grasped, but lightly, with the tips of the fingers. The knife is not for pressing. It is for drawing across the field of skin. Like a slender fish, it waits, at the ready, then, go! It darts, followed by a fine wake of red. The flesh parts, falling away to yellow globules of fat, even now, after so many times, I still marvel at its power—cold, gleaming, silent. More, I am still struck with a kind of dread that it is I in whose hand the blade travels, that my hand is its vehicle, that yet again this terrible steel-bellied thing and I have conspired for a most unnatural purpose, the laying open of the body of a human being.

A stillness settles in my heart and is carried to my hand. It is the quietude of resolve layered over fear. And it is this resolve that lowers us, my knife and me, deeper and deeper into the person beneath. It is an entry into the body that is nothing like a caress; still, it is among the gentlest of acts....

Richard Selzer, M.D.
"The Knife,"
Mortal Lessons

If you look at zero you see nothing: but look through it and you will see the world. For zero brings into focus the great, organic sprawl of mathematics, and mathematics, in turn, the complex nature of things. From counting to calculating, from estimating the odds to knowing exactly when the tides in our affairs will crest, the shining tools of mathematics let us follow the tacking course everything takes through everything else-and all of their parts swing on the smallest of pivots, zero.

With all these mental devices we make visible the hidden laws controlling the objects around us in their cycles and

APPLICATIONS OF CREATIVE NONFICTION / 269

swerves. Even the mind itself is mirrored in mathematics, its endless reflections now confusing, now clarifying insight.

Zero's path through time and thought has been as full of intrigue, disguise and mistaken identity as were the careers of the travellers who first brought it into the West.

Robert Kaplan
The Nothing That Is: A Natural History of Zero

POPULAR CULTURE

Writers like Tom Wolfe and Joan Didion have inspired a generation of other fine writers who keep us abreast of another world, that of our rapidly changing and wonderfully diverse popular culture. Sometimes these writers give us our first insights into what's happening to us as a people right now. We see our foibles, our fads, and our lives, sometimes distressingly clear, through their marvelously refractive eyes and quick intelligence. We all like to read about ourselves, thus opening a wide field for good writing about popular culture.

The Christmas party at the new Manhattan town house of Robert Soros and his wife, Melissa Schiff-Soros, was in full swing. As adults sipped Champagne in the candlelighted parlor, children raced upstairs to experience the electronic high life in its latest flowering: a home theater screening of the Disney classic, "Peter Pan."

The large screen descended from the ceiling with an extra-terrestrial hum, but the house lights refused to dim—despite a horde of caterers stabbing frantically at a panel of small buttons on the wall.

As bright spots flashed and faded overhead, Mr. Soros, an investment manager and philanthropist, bent prayerfully over a control panel, playing its glowing touch-screen like a pipe organ as he tried to raise the volume on Tinkerbell. He had given up when the sound suddenly surged to Imax level. Children screeched.

"I would give anything to go back to good old toggle switches," his wife, a filmmaker, said later, sighing at the memory.

On their own living room wall in upstate New York, John Markus, a screenwriter and television producer, and his wife, Ardith Truhan, an artist, have 14 buttons that control lighting; 22 buttons for the stereo and CD player; and four buttons for the window shades. Another panel operates the DVD, satellite service, and laser discs in their home theater system. Six lines accommodate the couple's telephones, fax machines and modems. By phoning the control "brain," Mr. Markus can regulate every device even from the middle of a studio set in Los Angeles.

Julie V. Iovine
"House & Home,"
New York Times (January 13, 2000)

Every decade seems to end, if not begin, with a handle—the "flapper era," the "Vietnam period," the "me generation"—all related to some outstanding event or popular practice. These are not official designations assigned by the government. They are usually invented by some writer about popular culture, someone like Tom Wolfe or Joan Didion, who seem to see more clearly, and earlier, some of our human foibles and behavior patterns. I've written in more detail about this in earlier chapters on the realities of group life, individual lives, and realism in general.

A writer capable of seeing changes, new directions, new behaviors, new loves, and new fads before most of us can carve out a writing niche for him or herself. Usually, these writers about popular culture point out our foolishness with humor and affection, but others will sometimes write with snide, nasty, elitist commentary. Unless this latter type write in a masterfully clever way, they usually lose their audience to those who write with affection and understanding. E. B. White, for example, might point (with a slightly embarrassed finger) at the latest fad, but always with good humor, wit, and in a graceful style that makes us love him for pointing out our weakness.

I was wearing jeans, a blue shirt, a brown knit tie, a dark-blue sport coat, and Weejuns. We walked into a huge suite of rooms. Lynette Bernay, a wardrobe woman, said, "You're not going to wear jeans on Miami Vice."

"I know that," I said. Did she think I was stupid? "I have another pair of pants up in my room."

"What kinds of pants?" she said.

"Brown corduroys," I said.

She shook her head. "Sorry," she said. "No earth tones."

She led me into the complex of rooms where the Miami Vice costumes were kept. I had never seen anything quite like it. The first section I ran into contained ties—more ties together than I had ever witnessed in my life. There were lime-green ties, pink ties, and aqua ties, and light-blue ties, and bright-yellow ties, and ties with birds on them. Beyond the ties were shirts and jackets and pants and dresses—all in the same dizzying array of pastel shades. The clothing stretched on as far as the eye could see. At one end of the room was the shoe department. Eleven rows of long shelves, all displaying men's shoes. White shoes, gray shoes, pink shoes—not the kinds of shoes you would ever wear in the regular world. Lynette Bernay pointed out one pair of shoes to me. "Phil Collins wore these on the show," she said.

Bob Greene
"Vice Capades,"
Esquire (July 1986)

Those evenings were high drama. There on a low platform before a large fireplace in the lodge was a white-bearded Old Testament-like prophet in a white jumpsuit asking if anyone wanted to volunteer to work with him. To the amazement of those who wouldn't dare submit themselves to such an ordeal, fully a third of the fifty to a hundred people usually present, would raise their hands, eager to sit in what Perls called the "hot seat" and have their psyches laid bare for all to see. Perls distrusted long-term therapy. Sometimes in a matter of minutes, employing a keen theatrical sense and a surgeon's skill, he would cut away every prop that his "victim" habitually used to bolster his or her neurosis, even charm and humor, until nothing was left but the opportunity for an existential leap into a new way of being. At this point, as the victim sat paralyzed on the edge of an abyss, Perls would turn to his audience and, in a thick German accent, utter a classical aside: "Ah, ze impasse." It was stunning. It was just what the people who came to Esalen wanted.

George Leonard
"Encounters at the Mind's Edge,"
Esquire (June 1985)

Gene Tulich, seventy-three, a consulting engineer: "I've been commuting to Manhattan since December 1945. When I started, I was coming from Poughkeepsie, a two-hour ride up the Hudson River. I did it because I was a licensed engineer, just back from the war, and New York was where the jobs were. After forty years we still have the unwritten rules of commuting, and they haven't changed much. The main one is: No talking. Especially in the morning. You say hello to the people who sit in the same seats around you every day, then you read your *New York Times*. If someone new comes on and they're chattering away, you still don't say anything, but you give them, you know, the Look.

"And then there's a rule about the three-seater: the person on the aisle absolutely never slides over to let someone else in; he stands up, and if you want to sit by the window or in the middle, you've got to squeeze by. It's awkward, but once you've staked out your seat, it's your territory. Once, years ago, my wife rode down with me and took up a seat that normally belonged to someone else, and boy, did she get the Look. People will abandon their regular seats only in very unusual circumstances, such as when the person next to them slumps over suddenly, sick or dead, which has happened a few times on trains I've been on. After a few stops the conductor would see a lot of empty seats around this one fellow, and he'd call for an ambulance...."

Charles Leerhsen
"Life on the 6:55,"
Esquire (June 1986)

This series of examples ends with one by Red Smith, who could always see the minor absurdity where others saw only the major reality.

A visit was made to the [Madison Square] Garden for the dual purpose of schneering at the other dachshunds and admiring the ladies who are led across the ring by toy breeds. It is a scientific fact that the ladies tethered to the tiny toys are invariably the most magnificent members of the species. No exception was taken in this case; the smallest pooch noted was towing the largest handler, a celestial creature measuring seventeen and a half hands at the withers, deep of chest, with fine, sturdy pasterns.

Red Smith
"In the Doghouse,"
The Red Smith Reader

SELECTED BIBLIOGRAPHY

Alexander, Caroline. *The Endurance: Shackleton's Legendary Antarctic Expedition*. New York: Alfred A. Knopf, 1998.

Allen, Moira Anderson. *writing.com: Creative Internet Strategies to Advance Your Writing Career*. New York: Allworth Press, 1999.

American Nature Writing 1995. Edited by John Murray. San Francisco: Sierra Club Books, 1995.

Baker, Russell. *Growing Up*. New York: New American Library, 1982.

Baker, Russell. *So This Is Depravity*. New York: Congdon and Lattès, 1980.

Baldwin, James. *Nobody Knows My Name*. New York: Dial Press, 1961.

Best Newspaper Writing 1985. Edited by Roy P. Clark. St. Petersburg, Fla., Modern Media Institute, 1985.

Beston, Henry. *The Outermost House*. New York: Penguin Books, 1949.

Boorstin, Daniel. *The Discoverers*. New York: Random House, 1983.

Bryan, C. D. B. *Friendly Fire*. New York: Putnam, 1976.

Bryson, Bill. *A Walk in the Woods: Rediscovering America on the Appalachian Trail*. New York: Broadway Books, 1998.

Carson, Rachel. *Silent Spring*. Cambridge, Mass.: Riverside Press, 1962.

Carver, Raymond. *Furious Seasons*. Santa Barbara, Calif.: Capra Press, 1977.

Catton, Bruce. *A Stillness at Appomattox*. Garden City, N.Y.: Doubleday, 1953.

Chatwin, Bruce. *In Patagonia*. New York: Summit Books, 1977.

Churchill, Winston. *A History of the English-Speaking Peoples*. New York: Dodd Mead, 1956–58.

Connell, Evan S. *Son of the Morning Star*. San Francisco: North Point Press, 1984.

Conway, Jill Ker. *The Road from Coorain*. New York: Alfred A. Knopf, 1989

Davidson, Sara. *Real Property*. Garden City, N.Y.: Doubleday, 1980.

Didion, Joan. *Salvador*. New York: Simon and Schuster, 1983.

Didion, Joan. *Slouching Towards Bethlehem*. New York: Farrar, Straus, and Giroux, 1968.

Dillard, Annie. *Encounters with Chinese Writers*. Middletown, Conn.: Wesleyan University Press, 1984.

Douglas, Justice William O. *My Wilderness: The Pacific West*. Garden City, N.Y.: Doubleday, 1960.

Edel, Leon. *Writing Lives: Principia Biographica*. New York: Norton, 1984.

Eiseley, Loren. *All the Strange Hours: The Excavation of a Life*. New York: Scribner, 1975.

Eiseley, Loren. *The Night Country*. New York: Scribner, 1971.

Eiseley, Loren. *The Unexpected Universe*. San Diego: Harcourt Brace Jovanovich, 1969.

Frazier, Ian. *On the Rez*. New York: Farrar, Straus and Giroux, 2000.

Heat-Moon, William Least. *Blue Highways*. Boston: Little, Brown, 1982.

Heat-Moon, William Least. *River-Horse: Logbook of a Boat Across America*. Boston: Houghton Mifflin Co., 1999.

Herr, Michael. *Dispatches*. New York: Alfred A. Knopf, 1977.

Kaplan, Robert. *The Nothing That Is: A Natural History of Zero*. Oxford: Oxford University Press, 2000.

Kidder, Tracy. *House*. Boston: Houghton Mifflin, 1985.

Kramer, Jane. *The Last Cowboy*. New York: Harper & Row, 1977.

Logan, Ben. *The Empty Meadow*. Madison, Wis.: Stanton & Lee, 1983.

Lukas, J. Anthony. *Common Ground: A Turbulent Decade in the Lives of Three American Families*. New York: Alfred A. Knopf, 1985.

Mailer, Norman. *Of a Fire on the Moon*. New York: Grove Press, 1970.

McCourt, Frank. *Angela's Ashes*. New York: Scribner, 1996.

McGinniss, Joe. *Going to Extremes*. New York: Alfred A. Knopf, 1980.

McGinniss, Joe. *The Selling of the President*. New York: Penguin Books, 1969.

McPhee, John. *A Roomful of Hovings*. New York: Farrar, Straus, and Giroux, 1968.

McPhee, John. *La Place de la Concorde Suisse*. New York: Farrar, Straus, and Giroux, 1984.

McPhee, John. *Table of Contents*. New York: Farrar, Straus, and Giroux, 1985.

McPhee, John. *The Pine Barrens*. New York: Farrar Straus, and Giroux, 1981.

Michener, James. *Iberia*. New York: Random House, 1968.

Morison, Samuel Eliot. *Spring Tides*. Boston: Houghton Mifflin, 1965.

Morris, Jan. *Destinations*. New York: Oxford University Press, 1980.

Morris, Jan. *Journeys*. New York: Oxford University Press, 1984.

Morris, Jan. *The Great Port: A Passage Through New York*. New York: Oxford University Press, 1969.

Olson, Sigurd. *Reflections from the North Country*. New York: Alfred A. Knopf, 1976.

On Nature: Nature, Landscape, and Natural History. Edited by Daniel Halpern. San Francisco: North Point Press, 1987.

Orwell, George. *Down and Out in Paris and London.* New York: Harcourt, Brace, 1933.

Pirsig, Robert. *Zen and the Art of Motorcycle Maintenance.* New York: Morrow, 1974.

Plimpton, George. *Paper Lion.* New York: Perennial Library, 1966.

Quammen, David. *Natural Acts: A Sidelong View of Science and Nature.* New York: Schocken Books, 1985.

Rawls, Thomas H. *Small Places: In Search of A Vanishing America.* New York: Little, Brown, 1990.

Reed, Rex. *Do You Sleep in the Nude?* New York: New American Library, 1968.

The Reporter As Artist: A Look at the New Journalism Controversy. Edited by Ronald Weber. New York: Hastings House, 1974.

Rhodes, Richard. *The Inland Ground.* New York: Atheneum, 1970.

Rice, Clyde. *A Heaven in the Eye.* Portland, Or.: Breitenbush Books, 1984.

Sandburg, Carl. *Abraham Lincoln: The War Years.* New York: Harcourt, Brace & Company, 1939.

Schulberg, Budd. *The Harder They Fall.* New York: Random House, 1947.

Selzer, Richard. *Mortal Lessons.* New York: Simon and Schuster, 1987.

Selzer, Richard. *The Rituals of Surgery.* New York: Simon and Schuster, 1974.

Sims, Norman. *The Literary Journalists.* New York: Ballantine Books, 1984.

Steinem, Gloria. *Outrageous Acts and Everyday Rebellions.* New York: New American Library, 1983.

Surmelian, Leon. *Techniques of Fiction Writing: Measure and Madness.* Garden City, N.Y.: Doubleday, 1968.

Talese, Gay. *Fame and Obscurity.* New York: Ivy Books, 1970.

Talese, Gay. *Honor Thy Father.* New York: Ivy Books, 1971.

Talese, Gay. *The Overreachers*. New York: Harper & Row, 1965.

Theroux, Paul. *Sunrise with Seamonsters: Travels and Discoveries*. Boston: Houghton Mifflin Co., 1985.

Thomas, Lewis. *Late Night Thoughts on Listening to Mahler's Ninth Symphony*. New York: Viking Press, 1983.

Thomas, Lewis. *Lives of a Cell: Notes of a Biology Watcher*. New York: Penguin Books, 1974.

Thompson, Hunter S. *Hell's Angels: A Strange and Terrible Saga*. New York: Random House, 1967.

Toffler, Alvin. *The Third Wave*. New York: Morrow, 1980.

Wambaugh, Joseph. *The Onion Field*. New York: Delacorte Press, 1973.

Warner, William. *Beautiful Swimmers: Watermen, Crabs, and the Chesapeake Bay*. New York: Penguin Books, 1976.

Wheeler, Sara. *Travels in a Thin Country: A Journey Through Chile*. London: Little, Brown, 1994.

White, E. B. *One Man's Meat*. New York: Harper & Row, 1944.

White, Theodore H. *In Search of History*. New York: Harper & Row, 1978.

Wolfe, Tom. *The New Journalism*. Harper & Row, 1973.

Wolfe, Tom. *The Right Stuff*. New York: Farrar, Straus, and Giroux, 1983.

Wolff, Tobias. *This Boy's Life: A Memoir*. New York: Atlantic Monthly Press, 1989.

Young, Alfred F. *The Shoemaker and the Tea Party: Memory and the American Revolution*. Boston: Beacon Press, 1999.

Zinsser, William. *Willie and Dwike: An American Profile*. New York: Harper & Row, 1984.

AUTHOR–TITLE INDEX

GENERAL INDEX